The Novel as Church

The Making of the Christian Imagination

Stephen Prickett
general editor

OTHER BOOKS IN THIS SERIES

Rowan Williams, *Dostoevsky*
Kevin J. Gardner, *Betjeman*
Fred Parker, *The Devil as Muse*
Ralph C. Wood, *Chesterton*

The Novel as Church

*Preaching to Readers
in Contemporary Fiction*

David Dickinson

BAYLOR UNIVERSITY PRESS

© 2013 by Baylor University Press
Waco, Texas 76798-7363

All Rights Reserved. No part of this publication may be reproduced, stored in a retrieval system, or transmitted, in any form or by any means, electronic, mechanical, photocopying, recording or otherwise, without the prior permission in writing of Baylor University Press.

Jacket Design by Andrew Brozyna, AJB Design, Inc.
Jacket Illustration: "Mr. Slope Preaching," from p. 51 of Anthony Trollope's *Barchester Towers*, edited by Michael Sadleir and Frederick Page, with illustrations by Edward Ardizzone (OWC, 2008). © Oxford University Press, used by permission.

Library of Congress Cataloging-in-Publication Data

Dickinson, David, 1956–
 The novel as church : preaching to readers in contemporary fiction / David Dickinson.
  232 p. cm. -- (Making of the Christian imagination series ; 5)
 Includes bibliographical references (p. 197) and index.
 ISBN 978-1-60258-682-6 (hardback : alk. paper)
 1. English fiction—20th century—History and criticism. 2. English fiction—21st century—History and criticism. 3. Preaching in literature. 4. Sermons in literature. 5. Religion in literature. I. Title.
 PR888.R5D53 2013
 823'.9109382--dc23
                        2012028956

Printed in the United States of America on acid-free paper with a minimum of 30% post-consumer waste recycled content.

In memory of Jacqueline Dickinson,
> with whom one of my last long conversations on a walk around Buttermere was about sermons in novels,

and with love for Yvette,
> who encourages me in all things and whose patience must have been stretched many times as I fretted over this task.

Series Introduction
by Rowan Williams

The current rash of books hostile to religious faith will one day be an interesting subject for some sociological analysis. They consistently suggest a view of religion which, if taken seriously, would also evacuate a number of other human systems of meaning, including quite a lot of what we unreflectively think of as science. That is, they treat religious belief almost as a solitary aberration in a field of human rationality; a set of groundless beliefs about matters of fact, resting on—at best—faulty and weak argumentation. What they normally fail to do is to attend to what it is that religious people actually do and say—and also to attend to the general question of how systems of meaning, or "worldviews," work.

Systems of meaning—philosophies of life, if you must, though the term sounds immediately rather stale—seem to operate by allowing us to see phenomena in connected instead of arbitrary ways. But this means the capacity to see things in terms of other things: it means abandoning the idea that there is one basic and obvious way of seeing the world which any fool can get hold of (and which some people then insist on dressing up with unnecessary complications), and grasping that seeing the world and being able to talk about what it is that we encounter is something we have to learn, a set of skills that allows us to connect and to see one event or phenomenon through the lens of another. At the most severely pragmatic level, this leads to observational generalizations about laws; at a quite different but no less important level, it leads us into the world of metaphor. And in case anyone should think that these are radically separate, consider that "law" itself is a metaphor in the context of natural process. . . .

Metaphor is omnipresent, certainly in scientific discourse (selfish genes, computer modelings of brain processes, not to mention the magnificent extravagances of theoretical physics), and its omnipresence ought to warn us against the fiction that there is a language that is untainted and obvious for any discipline. We are bound to use words that have histories and associations; to see things in terms of more than their immediate appearance means that we are constantly using a language we do not fully control to respond to an environment in which things demand that we see more in them than any one set of perceptions can catch.

All of which is to say that no system of perceiving and receiving the world can fail to depend upon imagination, the capacity to see and speak into and out of a world that defies any final settlement as to how it shall be described. The most would-be reductive account of reality still reaches for metaphor, still depends on words that have been learned and that have been used elsewhere. So it should not be too difficult to see that a map that presents the intellectual world as a struggle between rival pictures, well-founded and ill-founded ways of describing things, literal and fanciful perspectives, or even natural and supernatural vision, is a poor one and one that threatens to devour itself in the long run, if the search is for the unadorned absolute. How shall we move the cultural discussion on from a situation in which religious perspectives are assumed to be bad descriptions of what can be better talked about in simpler terms?

This will involve the discipline of following through exactly what it is that the language of a particular religious tradition allows its believers to see—that is, what its imaginative resources are. When believers are engaged (as they routinely are, despite what may be assumed by the critics of faith) in society and politics and the arts in ways that are recognizable to nonbelievers, how are their perceptions actually and specifically molded by the resources of their tradition? This is not—*pace* any number of journalistic commentators—a matter of the imperatives supposedly derived from their religion. It is about what they see things and persons in terms of, what the metaphors are that propose further dimensions to the world they inhabit in common with nonbelievers.

Characteristically this repertoire of resources—in any religious tradition—is chaotically varied, not just a matter of a few leading ideas or doctrines. It includes the visual and the aural—what is sung and seen as well as said. It includes formative practices, rites, which leave their semantic traces in unexpected settings. And it includes the legacy of others who have engaged the world in the same ways, at various levels of sophistication. The forming of a corporate imagination is something that continues to be the more or less daily business of religious believers, and it needs to be acknowledged that this is a process immeasurably more sophisticated than the repetitive dogmatism so widely assumed to be the sole concern of those who employ religious language.

The way to demonstrate this is to lay out what it means in the practice of specific people; this series is an attempt to exhibit a common imagination at work—and in the process of further refinement and development—in the labors of a variety of creative minds. Because we are in danger of succumbing to a damaging cultural amnesia about what religious commitment looks like in practice, these books seek to show that belief "in practice" is a great deal more than following out abstract imperatives or general commitments. They look at creative minds that have a good claim to represent some of the most decisive and innovative cultural currents of the history of the West (and not only the West), in order to track the ways in which a distinctively Christian imagination makes possible their imaginative achievement. And in doing so, they offer a challenge to what one great thinker called the "cultured despisers" of Christian faith: in dismissing this faith, can an intellectually serious person accept confidently the simultaneous dismissal of the shifts, enlargements, and resources it has afforded the individual and collective imagination? What, finally, would a human world be like if it convinced itself that it had shaken off the legacy of the Christian imagination? The hope of the authors of these volumes is that the answer to that question will be constructively worrying—sufficiently so, perhaps, to make possible a more literate debate about faith and contemporary culture.

Contents

Acknowledgments		xiii
Introduction		1
1	Sounding the Depths of Dissonance	9
2	Have We Heard the End of the Sermon?	23
3	Amen: The Assumption of Authority	43
4	Keeping Faith: The Troubled Preacher in Updike and Lodge	65
5	Heaven in Ordinary: Religious Experience in Fictional Sermons	83
6	Words: Poison in the Ear, a Game with Language, or Naming Truth?	103
7	Shaping Paradise through Preaching	127
8	Memory and Imagination	153
Epilogue		173
Notes		177
Bibliography		197
Index of Biblical References		213
General Index		214

Acknowledgments

Although my name stands alone on the title page and work on *The Novel as Church* has included many solitary hours in the study, I am conscious that writing is not an isolated task; as an act of communication, it is at heart a communal exercise. I am aware, therefore, of my indebtedness to the implicit and actual collaboration of many people in the completion of this book. From the point of view of those whose contribution I am acknowledging, uniform gratitude must seem unfair—they must feel like vineyard laborers in the Matthean parable—but, from my point of view, the fact is that I am equally grateful to anyone who has helped me in whatever way.

Thank you to . . .
— Writers—novelists, poets and essayists—whose ideas, characters, and dialogue fund my theology, inform my preaching, and sustain my Christian faith.
— The congregations I have served in British Methodist churches who have listened to more of my sermons than I am able to remember and who have courteously engaged with them. Some of these church members were the audience I imagined as I wrote this book. I hope they recognize in its author the preacher they heard week by week.

— Professor Elisabeth Jay, until recently Associate Dean of Arts and Humanities at Oxford Brookes University, with whom I worked on preaching in British fiction in the early years of the last decade.
— The editors at Baylor University Press who have carefully nursed the manuscript through its various stages, especially the general editor of the Making the Christian Imagination series, Professor Stephen Prickett, who encouraged me at the very beginning, and Dr. Gladys S. Lewis, who took it through the preproduction stage and helped me to see that the study of sermons in contemporary fiction is instructive for readers, writers, preachers, and believers.
— Members of the International Society for Religion, Literature and Culture with whom I have enjoyed many illuminating conversations, both face to face at conferences and in print. Their ideas have helped shape this text and this author.
— Friends and family whom I may have bored with accounts of fictional sermons on many occasions. Some of these were intended to be parties!

These—and others I have inadvertently failed to mention—are the people who deserve credit for anything that is good in this work, while I am responsible for its inadequacies.

Introduction

The fictional preacher appears in novels in many guises. A study of preachers in English fiction of the late twentieth and early twenty-first centuries shows how fictional preachers have shaped contemporary readers' understanding of Christianity. Their sermons, as foregrounded authoritative performed texts, have colored readers' views of the Christian faith as readily as actual sermons teach believers their theology. Sermons are more common in contemporary fiction than might be expected at a time when preaching is in crisis caused by a revolution in communications during an age of distrust of any claims for authoritative truth. At the turn of the twenty-first century, the quadrilateral of authorities on which preaching is based—the Bible, tradition, experience, and reason—is openly questioned, and the church is both formally and informally decentered to such an extent that univocal preaching that takes no account of other voices is untenable: a minority church on the margins of society is unable to voice the kinds of certitudes that once sustained Christian hegemony.[1]

Partly in response to this crisis, within the western Christian church, preaching is undergoing many changes. It is no longer seen as the authoritative expression of religious truth but as an offering laid before people to select what they want from it, all of which panders to the way in which reasonable religion has been compromised by misplaced confidence in what we chose to believe and the desire of so many people to be comforted and affirmed in what they have decided

The Novel as Church

is truth. More positively, recent years have witnessed what some have called the New Homiletic, in which sermons are seen as "creative events" rather than "delivered messages," and preaching is representational rather than propositional.[2] This has encouraged the development of new styles of preaching based on the use of story, imagination, or empathy in ways that acknowledge the variety of literary forms in the Bible, the range of hermeneutical techniques available, and the diversity of ways in which Christian belief is expressed.[3] In Britain, congregations are increasingly receptive to sermons offering alternative interpretations of the Christian story—from, for instance, feminist perspectives with the increase in women preachers and from black, third world and other non-European perspectives with visiting ministers through the World Church in Britain program. All of this has been called "funding the imagination";[4] rather than telling people what to think, it is "showing." Notwithstanding these changes, the future of preaching in fictional form is threatened because the experience of both preaching and listening to sermons is less well known and less well documented. Novelists and readers must increasingly depend upon a remembered genre, belonging to a former age, which may not best reflect the style and content of current preaching.

This dissonance is both cultural and literary. In a world where both official and unofficial discourses of Christianity have been pushed to the cultural margins, preaching is thought of as either a waste of words, humorous, or inflammatory. The Beatles make a rare reference to sermons in popular culture. One of the lonely people in "Eleanor Rigby," a song released in 1966, is Father Mackenzie:

> Father Mackenzie writing the words
> to a sermon that no one will hear.
> No one comes near.
> Look at him working
> darning his socks in the night
> when there's nobody there.
> What does he care?

At the end of the song, he walks away from Eleanor Rigby's grave. No one else has attended her funeral—and no one was saved. Thus the generations who have listened to the Beatles since 1966 have been led to assume that sermon writing is a lonely and purposeless occupation and that preaching sermons is equally purposeless because nobody listens. Popular culture also portrays preaching as comedic. In Britain, in the 1960s Alan Bennett in *Beyond the Fringe*, in the 1970s the Irish comedian Dave Allen, and in the 1990s Dawn French as *The Vicar of Dibley* and Rowan Atkinson as the vicar in both *Four Weddings and a Funeral* and *Keeping Mum* have sustained a portrait of preaching whose humor often depends upon the utterance of ineffectual inanities or the expression of inapt similes such as Alan Bennett's, "Life, you know, is rather like opening a tin of sardines. . . ."[5] Furthermore, in popular perception, preaching is readily associated either with the inflammatory promulgation of dogma by fundamentalist extremists and fanatics or with the ruthless manipulation of vulnerable people by charismatic self-acclaimed healers and television evangelists. These popular images have moved preaching away from the central pedagogical role it enjoyed in the centuries when people's experience of actual preaching nurtured the development of literary sermons to such an extent that the preponderance of the output of print culture in the nineteenth century was sermons.[6] Of course this is no indication of whether published sermons were read. Perhaps we should heed Samuel Butler's cynical but perceptive comment about the volumes of sermons that are given unread by the donor, accepted and shelved still unread by the recipient. Nowadays interest in religious matters has waned to the extent that volumes of sermons are rarely bought and preaching is no longer regarded as an important feature of society's discourse.

Further to this cultural dissonance, fictional sermons have a literary strangeness resulting from at least four factors. Expressed simply, these are, first, that sermons have a particular rhetoric and that fictional sermons are embedded within novels with different rhetorical strategies. Received wisdom tells us that the primary purpose of fiction is to show and that novelists should not preach, yet both sermons in their telling and novels in their showing enable hearers and readers to imagine alternative versions of their world. As a result, both alternate and companion worldviews coexist in the conflicting rhetoric of sermons included in fiction. Second, fictional sermons are intratextual performances in that they are contained within, and usually constrained by, a text. The sermon on the page is less than the sermon performed. This relates to the third aspect of literary strangeness which is that, when included in a novel, the essential original orality of a sermon has been transferred to a literary text, which results in a loss of important phonetic qualities. Fourth, sermons are avowedly attitudinal in that they purport to give moral, religious, theological, or spiritual insight with a directness that is not usually associated with fiction.

This brings sermons into a conflict of intentionality when they are placed in novels. Making a distinction between showing and telling has become important to modern novelists and their critics, for whom didacticism is the mortal enemy, and mimesis, or the convincing representation of nature or human behavior, is a holy grail.[7] Is it ever appropriate for novelists to preach to their readers? When an author's voice, opinions or creed are too obvious in a novel, the accusation of "preachiness" is often leveled as negative criticism. Here lies the problem for sermons in fiction: preachiness may be avoided in novel writing, but how can it ever be excluded from preaching? Do sermons in novels give authors an excuse to tell rather than show? Do sermons in novels provide authors opportunity to intrude into the narrative? Are they "cheap tricks" that let authors express their own judgment or their own philosophy?

None of this dissonance has prevented the development of a long literary tradition of both straight and satirical sermons in British literature with which Judeo-Christian readers have become familiar. Well within two hundred years of the publication of Alain de Lille's *Ars praedicandi*, which has been called the most significant contribution in British culture to the development of literary preaching,[8] literary preaching was present in Geoffrey Chaucer's *Canterbury Tales*.[9] Furthermore, Chaucer's contemporary, Langland, was preaching both directly and through his characters in *Piers Plowman*.[10] Thereafter, the traditions of straight and satirical literary sermons were combined in George Eliot's *The Sad Fortunes of the Rev Amos Barton*[11] and employed in the novels of both Anthony Trollope and Charles Dickens, most notably in *Barchester Towers* and *Bleak House*.[12] Almost a century earlier, a straight sermon constituting an entire chapter had felt natural in Oliver Goldsmith's *The Vicar of Wakefield*.[13] And in the early years of the twentieth century, the traditions of straight and satirical literary sermons were still strong enough for both Evelyn Waugh and

James Joyce to employ.[14] This long literary tradition was sustained because it was embedded in the assumption that the majority of readers were already educated in the traditions of Christianity and that many attended church. Now that this presupposition can no longer be held, it is surprising that this literary tradition persists among novelists, whether or not their novels deal primarily with religious, spiritual, or theological themes.

Fictional preaching in contemporary novels persists as a discourse still capable of effectively forging theology (or making the Christian imagination). This includes the sermons of John Wroe, Michael Mompellion, and John Ames in novels that use preaching to contextualize historical action, those of Blair Ashley and Huxley Grieve that form part of a novel's satire, and those of Gideon Farrar, Bill Potter, and "Mr." Ellenby that track the passage of time in a chronicle of four novels. Some fictional sermons cannot be trusted, such as those of the unreliable and disreputable preachers Jethro Furber, Thomas Marshfield, and Jack Eccles, while another is almost too honest for his own and his vocation's good—the troubled Catholic Austin Brierley. Some fictional preaching represents a nonconformist streak and tradition, for instance that of Pastor Finch, Richard Misner, Simon Carey, Senior Pulliam, and Brackett Omensetter. These are the creatures of novelists such as Michael Arditti, Geraldine Brooks, A. S. Byatt, William H. Gass, David Lodge, Toni Morrison, Marilynne Robinson, Jane Rogers, John Updike, and Jeanette Winterson.

What an assortment of characters' names! Wroe's is the name of an historical figure and Mompellion's is a thinly disguised historical figure, too, but almost all other preachers' names alert readers to aspects of their styles, storyline, or behavioral characteristics. Finch, birdlike, nags his congregation, beating into them both their sense of worthless sinfulness and their sense of superiority over the Unsaved. Grieve and Ashley are the careworn vicar and curate of a parish whose church is a charred ruin on Easter morning. Others, such as Brierley, are prickly characters who are destined to scratch at any religious certitudes congregants might have and for whom progress through life will always be complicated by its thorny issues. Ames, the surname of three generations of preachers in Robinson's novels, carries sufficient implications to be appropriate for three quite different preachers: it speaks of love, of goals, and of purposefulness. Pulliam employs a bullying manipulative style in the pulpit, whereas the newcomer Misner is miserly with his words. Updike gives his preacher a name similar in construction to his own: Marshfield is bogged down in his obsessive fascination with women and his inability to stand firm in theistic belief. The correct pronunciation of Brackett Omensetter's first name is a key moment in Gass' novel, but this does not detract from the significance of his given surname: Omensetter, with his claimed secret knowledge, predictions, and "luck," poses a grave problem for many of his neighbors. And, in an extreme case of nominative determinism, there is a bishop called Bishop.

Some of these preachers bolster traditional models of Christianity; others wrestle with problematic aspects of religious belief, sexuality, or ethnicity; yet others, inadequate and unscrupulous, who preach shallow and cliché-ridden sermons fail to engage with issues of contemporary life, and effectively subvert the integrity of Christian faith. Because any of these forms of sermon in contemporary fiction may represent the intrusion of the authorial voice, even to the point at which the fictional preacher risks taking on the identity of the novel's author, it is important both for the future of novels that deal with religious, theological, and spiritual themes and for the authenticity of the preacher's voice to consider to what extent authors use their characters' preaching to propagate their own views, to what extent the aims, voices, or interests of the author and the fictional preacher are in conflict, to what extent the character is aware of either toeing the party line or struggling with personal doubts in the sermon, and to what extent the preachiness of preaching is made "acceptable" to readers, who usually dislike preachy texts. One of the criteria on which the sermons discussed in these pages have been selected is that they are significant features of the structure, theme, or style of the novel in which they appear. They also represent the three main divisions of Christianity in Britain and America—Catholic, Anglican, and nonconformist.[15] Discussion of these sermons is informed by the analytical tool of rhetorical narratology, which uses four aspects of classical rhetoric, namely *pathos, ethos, logos*, and *praxis* to analyze the audience, the preacher, the sermon itself, and the language of the rhetorical act. The critical discipline of rhetorical narratology is therefore eminently suitable to engage with fictional

Introduction

preachers preaching to readers. Reliance on the conventional aspects of classical rhetoric will expose fictional preachers in their roles in such a way that the reader will understand the message and be caught up in it. The chapters of *The Novel as Church* will examine the various dimensions of the preachers, their reading audiences, and the results of the interchanges. This examination will be achieved primarily by exploring the complications and implications of the dissonances created by placing sermons in fiction, namely questions of authority, faith, experience, language, and community. The next chapter will consider the cause of these literary dissonances.

I

SOUNDING THE DEPTHS OF DISSONANCE

The cultural dissonance of sermons in contemporary fiction finds expression in two of John Updike's stories.[1] A sentiment expressed in the sermon-like interior monologue that constitutes John Updike's short story "Lifeguard," in which the lifeguard preacher remarks, "I don't know why people no longer go to church," is reminiscent of a similar sentiment in a companion story "Packed Dirt, Churchgoing, a Dying Cat, a Traded Car," where Updike shows disdain for churchgoing and preaching. He says in this story that preachers, hopelessly compromised by words, are capable of only halting accounts of fleeting glimpses of God. Yet, in his own work and in various ways, Updike relies heavily on sermons. He thus epitomizes the phenomenon of the persistent use of sermons in fiction despite readers' reduced experience of actual preaching. His view, expressed in these stories, if not throughout his massive oeuvre, that preaching is of limited effectiveness prompts two questions: How do novelists imagine preachers and what picture of religious faith do fictional preachers give to readers of novels written in the last fifty years?

Questions of this nature also come to mind when considering the prominent role of three sermons in Iris Murdoch's fiction. Although these are the only sermons present in her novels, they are extremely important: two provide the frame for a debate that recurs throughout Murdoch's novels, and the other is at the heart of Murdoch's novelistic exposition of godless religion.

The Bell, the first of Murdoch's novels to be fueled by Platonism, is set in Imber Court, a lay religious community based in a Benedictine abbey whose putative leader is Michael Meade, a failed priest and schoolmaster forced to retire fourteen years before the action of the novel because of an unconsummated affair with an adolescent schoolboy. Quietly challenging him for leadership of the community is James Tayper-Pace, the younger son of a military family. The conflict between these two characters is described in a strange stilted debate in the form of two sermons delivered a week apart, each beginning with the exact same words: "The chief requirement of the good life is . . ." (132).[2] Each also uses the image of the bell. In the first, citing Christ's injunction "Be ye perfect," St. Paul's observation in his letter to the Galatians that the good person lives by faith, and Milton's refusal to praise a fugitive and cloistered virtue in *Areopagitica*, James argues that we should live without any image of ourselves. He shows himself to be a rigid moralist who sees the good life as unthinking obedience to rules and duty. He uses the bell, a simple instrument with no complex hidden mechanism and with a clear purpose to speak out, as a symbol of innocence. A week later, in contradiction to James, Michael suggests that there is a hidden mechanism in the swing of a bell: this is spiritual energy, which he likens to the wisdom of serpents. Although Michael claims to be adding to James' comments, his argument is quite different: the good life begins with self-knowledge and continues as we live in awareness of our moral capabilities, for knowing our strengths and weaknesses is necessary to avoid temptation. As Father Bob Joyce leads the community in prayer after the sermon is over, Michael reflects on James' previous contention that sodomy is not deplorable but just forbidden; and, although he questions the absoluteness of morality, he wonders whether the sermon he has just preached was successful or appropriate as "a commendation of the second best act." Overseeing Imber Court, like an author narrating her text, the abbess had earlier expressed balance between Michael's and James' opposing views when she spoke of seeking a place where one's spiritual life can flourish. That, she says, requires divine cunning, "As wise as serpents, as harmless as doves." Hers is the most authoritative voice in the book; the reader's suspicion that it is also the authorial voice is confirmed when Murdoch later admitted in an interview that she identified with her.[3] These two sermons first brought to the fore a tension at the heart of most of Murdoch's work, including not only her philosophical works but also *The Time of the Angels*, the novel in which her other sermon occurs; this is the tension between choosing to attempt the best act you know or settling for the second best you are confident you can achieve, a tension Murdoch called the conflict between saint and artist.

The Time of the Angels is an obviously religious novel, yet it is Nietzschean in thought and mood. Its central character is Carel Fisher, the eccentric rector of a nonexistent city church whose tower designed by Wren, itself later demolished, is all that survives after wartime bombing. He seems to lead an isolated, fog-bound, underground existence in perpetual wintry darkness.[4] His "unhoused spirituality" could be one move away from organized religion toward either religionless theism (belief in God held without any religious observance) or atheistic religion (ritual without belief in an Ultimate Other). Readers discover it is the latter. Carel's eccentricities, exaggerated after the death of his wife, have already included contemplating beginning a sermon, "What if I told you there's no God?," and the idea-play of the novel culminates in an antisermon that Carel delivers to his faithful younger brother, Marcus. Parodying Murdoch's own views,[5] Carel declares that all philosophizing and theologizing are futile attempts to tame that which is feral and to explain that which is unfathomable. He makes what he subversively believes would be the most religious statement that can be conceived of—that there is no God (171)—states that the single Good of the philosophers is illusory (172), and asserts that his vocation is to be "the priest of no God" (170). At the end of Carel's atheistic sermon, his addressee is left with his mouth gaping ready to cry like Adam banished from Eden (174); indeed, Carel soon dismisses Marcus from the rectory. The appalled dissonance between preacher and hearer, between the atheist priest and the faithful brother who pities him, not only sets up an exploration of godless religion that pervades all of Murdoch's fiction but also warns of the literary dissonance that sounds almost every time a sermon appears in fiction.

Renewed interest in recent decades in the study of rhetoric, in particular at the interface between rhetoric, theology, and homiletics, has led to an increasing acknowledgment of the role played by preaching in the development of theology. These studies also offer insights into what happens to sermons when they are embedded in fiction. Rhetoric is almost everywhere; one of the few exceptions may be a telephone directory, which is entirely rhetoric-free, whereas *The Yellow Pages* is a rhetorically nuanced interpretation of a directory. Considering obviously sermonic biblical texts, it is clear that Christian preaching was originally proclamation rather than persuasion. Two New Testament passages demonstrate this. The first is Stephen's martyrdom speech in chapter 7 of the Acts of the Apostles, comparable with both Jewish homily and Joshua's speech reported in the final chapter of the book of Joshua (24:2-15), and the other is Paul's efforts to explain why some people respond to God while others do not in chapters 9 and 10 of the Epistle to the Romans (9:30-33 and 10:11-17). These suggest that the Christian message is proclaimed rather than proved; it is persuasive only to those whom God calls.

These first instances of Christian preaching exemplify four major forms. The first of these is the missionary sermon, examples of which are to be found in Acts. The first is Peter's Pentecost sermon (2:14-36), and there are others by Paul, among which the sermon preached in Athens (17:22-31) is distinctive for the manner in which the preacher adapts his material to accommodate Greek hearers' thought forms. Then there are examples of prophetic speaking such as that found in the Second Epistle of Clement to the Corinthians, the work of an anonymous author dated no earlier than circa 140 CE and wrongly attributed to Clement who died circa 99 CE. The third form, homily, was intended to interpret Scripture and exhort hearers to live in accordance with its teaching. These homilies tended to project Scripture's eloquence more than the preacher's. Finally, from the fourth century CE onwards, panegyrical or epideictic sermons developed, in relation to which some of the Latin Fathers, most notably Jerome circa 343–420 CE, warned against using Ciceronian rhetoric in the service of Christianity, which, it was argued, did not need to resort to secular techniques.[6] It was Tertullian (160–225 CE), however, in *De praescriptione haereticorum* who had much earlier phrased the famous question, "What has Athens to do with Jerusalem? What concord is there between the Academy and the Church?"[7] Ironically, Tertullian was himself an expert in rhetoric and a preacher of renowned burning eloquence.[8] Authoritative approval of the use of rhetoric in sermons was later found in the acclaimed ministry of John, bishop of Constantinople from 398 to 403 CE, who earned the accolade Chrysostom, meaning "golden-mouthed," and in Augustine, bishop of Hippo from 396 to 430 CE, who refashioned the teaching of Cicero for the Christian preacher and suggested in *De doctrina christiana*[9] that the duties of a preacher are to teach, to please, and to move. From such a connect-the-dots drawing, this much is clear: for much of Christian history there has been at best an on-and-off romance between the study of rhetoric and preaching.

The preface to the *Bay Psalm Book*, in 1640 the first book published in English in America, succinctly expressed this uneasy relationship as "God's altar needs not our polishings."[10] These early American settlers were profoundly aware of the power of words. They made crimes of blasphemy, cursing, slander, lying, and all other manners of improper speech. They also controlled the development of good language, beginning in the classroom with primers such as the *New England Primer*. They were suspicious of rhetoric and so keen not to polish God's altar with fancy speech because they were aware of the power of words both to convince and to lead astray.

On the other hand, language shapes theology. Speaking about God requires words. Preaching and the rhetoric employed by the orator are integral components of theology. Jerusalem needs Athens. Because theology is always an act of proclamation, preaching is not a theological sideshow after "real" theology has been done; rather, both "textbook theology" and "rhetorical theology"[11] are proclamatory and suasory. That which is proclaimed in the pulpit contributes to our understanding of what we mean when we think of God just as much as what is taught by the seminary and theology faculty, perhaps more so because it is more immediate and more directly influential on the lives of people in the churches' congregations. Theology forged on the anvil of the preacher's pulpit is always contextual and is usually based on practical methods and public discourse. It inevitably expresses opinions and takes sides in argument. Some homileticians[12] have suggested that contemporary discontent with the homiletical task is due to most preaching being *logos*-centered and that recovery for preaching will come through a rediscovery of *pathos*-centered, that is, audience-focused, preaching. True though that may be, there is nevertheless a danger that rhetoric will woo and court the audience so much that it merely reaffirms the hearers' existing values without altering them.[13] Resisting that danger, preachers recognize that the pulpit is a proper place for doing theology, inasmuch as sermons are common sites for both believers and agnostics to engage with the intersection of the quotidian world and classical faith. Pulpits are where "an ongoing argument between the voice of God and the voices of the world"[14] is conducted. This is not a task reserved for the academic theologian. Indeed, one of the preacher's tasks is to bring the worlds of belief and experience together in meaningful and change-permitting discourse. This confessional theology is "a discourse of rhetorical performance" in which the preacher employs rhetoric and its powers of persuasion.[15] It is a vital, contextual theology.

Preaching's vibrant theology-shaping rhetoric conflicts with the rhetoric of its context when sermons occur in novels, causing a disjunction that can be disturbingly jarring. It can either reduce the sermon to a dead quotation or make the novelist into an intrusive preacher invading her own story. More than fifty years ago, Wayne Booth demonstrated that rhetoric in fiction is inescapable. Although the author is often encouraged not to be intrusive and authorial preaching is discouraged, the author is unable to disappear from the text entirely.[16] Just as the readers cannot claim that they are not reading a novel, so the audience grants the authors permission to know and be present in what they are writing about.[17] So, readers allow some signs of an author's presence, telling things unknowable, such as a character's motives and, in the case of fictional sermons, insight into the preacher's self-perception. Despite disjunction between the rhetoric of fiction and the rhetoric of preaching, the suggestion that preaching is an act of imagination by which hearers are invited, encouraged, or persuaded to consider the plausibility of alternative scripts that enable them to tell their lives differently[18] shows that there is nonetheless an interesting correlation between the purpose of fiction to show and the purpose of preaching to show and tell. Like sermons, novels enable readers to imagine alternative versions of their world. There is, however, a rhetorical difference. In the case of sermons there is what Walter Brueggemann calls rhetorical "density." This density is the product of a dense text, a dense subject, and what we cautiously call "dense" hearers. Like any other text, sermons are subject to intertextuality; this

Sounding the Depths of Dissonance

makes them rich, multi-layered, or 'thick' texts, pointing beyond their immediate referents. Like the hearers or readers of any text, those who listen to sermons listen with multidimensional memory; this gives both individual listeners—and the church as a collective listener—what we might think of as breadth or depth of listening. Moreover, unlike some other texts, sermons usually claim the "density" of pointing beyond themselves to what (or whom) Brueggemann often calls the "Primal Character," a divine being. Naming the divine being the Primal Character is unusual for a theologian and biblical scholar, but it is fortuitous for our literary purposes in that it establishes the role of the Other, the Ultimate, or the Divine as some form of protagonist in novels similar to that of human characters. The referent for most preaching is a Character. Novels, of course, need not be theistic, whereas most, but not all, sermons are. The contrasts between the rhetoric of preaching and the rhetoric of literature are not absolute. There is sufficient common ground for novelists to succeed in dealing with the dissonance. Moreover, when reading fictional preaching, the audience should be sensitive to authors' difficulties in successfully establishing the rhetorical density of sermons as distinct from novelistic intertextuality. Only then will sermons in fiction successfully represent convincing discourses.

The second dissonant feature of fictional sermons is that they are performances. The verbs most usually associated with the delivery of sermons are "give," "deliver," and "preach," while "perform," though rarely used, may be as appropriate because preaching is a reluctantly recognized category of performing art. The performative aspect of preaching, such as necessary rehearsing to hone the artistry and effectiveness of preaching, is played down because performance has come to suggest the spectacle of theatricality, which foregrounds the actor rather than the word. Thomas Hardy's short poem "In Church,"[19] in which a preacher who has mesmerized and thrilled a packed church retires the vestry and, thinking he is out of sight, rehearses some of his moves, only to be seen by a pupil whose admiration for the preacher is firmly dashed, gives succinct expression to the dangers of theatricality in the pulpit. Hardy offers no express judgment of the preacher's behavior in the vestry; instead the poet leaves the reader to see the ironic contrast between the pupil's adoration of her idol and his deft dumb show. His preaching is practiced show, which he clearly enjoys performing, and his dumb show makes readers doubt the sincerity of his earlier thrilling speech; his performance is dumb, thereby emptying and silencing the Word that should be central.

Nevertheless, performativity, which is to be carefully distinguished from purposeful theatricality, cannot be avoided. Broadening out the observations of gender studies theorists that gender has no pre-existing identity[20] but is constructed by performances or expressions of gender,[21] most aspects of human personality, such as societal role and individual identity, are also performed. People cannot help but *perform* who they are. Preachers *perform* preaching. Indeed, preachers are defined by their performance of preaching. The problem is that people are also defined by other attributes such as age, race, education, and social class, so the fit can never be perfect. Moreover, this is complicated by our use of language in these performances. Mikhail Bakhtin, the Russian scholar of linguistics whose work on speech genres (including sermons) has influenced many later literary studies and has implications not only for our understanding of the way language works in literature and in oral utterances but also for what happens when writers insert speeches in their novels, observes that our language is never unitary but stratified in several ways. It is stratified generically, professionally, socially, and historically,[22] and there are many of these strata to a preacher's discourse. Preachers are constructed as both more than—and other than—their preaching, and this study of fictional preachers will confirm any suspicion that in this area of excess and discrepancy trouble lurks. In terms reminiscent of the on-and-off romance between rhetoric and preaching, critic and philosopher Paul Ricoeur dismisses oratorical histrionics and argues that we must not lose sight of Plato's condemnation of rhetoric, which is often seen as "belonging to the world of the lie, of the 'pseudo.'"[23] It is no more than "cosmetic flattery, a simulation of art."[24] This perception of rhetoric has resulted in performance phenomena being rarely understood as "truthful" or authentic among preachers.[25] This is why performativity, which is unavoidable, should be distinguished from theatricality, which is when performance has become hyperbolic. For instance, it is his theatricality, rather than his self-consciousness as a performer, that arouses our suspicions about the preacher in Hardy's poem, and it is the Pardoner's theatricality that distinguishes him from the Parson in Geoffrey Chaucer's *Canterbury Tales*. Each of their messages is worthy, but the Pardoner's is compromised by the histrionics that draw our attention from the message to the messenger, whereas Alain de Lille's thirteenth-century handbook for actual preachers, *Ars praedicandi*,[26] argues that performance should be used to deny the suggestion of acting.[27] Similarly, the contemporary novelist Barry Hannah risks the reputation of his fictional preacher in *Yonder Stands Your Orphan* but rescues it by matching his words with action. Byron Egan is a reformed criminal who pulls no punches when he preaches. On one occasion he rolls up his sleeve, ties off his arm with a necktie, plunges a hypodermic needle into a vein, and draws some blood. "This is what God gave us," he yells, "not the green, gray dirty thing we call cash." The reader would be tempted to dismiss this theatricality as nothing but showmanship if Egan did not also scorn the moral hypocrisy of false evangelists, confront the evil that he sees in Man Mortimer, and seek to rescue people from the gambling casinos of Eagle Lake. He knows at firsthand what he rails against.[28]

Many literary works have two distinct modes of existence, one as text, the other as performance.[29] Think of the relationship between books and audiobooks. For instance, an actor's reading of a Dickens novel, both in the ephemeral form of a radio broadcast and in the more permanent form of a compact disc, differs from the way a reader customarily encounters a Dickens novel as a bound book of printed pages, but it is in keeping with Dickens' own presentation of his work in public readings. Yet even when privately reading a book, there is an element of performing to an audience in that words on the page come alive when the reader becomes his or her own audience in silent reading. In the case of an actor's recorded performance of a text, the words have been said in particular ways, in a particular place and time, and performed to an (imagined) audience, probably in a cultural context and perhaps accompanied by (unseen) gestures. Clearly, this is more than merely text on the page; it enhances and offers an interpretation of the text. In performing the text, "a contractual relationship between performer and audience based on shared knowledge" has been established.[30] In the case of sermons, their performance suggests situated behavior in a compact between the preacher who performs and the audience to whom the performance is presented.[31]

This situated behavior involves interplay among many factors such as setting, sequence, and the ground rules of performance. The smallest detail in these and other factors at play in a text may be significant to an audience when a text is performed, so if a performed text is displaced from its setting, there is a consequential disturbing alteration of performance frames that leads to a truncated, impoverished, or summarized form of the text, for which another linguistics scholar coined a memorable phrase: "performance in a perfunctory key."[32]

Perfunctory performance is the second problem for sermons in fiction in two respects. First, the sermon on the page is always other than—and usually less than—the actual sermon in performance, and, second, self-conscious and well-prepared performances within novels too readily imply the meretricious, and this may be especially so in a discipline where practicing what you preach is proverbially expected. Research reported in a book on Christian preaching examined this risk of theatricality:[33] using a *New York Times* article and an extract from an Iris Murdoch novel, both containing discrete and recognizable illocutionary speech acts, the researcher showed that when readers recognize that someone is pretending or performing, they adjust or suspend their response to the force of the illocutionary speech act. Audience response is less immediate; the speech act loses some or all of its effectiveness. Clearly, the loss or reduction of any of a speech's performative elements puts the text at risk. This is to say that, in the case of preaching, removing any of the traditions associated with the sermon genre may mean that the discipline either loses its *raison d'être* or becomes devalued as merely part of the residual culture.[34] This is a critical issue for fictional preachers. How do authors retain a sense of preaching as performance, and how do they use sermon performances to indicate the preacher's reliability or lack thereof? How do novelists avoid perfunctory performance, when the displacement of sermons and their insertion in a novel where the conditions for appropriate or full performance no longer prevail, inevitably tends toward their being played in a perfunctory key?

The third characteristic of sermons causing dissonance when placed in novels is that, despite the availability of some published sermons, their most usual form is oral. In the nineteenth century, people's familiarity with sermons was in both oral and written forms, for we are given to believe that, having attended preaching services on Sunday mornings and before attending evening preaching services, they read published sermons as a devotional exercise on Sunday afternoons and during the week. This did not always have the desired effect: in a well-known episode in *Wuthering Heights*, the young Catherine and Heathcliff use the devotional texts they have been given to lighten a wet Sunday afternoon as weapons in a physical fight.[35] A study of three nineteenth-century preachers reveals the coexistence of three different traditions or techniques of preaching: Charles Spurgeon, a Baptist, preached extemporaneously; John Henry Newman, an Anglican turned Catholic, preached from a manuscript; and George MacDonald, an ex-Congregationalist preacher with a dual vocation, wrote his sermons in novels.[36] This suggests that sermons, although essentially oral, are in the center of the orality–literacy continuum. Spurgeon's preaching ministry can be regarded as a form of "secondary literacy," in that he cultivated spontaneity but his sermons were later transferred from extemporaneous public speaking to print.[37] Newman's preaching can be regarded as "secondary orality," in that his oral performance in the pulpit was grounded in writing beforehand and in print afterwards.[38] George MacDonald was the most unusual of the three in that his "primary literacy"[39] circumvented or excluded the oral element of preaching. As his career as a novelist flourished, he appeared less frequently in the pulpit, with the effect that many of his sermons were never preached orally but only to those who read his books, some of which were in effect sermon-novels. Many remained "unspoken sermons."[40] Despite this variety of techniques and traditions, it remains true that both before and after this "golden age of the sermon" that is the nineteenth century and the few decades each side of it, sermons are usually regarded as part of oral culture.

What happens when something essentially oral migrates into the literary world is a process of defamiliarization; the dislocation is transformative and disruptively so. Walter Ong famously argues that, because writing is artificial whereas the spoken word is full of vitality,[41] when speech migrates from orality to literature, this vitality is lost. Words inevitably lack their full phonetic qualities, they lose intonation, and the reader is unable to hear the speaker's tone of voice.[42] As any actor preparing a performance or any reader preparing an audiobook knows, there may be grammatical cues for appropriate intonation of the text, but there is no expressive intonation expressly written on a page.[43] Perhaps, then, the ideal performer of an audiobook is its author. For evidence of this, listen to President Obama's own reading of his memoirs. Professional preachers writing sermons often lard them with intonational cues so that on delivery they can recall the pre-planned rapidity of some phrases, the deliberate emphasis of others, pauses and stresses. In the cases of Peter Marshall, the Scottish-born preacher who twice served as chaplain to the United States Senate before his premature death in 1949, and John Bell of the Iona Community, whose fame as a preacher extends beyond his native Britain, the cues in their printed sermons are exaggerated by an unorthodox page layout.[44]

When sermons are placed in a novel, they have migrated from an intended oral culture to the chirographic, or written, world of a literary construct; they are set within the novel as an inserted, embedded, or ingested genre, often losing some aspects of their essential spokenness. Thus an inevitable tension between the original, imagined, spoken form of the speech and its final written form, between the sermon's fictive orality and actual literacy, arises. The tension is a troubling disjunction, but it is also part of the stratification of language of daily life. A character's speech in a novel is likely to have several strata, and, in the case of fictional sermons, these are likely to include the voices of the preacher, intratextual hearers, extratextual readers, and the author as well as those of the Bible, creeds, and any other authoritative texts cited in the sermon. Again, the challenge for the author is how to let these voices be heard and avoid the sermon's reduction to a dead quotation.[45]

The fourth problem of dissonance with fictional sermons is that it is usually assumed that sermons are attitudinal. This is to say either that preaching is expected to give religious or moral insight or instruction or that it is committed to an acknowledged outlook. Most preaching is associated with confessional theology, which typically begins with the symbols, narratives, creeds, hymnody, or dogmas of a particular church tradition then expresses either the church's faith or the preacher's affirmation of, or dissension from, that tradition. Although sermons are often heard as the voice of ultimate authority and ultimate reality, and, although they are usually monological in form, any sermon will unavoidably have many voices. As well as the preacher's voice, there will be the voices of the preacher's predecessors, the voices of the listeners adding their understanding, incomprehension, or resistance to the sermon's text, and the absent (or silent) sacred voice. Furthermore, when sermons are put into novels, the number of these voices swells to include characters' voices, readers' voices, and the voices of the literary tradition to which the novel belongs. A noteworthy literary antecedent to all the polyvocal sermons discussed in this book is Laurence Sterne's sermon on the Levite's concubine, sermon 18 in *The Sermons of Mr Yorick* in which Sterne conducts a conversation with his imagined hearers and actual readers by repeatedly anticipating their responses to what he says, which effectively destabilizes their reading of the text and adds a novelistic tinge to his account of the biblical story. At the beginning of the sermon, the composite preacher who is both Sterne and his creature Parson Yorick says:

> A Concubine!—but the text allows for it; "for in those days there was no king in Israel"; and the Levite, you will say, like every other man in it, did what was right in his own eyes;—and so you may add, did his concubine too,—"for she played the whore against him, and went away."—
>
> Then shame and grief go with her; and wherever she seeks a shelter, may the hand of Justice shut the door against her.—
>
> Not so; for she went unto her father's house in Bethlehem-judah and was with him four whole months—. . . I see the holy man upon his knees,—with hands compressed to his bosom, and, with uplifted hands, thanking Heaven that the object which had so long shared his affections was fled!
>
> The text gives a different picture of his situation. . . .[46]

There is much more going on here than a straightforward dialogue between the preacher and his hearers. A good commentator chips in with the observation that "shame and grief go with her" before the text offers a dry corrective. This is but the beginning of a multifaceted conversation within the sermon as, later, aspects of the readers' minds, in the form of spleen, prudery, candor, courtesy, the heart, and the opinions, are given opportunities to contribute.[47]

As in this famous literary sermon, many such phantom voices can be heard in the sermons embedded in contemporary fiction, but, over and through all these sometimes dissonant voices, there runs the assumption that the preacher's voice has "attitude"; unlike the novel itself, the preacher within it is expected to adopt and present a confessional stance. How can this be done without compromising the principle of the open book or the notion that novels should not preach?

Fictional sermons have a vulnerable existence in contemporary novels as a result of the dissonances sounded out in this chapter. Their current status is jeopardized because their presence in novels raises serious theological questions about religious authority and spiritual integrity, literary questions about the representation of religious experience, linguistic issues about sermons as context-shaping signifiers, and at least one religio-literary question about the shaping of readership communities. These questions will articulate the concern in forthcoming chapters after the next chapter tests fictional sermons for vital signs.

2

Have We Heard the End of the Sermon?

Pictures of two preachers hang above the desk upon which this book was written. One, a cheap souvenir bought with a few drachmas, is a small crudely painted figure of a Greek priest; the other, much more valuable, is a specially commissioned Edward Ardizzone print of a pen-and-ink drawing of Mr. Slope from the *Oxford Illustrated Trollope* published by the Oxford University Press in the 1940s. The Greek priest and the fictional Anglican cleric represent two of the many possible models of preaching. Inasmuch as the worlds constructed in novels serve as models for the quotidian world, so the preachers encountered in novels offer models for preaching. Some are helpful; others are not. Common to many of them is the impression that preaching is a troubled occupation nearing its natural end, and this is seen most dramatically when a fictional preacher, almost always a man, finds himself unable to preach.

One such troubled fictional preacher, from an era in fiction and politics fascinated with fallen women, is the crook-backed but morally upright Dissenting minister Thurstan Benson in Elizabeth Gaskell's *Ruth*. His only wrongdoing is to pass off a rescued fallen woman as a distant widowed relative. In every other respect, he is a solid representative of Christian charity in Gaskell's novel. Loved and respected by the members of his church, his relationship with them degenerates when one, the wealthy and influential Bradshaw who had employed her as governess, discovers Ruth's true identity. The coincidence of Benson's initial encounter with Ruth, when he was on extended leave in Wales and when she, still only sixteen years of age, was seeking refuge after her seduction by an archetypal Victorian cad, Henry Bellingham, does little to explain Benson's unsolicited decision to give Ruth a home with him and his sister; as a result, Ruth's story becomes one of twists and turns rather than one of unrelenting decline into poverty, servitude, petty crime, and prison, such as that which Gaskell had seen in the real-life case that inspired the novel. Frequent biblical allusion and the depiction of compassionate, countercultural Christian charity in the face of the strict—and often duplicitous—moral code respectable society sought to impose, are perhaps to be expected of a novelist who was herself married to a Unitarian minister. Bellingham's double standards and Bradshaw's inflexible moralism are easy targets for Gaskell, whose plea in the novel is not for sexual permissiveness but that sympathy be shown toward those who have sinned. *Ruth*'s morality, however, is not simplistic, because the moral theme of the novel achieves greater complexity by its warning not to do evil with the intention that good may come of it. Despite the moral thrust of the novel, Gaskell expected readers and reviewers to be shocked by the narrative, whose suitability for published fiction she had herself questioned. She would not allow a happy ending for the novel. Instead, additional twists of coincidence and fate involving Ruth's exemplary self-denial result in Ruth's becoming fatally ill, having caught the illness from Bellingham, who almost miraculously recovers.

The final chapter tells of Ruth's funeral, at which there is an unspoken and unread sermon, for Thurstan Benson is so distraught that he is unable to preach the sermon he has carefully prepared. He had destroyed sheet after sheet of paper as he discarded sentences and paragraphs that were not quite good enough for the occasion, and he often had to break off from writing as his eyes filled with tears at the remembrance of yet another aspect of Ruth's sweetness and humility. This was to be "his great, last effort" (457) for Ruth, his final tribute to one we suspect he regarded as a true Christian heroine, but as he opens the sermon he looks over to the attentive congregation and he finds he cannot preach. His voice had already trembled as he prayed; a mist veils his sight, and all he can see is "Ruth as she had been . . . a woeful, hunted creature!" (457). He sits down to compose himself and chooses instead to read the last four verses of chapter 7 of The Revelation of St. John, referring to all nations appearing before the throne of God, which Gaskell quotes in full. The aborted sermon is replaced by apt scriptural quotation, which in the congregation's judgment is "more appropriate than any sermon could have been" (457). Yet one of the congregants, the Bensons' housemaid who had treated Ruth most unkindly when she was first taken in, comments that the minister preaches effective sermons sometimes: "I make no doubt," Sally says, "there was as grand a sermon in yon paper-book as ever we hear in church" (458). The problem for readers is that it remains in the paper-book, behind the text of the novel. Like that in the Lennon and McCartney song, this is a sermon no one will hear. Instead, readers are given what can be regarded as either a different sermon or a different fiction, for Gaskell's usage of Scripture in this way points to two unconventional but creative ways to read the Bible—as sermon and as fiction. The scene in St. John's apocalyptic vision is a sermon in that it proclaims what the mystic understood to be the Christian Gospel. It can also be read as fiction liberating the New Testament narrative from a purely historical perspective into applicability to all times and all places, giving account of the real world and religious belief. Other parts of the Bible are also sermons: the books of Kings and Chronicles, for instance, are unashamedly nuanced history with theological intentions, the Old Testament prophets' claims for direct inspiration—"the word of the Lord that came to the prophet Jeremiah"—are akin to the preachers' claim for inspiration in the study and pulpit, and the Gospels are not biography but sermonic proclamations of a message of good news based on the story of Jesus' birth, life, death, and resurrection. Within the Gospels there is much evidence to suggest that Jesus was a storyteller, yet not all the stories attributed to him by the evangelists originated with him. Some, such as the parables of the Parousia, began in the early church, whose members told the stories as sermons reflecting on the sayings of Jesus, thereby keeping them firmly within the Jesus tradition. As a single instance from among many, Luke's parable on the returning master interprets Jesus' saying about being ready for action with your robes hitched up and your lamps alight earlier in the same chapter of the Gospel (12:35).

Through the loss of Thurstan Benson's intended sermon, silenced by emotion, Elizabeth Gaskell, although sympathetic to Christianity and in particular to the tradition of nonconformist preaching, shows the inadequacy of sermons in some circumstances. Although Thurstan Benson had labored over it, his will not suffice. Toni Morrison will play a similar trick or deploy a similar tactic to more positive effect in *Paradise*. Whereas Morrison's silenced sermon demonstrates the continuing vitality of the imagined sermon, in *Ruth* readers are left asking themselves whether sermons can ever find their voice again after such a silencing. Was Gaskell's implied pronouncement of the end of the sermon in literature premature or timely?

Sixty years later, the fictional sermon was still showing vital signs when another suppressed novel, James Joyce's *A Portrait of the Artist as a Young Man*, was published in America in 1914. The sermons therein could be the last famous sermons in fiction. In honor of St. Francis Xavier, described by the rector as "a great soldier of God . . . a great fisher of souls," three sermons are given at a three-day Jesuit retreat at Belvedere College. Despite the authority and enthusiasm with which the event is announced, anticipation of the retreat withers Stephen Dedalus' heart like a desert flower feeling the chill night air that will not open again until a later vision of loveliness, a wading girl, fills his soul like "an opening flower" (173). His former master at Clongowes Wood School, Father Arnall, is a preacher whose gleeful depiction of the horrors of hell in the sermons terrorizes the reader as much as it abuses the individuality and integrity of those who listen to the sermons, in the process killing off in Joyce any remnant of sympathy for organized Christianity and pushing the preacher into the realm of oblivious delusion. The vitality of these sermons lies ultimately in their engagement with the reader, for what they do to Stephen they also do to readers. He, with the other boys from his school, is coerced into being a passive receptor, devouring his individuality as he is encouraged to throw in his lot with the hopelessly depraved human race, stunting his growth into mature humanity and resulting in his voicing aloud his exaggerated guilt. That Catholicism, as represented by Father Arnall in the novel, attempts a cohesive worldview based on a simplification of human experience, and a totalizing narrative is established in the first of the Belvedere sermons, which stresses the collectivity of the occasion. It emphasizes that the boys have withdrawn together "away from the busy bustle of the outer world" (109), that they are assembled as a single congregation in the chapel, and that they are doing what college boys have done for generations since long before anybody present can remember.[1] In short, they are part of a tradition. Implicitly, this first sermon makes the reader conscious of the social act of reading. Although readers are not actually participating in the traditional retreat, reading the text establishes dialogues between the reader and the narrator, between the reader and the preacher, between the reader and the writer, and, potentially, between the reader and other readers. These dialogues become stronger and louder in the accounts of Arnall's later sermons. Their appallingly abhorrent imagined descriptions of the prison house of hell with which the preacher casts fear into the hearts of his hearers. He says, "The prisoners are heaped together in their awful prison, the walls of which are said to be four thousand miles thick: and the damned are so utterly bound and helpless that, as a blessed saint, saint Anselm, writes in his book on similitudes, they are not even able to remove from the eye a worm that gnaws it" (120). The language suggests the preacher is an omniscient narrator speaking on behalf of the church, with his priestly authority bolstered by direct quotation of the Bible and the saints as well as a strong sense of the *Spiritual Exercises* of Ignatius of Loyola as an intertext.[2] Arnall ruthlessly manipulates the boys as he preaches, and there can be little doubt that Stephen continues to be disturbed by the preaching long after the sermons have ended. Tormented by the "leprous company of his sins" (137), he is in a living nightmare as he feels that God allows him to see the hell reserved for his sins, "stinking, bestial, malignant, a hell of lecherous goatish fiends" (138), until he rushes through Dublin into a church to unburden himself in the confessional, repeating the Confiteor "in fright" (144).

Above and beyond the text's fictional preacher and audience, Arnall and Stephen, are Joyce and his intended audience, the readership. Beginning with the sense of a discourse community that the first sermon established, Joyce continues to involve readers in the later sermons, drawing them in so that they are simultaneously appalled by the portrait of God and invited to consider the state of their own souls. He achieves this by several means. First is the gradual disappearance of the preacher, named when he first preaches but, by the third sermon, becoming little more than a disembodied voice whose words are given in direct extended quotation, with reduced reference to anything other than the spoken words.[3] Similarly, the audience becomes less specific as early references to the addressees as "dear little brothers in Christ" (111) disappear from the text. As a result, the distinction between the imagined original orality of the sermon and its written report becomes blurred to the extent that the difference between spoken and printed address is almost lost. In this way, Joyce draws readers in to form part of the intended audience of sermons. They frequently embrace readers by using collective pronouns in phrases such as "let us imagine" and "shall we consider." As a result, the sermons overtly address readers within the text of the novel.[4] The dominant monologic authority of the preacher directly addresses and tries to impose itself upon those who read Father Arnall's sermons, but, because extratextual readers are able to see what is hidden from hearers within the novel, the effect is a little different. Although intended that readers will be as traumatized by this oppressive preaching as Stephen is—and as Joyce himself was—the audience is unlikely to rush to the confessional in fear. Joyce intends readers to recognize that there is no place in "good" religion for such brutality.

Seemingly, such a scathing attack on Catholic preaching would have killed sermons off. This book would then be an obituary announcing the demise of a long but now defunct literary tradition and regretting the sad loss of a good friend who is now to be found in fiction only as a remembered genre employing clichéd religious language, now either inert on the page or sounding discords as harsh on the ear as clanging cymbals. In short, the sermon appears to be an example of an authoritative text being reduced to a lifeless quotation when ingested into fiction. However, if, as readers readily believe, fiction can be at the vanguard of contemporary thought challenging outdated but accepted norms and if, as homileticians readily believe, preaching can express fresh avenues for theological exploration in countercultural ways, it would be strange if preaching within fiction had entirely lost its power to persuade.

The continuing effective power of the fictional sermon is evident in a controversial British novel recently published in the US. In *Easter* its author, Michael Arditti, announces the end of what he calls the fascistic sermon and makes plain the promise of the creative sermon forging contemporary theology on the anvil of experience. In this novel, contemporary Christianity is imagined through the honest preaching of characters torn apart in the cut and thrust of living faithfully in difficult times. The novel holds interest partly because it is a satire on the controversy about homosexual priests in the Anglican Communion at the beginning of the twenty-first century and, also, because it uses sermons both for satirical purpose and to allow three of its characters to make their formal response to the events of the novel. Arditti appears to regard *Easter* as an attempt to integrate sexuality with spirituality, and this makes the book as highly charged with a heady mix of religion and sex as James Baldwin's *Go Tell It on the Mountain* had been almost fifty years earlier. *Easter* attracted interest from reviewers in both the gay and the religious press and caused quite a stir, both of approval and disapproval. Reviewers variously suggested that it can be read as allegory, parody, satire, or chronicle; as comedic farce, tragedy, or tragicomedy; as comic fantasy or as having serious intent; as liturgy, drama, or a verbal triptych. Indeed, the novel's tripartite structure mirrors the structure of its inspiration, the Matthias Grünewald triptych for the altar at Isenheim. At its center is a first-person narrative, preceded by an initial account of Holy Week from the point of view of the unenlightened characters and followed by a final account of the same week through the eyes of the more enlightened ones. The novel also performs as midrash on the Christian credal statement, "I believe in the resurrection of the body."

Easter carries a strong sense of the allegorical. Its central character, Blair Ashley, a gay and HIV-positive curate at St. Mary's in the Vale, serves as a contemporary Christ figure. Christlike, Blair washes the feet of a tramp in a cemetery that doubles as the garden of Gethsemane. He drives the money lenders out of the temple when he disrupts the Queen's distribution of Maundy money. He shares a prison cell with Barry, a name that could be a diminutive of Barabbas, and his subsequent crucifixion by the press and church authorities sends him on a spiritual journey that culminates in his own rebirth in the faith. There are further elements of allegory in the novel: the Queen is an amalgam of Pontius Pilate and Herod, Blair is betrayed by a spotty adolescent Judas figure, and, when the archdeacon of Highgate is abandoned in a mock crucifixion sex scene, his mother helps him down in a manner that lampoons the Pietà.

The novel is carried forward through a series of sentences laid out like the rubric for a church service, supplying bare bones that the reader must animate and a liturgy the reader must celebrate, so that the liturgical observance of Holy Week and Easter also gives shape to the novel's structure. The novel is primarily satirical, yet the object of the satire is in question; for some, it is simply the church's tangle about bodies and sex, while, for others, the satire polarizes liberal and fundamentalist attitudes to this tangle. Arditti himself thought he was satirizing fundamentalism as personified in the novel's bishop, but some reviewers have felt that the target is liberalism personified in the vicar with his hand-wringing response to his curate's homosexuality.

There are three preachers and nine sermons in *Easter*—the bishop, amusingly called Ted Bishop, preaches twice; the vicar, Huxley Grieve, preaches five times; and the curate, Blair Ashley, also preaches twice, all in the course of *Easter*'s Holy Week. The vicar's five are a short sermon at the donkey procession on Palm Sunday, an address given at Daisy and Joe's wedding, the sermon at Julian's funeral, and sermons given at the Maundy Thursday foot washing and Good Friday's celebration of the Lord's passion. The bishop preaches at a healing service on the Monday of Holy Week and again on the morning of Maundy Thursday when he addresses the clergy of the diocese at a Eucharist with the blessing of oils. The curate's two sermons are given in the side chapel at Alice and Dee's lesbian wedding and outside the burnt-out church on Easter Day. Arditti reports most of these sermons in full, and they constitute a significant proportion of the book, but, because of the triptych form of the novel, they do not appear in the text chronologically. For instance, Arditti reverses the order of the bishop's sermons and places them far apart, with the earlier sermon preached on Holy Monday coming almost two hundred pages after the later sermon supposedly preached on Maundy Thursday.

A close reading of these sermons will show that the bishop's sermons represent the redundancy of this kind of preaching, which is no longer able to fund the contemporary Christian imagination, whereas those of the curate (and to a lesser extent those of the vicar) show how preaching has the potential to continue to be a resource for innovative and enriching theological thinking.

Both of the bishop's sermons are parodies of the sort of preaching Joyce portrayed in Arnall's sermon, unashamedly, anachronistically, and offensively using the lexis—or linguistic repertoire—of conflict and crusade as he announces war on liberalism. The effect of Arditti's reversal and separation of the two sermons is that the reader reads first the sermon intended for the wider audience that comprises all the clergy of the diocese. It is a sermon that introduces the new bishop and announces his perceived task. The lexis and the intertexts of both sermons underpin their satirical intention. Before the Maundy Thursday service begins, the bishop expresses the view that he has a strong sense of the sports hall changing room whenever he comes to the dean's vestry at St. Paul's Cathedral. Walking into the pulpit is, for him, like walking into the boxing ring. In the foregrounded rubric of the novel, Arditti's choice of verb to describe the bishop's entry into the pulpit—"mounts" (37)—reminds the reader of a jouster facing a valiant fight astride a charger. The Maundy Thursday service of the blessing of the oils in St. Paul's Cathedral is Ted Bishop's opportunity to address the clergy of his new diocese. Using the lexis of business management, which he himself uses when he addresses his diocesan "team," Ted Bishop sees himself as a senior executive, the highest-ranking of all the fictional preachers in this book. Before he preaches he prays that God's "written word may be [their] rule" (78). The clergy of the diocese expect that the newly appointed bishop will bring a new era of reconciliation and hope, but Ted Bishop feels himself called to purge the diocese of "pernicious liberalism." Readers wonder whether he is as misguided in this sense of call as he is in his belief that his closeted lesbian wife, keen to break free from his oppressive grasp, is his "dear lady wife." The sermon is an episcopal rallying cry in which he exhorts "ministers of the Lord" to raise the Holy Bible as a "sword and shield" above their congregations (80). He knows that for liberals this will be an embarrassment, for they regard the Bible as "just another volume in their library." At the conclusion of the sermon, his cry of "Hallelujah" is returned like a mating call, and, as the bishop holds up a Bible, he declares, "This is the witness of God. Amen."

Later in the novel, Ted's sermon at a healing service on Holy Monday begins in conventional style with the quotation of a text, Matthew

11:4-5, in which Jesus instructs his followers to report the healing miracles they have witnessed. The sermon, after an opening declaration that the Bible is the Word of God (267), quickly becomes an attack on humanists, atheists, and liberals, some of whom are characterized as people who read the Gospels "like a modern novel where nothing can be taken on trust":

> These atheists—humanists is too mild a name—are doubly culpable. They don't just deny Jesus; they deny Satan. They trot out their cocktail-stick arguments: the Devil is as mythical as the Loch Ness Monster; Christ's temptations were hallucinations (after forty days without food or drink in that heat, He was bound to start seeing things). And they laugh as though they've said something witty. They'll be laughing on the other side of their faces soon enough. And the rot reaches to the heart of the Church . . . (267)

Then the bishop implicitly denies any need to interpret the Bible for the modern age when he criticizes those he brands "liberals" for watering it down by translating it into modern parallels. Jesus' invitation for children to come to him has become like Lord Shaftesbury saving them from the mines, and Jesus casting demons from a young girl has become like Freud putting her on a couch. Thereafter Ted is careless, even liberal, in his use of the Bible, in that he makes leaps of interpretation without either acknowledging or making plain his hermeneutic. He asks who is more powerful, God or the devil, and asks why God created the devil. He answers his own question by referring to the legend of the fall of Lucifer, who was created as God's good creature, an answer he embellishes with the misogyny he seems unable to resist, for he says Lucifer had no woman to blame for egging him on (268). The bishop seems to be unaware that he owes more to Milton than to Scripture for the legend of Lucifer. The two biblical texts on which the legend of the fall of Lucifer developed are imprecise. The first is from a powerful taunt in Isaiah 14:12, written in the form of a lament on the death of an unspecified world leader, whose identity must remain a mystery, for there are no criteria within the poem by which it can be dated. The only clues are its eventual biblical context where it seems to apply to the king of Babylon. The taunt, "How you are fallen from heaven, Shining Star, son of the Dawn!" was taken up in Jewish tradition, and its application to Satan was strong enough to inform one of the seven visions of St. John the Divine in Revelation 12:7-9 where the seer imagines a battle in heaven in which the victors, Michael and his angels, throw down the serpentine dragon who had led the whole world astray. Both Protestant and Catholic New Testament scholars in their commentary on Luke's Gospel note that these texts are echoed when Jesus, in commissioning his disciples with the power to exorcise demons, says, "I watched Satan fall from heaven like a flash of lightning" (10:18). What seems to have happened is that two New Testament writers, independently of each other, but both writing within the tradition of Jewish legend, appropriated an unspecified political taunt, decontextualized it, and gave it mythological significance. Furthermore, in the 220s CE, Origen of Alexandria in book 4.22 of *De principiis*, arguing that the text has no "corporeal" interpretation by which it can refer literally to Nebuchadnezzar, sought a spiritual meaning. By twisting Isaiah 14:12, he established the Christian association of the Shining Star, or Lucifer, with Satan.[5] John Milton developed this in *Paradise Lost*, a text that British Protestantism has easily conflated with the Bible to such an extent that, although there is some biblical warrant for the legend for the fall of Lucifer, it could be argued that for many Anglicans, such as those in Ted Bishop's congregation, understanding of the legend is filtered through Milton and its authority is literary rather than scriptural. In failing to acknowledge the minority status of the biblical tradition of the fall of Lucifer, the bishop, who had earlier held a Bible aloft as "Word of God" above all other texts, becomes duplicitous in his speech and actions. Arditti's satire of the bishop is that he is a self-confessed biblicist who unwittingly blurs the margins of the Bible, failing to make specific the authorship of the authorities he uses.

In direct contrast with Ted Bishop stands the troubled curate Blair Ashley, and between them on the spectrum is the vicar Huxley Grieve. The five sermons Huxley preaches develop the novel's exploration of intimacy and embodiment as midrash on "I believe in the resurrection of the body." Huxley preaches his first sermon in unfavorable conditions—during a Palm Sunday procession on the way to church in the middle of a traffic roundabout. The author has already told readers that the vicar approaches services more like a choreographer than a priest (3), and one of the parishioners, Thea, has already observed that he is dressed in red like a circus ringmaster. Given that the distractions of the setting for this sermon include a squawking parrot and a braying donkey as well as honking cars, this is an appropriate comparison. The setting contrasts markedly with the desire to create sacred space, to preserve one's own space, and to establish conditions suitable for a holy and reflective pilgrimage. The main intertext for this sermon is the risen Christ's words to Mary in the garden, "*Noli me tangere*" (John 20:17). The church has cynically taken this specific instruction to Mary to mean that no one must be touched to the extent that, as Arditti himself remarked in an interview, that "the *noli me tangere* side of the church has become too dominant."[6] The Palm Sunday sermon introduces this theme through Huxley's attempts to encourage his congregation to move closer so they can hear, in contrast with the tendency of the church—although ecclesiologically described as the body of Christ—to keep space around its members. Bodies within the Body tend to keep their distance.

Huxley's sermon at Daisy and Joe's wedding on Holy Tuesday shows an attempt to encourage the congregation to tolerate alternative forms of human relationships. Huxley preaches on what *The Book of Common Prayer* calls "the matrimonial causes" in a manner intended to challenge society's conventional understanding of marriage, as readers will later learn that this marriage is a front to cover the blessing of a lesbian relationship. Arditti communicates much of the humor in the situation, a comedy of manners, through schema breaking and contextual performance frames, many of which are noticed by the disapproving groom's mother, Maureen. For instance, half the women guests are in jeans, and little care has been taken with the bride's hair and makeup. The Maori choral music reminds Daisy of her New Zealand home, but it strikes Maureen as odd, and when she chats with another guest about the choice of music, the timing of the wedding breakfast, and an unorthodox choice of date for the wedding, her husband, conscious of appropriate behavior at weddings, tells her to stop talking. This ironically reveals her inappropriate behavior. Her perceptions of what is right and proper are the schemata of wedding conventions—dress, cameras, a long-winded vicar, and churchly decorum—yet there is much in this section of the book that breaks readers' expectations of wedding protocol. At the beginning of the sermon, for instance, Huxley declares his intention not to take up too much of the congregation's time. He tries not to be the long-winded vicar. All around him are incongruities that variously disturb or amuse the reader. These include the guest breast-feeding her baby, the female groom's sponsor, the women in jeans, the lack of a honeymoon, the attempt by Daisy and Joe to keep the event as low key as possible, and the cuckolded Huxley's frequent, and unwittingly ironic, references in his sermon to his own long and happy marriage about which he feels fortunate and not in the least complacent. Even so, the established church, personified in the vicar of the parish with all the authority he enjoys, here acknowledges the validity of physical intimacy in relationships other than conventional heterosexual marriage. Toward the end of his sermon he says,

> Those of us (and I speak for myself), who know the blessing of a happy marriage, know that it is indeed a miracle. But that doesn't give us the right to disparage those who either cannot or have no wish to share our ideal. . . . We also know people who have loving relationships outside marriage. . . . We must reach out to those in other relationships just as the Church reaches out to those in other faiths, no longer trying to convert them but rather to discover our common ground. (61)

Thus, the sermon becomes a site of conflict not only in terms of the fictional parish politics but also in terms of contextualizing theology in the twenty-first century. In its acceptance of loving relationships outside marriage, it expresses an emergent worldview that challenges and supersedes residual expressions of the world order. It jars with the conventions expressed in the wedding service of *The Book of Common Prayer* and, in places, sounds dissonant.

Huxley's funeral sermon, a protest against premature death, shows a priest troubled by experience and verbalizing the perhaps unspoken doubts, questions, and fears of his congregation. Only the "not-so-dumb" parrot Stevenson, always brought to church by its owner Edith, squawks the question "why?" (69). The sermon begins conventionally enough—"We are gathered together to bury the body of Julian Blaikie and to commit his soul to God" (67)—but very soon the vicar must explain a break in convention because, while in the hospital, the deceased had requested that there be no eulogy at his funeral. Instead, the vicar's sermon aims to see Julian's death "within the broader context . . . [of] Holy Week" (68), and he argues that the value of a life bears no relation to the length of it. The sermon also expresses a theology of resurrection that evangelicals like the bishop would describe as reductionist: Huxley speaks of Jesus' disciples keeping his memory alive. This, however, in the context of the novel is to be seen as more than afterlife defined as merely the retention of happy memories of a deceased member of one's family. Rather, it is that the church, as the body of Christ, perpetuates the life of Christ. It remembers and re-members, holding together the members of Christ's body. The sermon describes resurrection as each believer having Christ in his or her heart: the church is an anamnestic or nonforgetting community that keeps the memory alive. Huxley's actions speak as loudly as his words as, in reaching out to touch the coffin during the funeral liturgy, he makes a further contribution to the novel's theme of embodiment.

The vicar's Maundy Thursday sermon, as on Palm Sunday, invites the members of the congregation to move closer, this time to remove their shoes and socks for the ritual foot washing and this time with some success. Even the journalists who are present to pick up news about the scandal of the curate's arrest respond to Huxley's gentle persistence and remove their shoes and socks. When Huxley bathes his wife's feet, Jessica feels that she does not want to share this man with anyone, "all the boundaries of her flesh dissolve . . . [and] such rapture is enough to restore her faith in God" (103). As far as Arditti's readership is concerned, this sermon marks the beginning of our awareness of Huxley Grieve's move away from the conventions of the Anglican Communion, for now his tension over the political and sexual behavior of his curate finds public expression in his preaching as he promises his love, support, and prayers for Blair Ashley as a man and a priest. Here the vicar is most closely aware of his priestly role, for he consciously "choose[s] to put on the apron of Christ in the Upper Room" and speaks of there being no division between the private man and the public persona but a vocation "truly [to] live our liturgy" (102). Huxley describes with unashamed erotic intimacy Jesus' readiness to "expose himself to another man's touch" (100) and his acceptance of Mary's devotion as she wiped his feet with her hair. He contrasts Jesus' lack of fear of male and female intimacy with the congregants' terror of intimate human contact. Huxley implies in his reference to swapping the pulpit for the hustings that this is a political point, inasmuch as Jesus' life was as political as Karl Marx's, Che Guevara's, or Margaret Thatcher's in his "lifelong challenge to our compromised humanity" (101). He knows he treads dangerous ground, but he will not be muzzled, and he warns that we should beware of "ideologues bearing Bibles" because what Jesus inaugurated was not the imposition of a tradition but a new commandment and a new world order in which we no longer define ourselves by difference but by points of contact. This strengthens the Christian congregation's sense of communality. The sermon also expresses a contrast between safe space and dangerous ground, as the sanctuary contrasts sharply with both Hampstead Heath and the exposure and wilderness of the cemetery where Blair prays alone.

In his final sermon of the week on Good Friday, using an image that asserts that the pulpit is an exposed place where preachers parade personal faith publicly, Huxley describes himself as naked before his parishioners, a clerical scarecrow stripped of all unnecessary baggage like the church stripped for Good Friday. Until now, he has been what he calls "a spiritual conduit" mouthing the words of others. In this sermon that aims to encourage mutual empathy and involvement, Huxley reflects on what he has experienced in Holy Week and acknowledges that he has faced questions of integrity. In the novel's final account of Palm Sunday in part 3, Huxley takes comfort from the thought that if a "white man can black up to play Othello," (though, in contemporary theater, there is a troubling inauthenticity about such productions) "then a sceptic can present the man of God" (246). When the Easter Vigil descends into an unholy fight, it becomes apparent that Huxley's Good Friday sermon is capable of being misunderstood as "denying [God's] very existence" (143). Of course, unlike Carel Fisher's atheistic sermon in Murdoch's *The Time of the Angels*, this is not what it does. Rather, it questions the claims made for the passion and resurrection of Christ. Huxley declares, "In the two thousand years since Christ died, I find no confirmation that His death altered anything. There's not a single sign that the world is either a better or happier place," and he repeatedly asks, "Is this a world transformed by the Resurrection?" (109). These are Huxley's blunt and honest reflections on his role as priest in which there has to be some connection between the office and the man (108); it shows that in the space of less than a week he has travelled a long way on his spiritual pilgrimage, from mouthing the words of others to finding his own voice and faith. The sermon expresses his shame that he uses the phrase "if I'm honest" (109), because it implies he has been dishonest in other sermons; in the sermon he looks for evidence of a world changed by Christ's involvement in it. In the course of this sermon, preached soon after Huxley learns of the scandalous events of the previous day and crying out from the gloom of Good Friday and the cheerlessness of a church whose altar is stripped and whose statuary is veiled, readers see Huxley dying to the mask of faithfulness, which in fact hides the crisis of skeptical faith, and rising to a realized faith that is honest enough to enable faithful living in troubled times.

The Christ figure at the heart of the novel, whose political and sexual behavior brings to a head the vicar's crisis of faith, is Blair Ashley, the curate. He preaches the two remaining sermons of the novel. One is preached on Holy Wednesday at the lesbian union of Dee and Alice, and the other is the sermon at the parish's Easter Eucharist. These make clear what other sermons in the book have merely hinted, that the church needs to find new ways of expressing its creed and create theology for the present age. Evidence of the need for change rests, in Huxley Grieve's case, because the preacher has been wrestling with expressing the Christian faith, and in the bishop's case, because the sermon has been, at best, conservative or, at worst, anachronistic. Although three days and four other sermons separate them, the emphasis resulting from bringing Blair Ashley's two sermons together as the last in the novel, allows the reader to sense their importance.

Both of Blair Ashley's sermons are preached on the margins of the church. Alice and Dee's lesbian union takes place behind locked doors in the side chapel, in a setting Blair describes as "integral yet independent." Arditti himself sees this as an image of gay culture, in that it is at the side, yet part, of the main body of the church. In his preaching at Alice and Dee's blessing, Blair is conscious that he sets himself up against the powers that be and, in particular, against the bishop who has already asked him to keep silence. However, he diminishes his own rebellious preacherly status when he describes all the people present as prophets, by which he means "poet[s] . . . who put the future into words" (283). Nevertheless, he is also conscious of God's approval and says that he is convinced that God is smiling over the ceremony. Taking up a phrase Huxley had employed in one of his sermons, Blair sees the blessing of this lesbian union as "living [a] liturgy," living with faithful integrity. Arguing partly through negatives, such as "the only sexual practice Christ condemns is divorce," he also justifies the event by alluding to "pioneering scholars [who] have shown that, although the Blessings of recent centuries have been exclusively heterosexual, the first thousand years of the Church's existence saw same-sex couples recognized in their own rites.... So ... we're historians, restoring to the future a sense of the past" (283). Similarly, the Easter Day sermon is preached on the margins, this time outside the church as the premises have been damaged by fire. This sermon has an intentionally Wesleyan motif. When the curate climbs on a tomb to deliver it, he follows the pattern of a more famous preacher, John Wesley, who in 1742 climbed onto his father's tomb to preach after he had been denied permission to preach in the church at Epworth. Blair encourages his hearers to think of themselves as "brands plucked from the burning" (376), a biblical phrase that Susanna Wesley also used to describe her son, John, after he had been rescued from a house fire as a child. Associating Blair with Wesley in these ways, Arditti indicates either that Blair has now discovered an evangelical zeal, in contrast with his earlier pulpit inhibitions, or that he no longer feels a need to dress up what he says in a form which will please traditionalists. It also emphasizes that Blair has moved outside the boundaries of the church to meet people where his words can be heard.

In both sermons, Blair appeals to tradition. In the first, he refers frequently to the liturgy of *The Book of Common Prayer,* the origins of the Church of England, the biblical stories of Ruth and Naomi and David and Jonathan, and the same-sex rites of the first thousand years of Christianity. He also points out that some histories have been suppressed and bemoans the fact that gay men and women have been forced to dress their ceremonies in other people's ill-fitting cast-offs: "Pages have been ripped out of prayer-books and history books alike" (283). Similarly, in the Easter sermon when Blair complains about the Church's preoccupation with sin and suggests that Christians should give up their obsession with the doctrine of original sin, he employs a provocative pun: "If we are to take a leaf out of Genesis, then let it be that one on which 'God saw everything that he had made, and behold it was very good'" (376). Thus, Arditti reminds us that Blair, like the other preachers in *Easter*, uses the Bible selectively. When the curate hints that he would like to remove the pages that tell of the fall, the inference is that he also wants to retain, indeed foreground, other pages. All preachers take leaves out of the Bible, in both senses of the punning phrase, and the important question to consider is whether they take a leaf out in order to dispose of it or to learn its lesson.

Full appreciation of this final sermon in *Easter* requires an answer to another question: For whom was this sermon written or preached? Blair's Easter sermon audience comprises the parishioners who are owed an explanation for Blair's actions:

> I know that I have offended many of you and the deferential side of me . . . says that I should ask your forgiveness. That way, I could bask in the warmth of your magnanimity and you in the joy of my gratitude. We could all consider ourselves good people. But it would be a mistake—or, at any rate, too easy. What I ask instead is your acceptance: of me with all my failings . . . of me in all my humanity. (375)

He encourages the parishioners to think of themselves as "brands plucked out of the fire" figuratively, although one young man had been literally rescued. Moreover, Blair encourages them to see this theologically or spiritually, also: "There's no stronger Easter message than that life triumphs over death" (376). Nor is there is any stronger message in *Easter*: life triumphs over the moribund and stultifying homophobic conservatism of the bishop's form of Christianity. The congregation is asked to recognize the essentially incarnational theology proclaimed by—and realized in—the experiences of this preacher:

> We must stop tormenting ourselves with our faults and see that humanity—even the messy bits—is a thing to honour not to revile. After all, the Word became flesh, not light or music or even bread or wine (at least not at first). . . .
>
> The truth is that Christ became incarnate not in order to redeem a sinful people who had cut themselves off from salvation but to reassure a suffering people of their unity with God. Or, to put it another way, the

> world was not in a state of sin waiting for Christ to rescue it; the world is in a state of grace, waiting for us to recognize it. (377)

The sermon also preaches to Arditti's readers who, in the final words of the novel, are dismissed with the familiar liturgical words, "Go in peace to love and serve the Lord in the name of Christ. Amen" (391). They are likely to read Blair's sermon as an honest re-expression of Christian belief that, as congregations are reminded whenever a bishop is installed in his or her diocese or an incumbent is inducted into his or her parish, "the Church is called upon to proclaim afresh in each generation." The theology of this sermon is what the novel's narrative has illustrated, that is, the presence of God in the messiness of life, the love of God in human relationships, and the contra-Augustinian "original blessing" of humanity.[7] This sermon on Resurrection Day expresses in fictional form Arditti's view, given in a *New Statesman* interview and echoing the words of an American controversialist John Spong, that the church must change by constructing an alternative theology or it must die.[8] It stands as a useful summation of the novel's implied theology, themes, and ecclesiastical critique and serves as a positive antidote to the book's satire.

Arditti's masterly use of sermons, both as a tool for the satire of his novel and as counterpoint to that satire, both to express false theology and to describe truth, both to carry the narrative and to comment on the action, ably demonstrates that we have not yet heard the last of sermons in fiction. The long tradition of literary sermons almost from the beginning of the publication of literature in English through to the middle years of the twentieth century has not been halted; it is not even in its death throes. It is, like actual preaching in churches, in a transitional stage. Literary sermons continue to serve satirical purpose, but they are also being employed by novelists to show the ability of theological thought to re-express itself, to align itself afresh to contemporary culture and to continue to be vibrant, meaningful, and resourceful. In short, literary sermons still contribute to the making of the Christian imagination. That is not to say, however, that their presence in fiction is without problem or danger. Sermons in fiction are not always comfortable in their surroundings; they tend to make discordant noises. One aspect of this dissonance is the conflict between different types of authority, and the next chapter will look more closely at the nature of authority in preaching and in fiction as well as the tension that arises when they are brought together on the page.

3

Amen
The Assumption of Authority

No one has more authority over a text than its author, until the publisher's editors make their marks. From then on the author lets it go. Once the text is published, the author's authority over the text has diminished to the extent that it is no greater than that of its readers and its critics. Readers can read it in any way they choose. Similarly, preachers compose and write their sermons with an author's authority over their text. Then, in the pulpit, they let them go, and, try as they might, they cannot control how their words are heard. The hearer is as entitled as the preacher to say what the sermon was about.

One conventional way preachers claim their texts is to end sermons with "amen." Liturgically, "amen" is a people-binding utterance,[1] by which, as bishop Cyril of Jerusalem said circa 350 CE, Christian congregations make a public act of prayer their own by sealing it with an amen. It functions as an audible indication of a congregation's response by which its members give assent to assertions or associate themselves with sentiments expressed within the liturgy. In the culture of some congregations, those who listen to sermons encourage preachers and express their accord with what is being said with murmurs or acclamations of amen during the sermon. Thus, authority is recognized in, or ascribed to, the preaching. But when preachers themselves say amen at the close of their preaching, two problems are introduced. First, this effectively transposes the term from its original liturgical usage to little more than an audible punctuation mark to indicate that the sermon is over, and, second, they are claiming authority for their own sermon, implying the absence of divine involvement in the creative process, even if they say amen with quizzical intonation as if inviting an affirming response from the congregation that these words have either divine origin or divine orientation.

Both the preacher's amen at the end of the sermon and the congregation's interposed amens are expressions of an assumed authority of the pulpit which originates in Christianity's foundation documents. The author of Matthew's Gospel, for instance, concludes the Sermon on the Mount by describing the crowd's astonishment at the authority of Jesus' teaching, which set him apart him from other teachers of the day. From this point forward in the Gospel, distinguishable from the other canonical Gospels by its presentation of Jesus as the new Moses, authority becomes a recurring theme. As a new lawgiver with new teaching, Jesus has authority to forgive sins, to heal disease, and to exorcise demons. Ultimately, Jesus claims that all authority in heaven and earth has been given to him. Many other New Testament books continue this concern for authority. For instance, when Paul uses his pastoral letters to Timothy and Titus to encourage them in their discipleship, he appeals to his own authority as an apostle of Christ, and, once he has reminded them of the themes of their teaching and preaching, he urges them to "argue them with an authority which no one can disregard." In line with Paul's general exhortation to Christ's followers to let the same mind be in you that was in Christ Jesus, it has been assumed ever since that Christian teachers are to teach as Christ taught and that Christian preachers are to preach authoritatively as Christ preached.[2]

The trouble with this in the twenty-first century is that people are suspicious of authority. Already evident in the postmodernism of the late twentieth century, distrust of authority came to a head in the catastrophic events of the attacks on the World Trade Center in New York and the Pentagon in Washington by religious fundamentalists whose fanaticism was bolstered by perverse readings of the Qur'ān. When, on September 11, 2001, terrorists, some reciting, others carrying, proof texts from the Qur'ān, targeted their peopled weapons at buildings representative of Western culture, this, thereafter, destabilized discussion of religious authority and authoritative texts. Now, "9/11" stands as an appalling symbol of conflict between religion and culture, where religions are regarded as absolutist claims on truth and culture is seen as an artificial interpretation of human experience and environment constantly in a state of flux. Such an impasse need not be so. The tendency toward fundamentalism in religion, the developing political aspirations of faith groups, and the increasing impatience with democracy as a means of attaining political change make discussion of authority in religion, literature, and society difficult, yet even more essential, if the bind twenty-first century religion is in is ever to be broken.

Literature remains capable of being an instrument of rescue from the clash of truth claims and the religious conflict of the present age, and this chapter will show that sermons—whose absolutist claims are compromised by their inclusion in novels, whose authority is different—play a part in retrieving truth from these clashing truth claims. The twenty-first century has seen a rapid rise in the sales and use of e-books to the extent that any claim that the West is a book culture is now dubious. This is fortunate for Christianity for, unlike most other world religions, it is not a religion of the book. It is less book centered than on first impression; its official doctrines allow for other authorities such as tradition, reason, and experience to interplay with Scripture in the formation of the Christian faith. Even so, the "dynastic relationship" of author and book is so strong that there is a close connection between the concept of authorship and Western economic principles of private ownership.[3] Books stamped "©" bear the mark of their creators; authorship implies ownership as well as a claim of authority. The author's interest in the book is literary, intellectual, and, in some cases, monetary. But a distinction can be made between books of which there are many authors and readers and the Book of which God is not just any author, but the Author of authors who is behind and within the Book of books.[4] Over and beyond its human authors is the divine author.

If preachers are authors and if sermons have a similar literary status to that which books have (and they do, whether or not they are ever printed or published), this understanding of authorship by extension means that all preachers defer to God, the divine Author, and all their preaching turns back to God's Book, Word, and Activity.[5] Discussion of religious authority in fictional sermons therefore orbits a family of words including "author," "authorship," "authorize," "authority," and "authenticity," each of which might be used in some way to refer to divine creativity and inspiration. The validity of the discussion does not depend on firmly establishing relationships within this family of words. Loose etymological relationships will suffice in that, in the case of sacred and religious texts, the authenticity of a text is often understood as undisputed authorship, the authorship of a text often permits some degree of authority over or through it, and an authoritative text may often become an authorized text. The scope of authority and authenticity is related to authorization and authorship, and what is said of books in this regard may also be said of the spoken words of religious leaders in their sermons.

That preachers derive their textual authority primarily from the Bible, their basic foundational text, and that the directional flow in the act of creating a sermon is "from text to sermon"[6] can be demonstrated by referring to a recent survey of the practice and theory of most currently published American homileticians that identified nine styles of preaching.[7] For each style, the survey gave two examples, each headed by a biblical passage, with some of the sermons actually beginning by quoting a biblical text. The inference to be drawn is clear. Even those styles called "imaginative," "narrative," "pastoral," and "topical" are preached *from* the Bible in that at least one of the aims of the sermons is to relate the cited Bible passage to the hearers' life experiences. They are all biblical preaching inasmuch as the creative dynamic of the sermons is from the biblical textworld via the text of the sermon to the audience textworld. The inferable assumption is that the Bible passages merit interpretation so that they can be successfully, helpfully, and appropriately applied to the present age; these preachers regard the biblical passages from which they preach as their authoritative texts. Despite the diversity of approaches to the homiletic task, homiletics teachers at the beginning of the twenty-first century are almost univocal in their assumption that the primary role of the Christian preacher is to interpret the Bible so as to appropriate its insights for Christians faced with the complexities of modern living. The preacher begins in the world of the Bible with the presumption that the gap of at least nineteen centuries requires bridging and, so, uses a range of hermeneutical tools to apply these ancient but authoritative texts to the contemporary world.

The authors and readers of fictional sermons are highly unlikely to start from the same premise of "from text to sermon," for, aside from a recent renewed interest in the retelling of Bible stories in biblical fictions,[8] the interpretation of the Bible will rarely be the primary concern of novels. However, no appraisal of fictional preaching would be complete without hearing the dissonance of clashing authorities resulting from the way the avowedly attitudinal and confessional rhetoric of the embedded sermon conflicts with the less opinionated, or less didactic and doctrinaire, fiction that embraces it. Does the preaching become a dead quotation? And, if not, in what way does it continue to be authoritative? The search for answers to these questions begins with an assessment of how novelists and their preachers employ the Bible in the creation of their fictional sermons. Because readers can see authoritative preaching most clearly in historical novels where the preaching of religious leaders is distanced from the complicating factors of twenty-first century competition between religious metanarratives, a focus on two historical novels featuring fictional preachers, based on real-life characters who enjoyed quite different kinds of authority in their time, will foreground the conflicting authorities present when sermons feature in novels. But, because questions about the authority of preaching are also raised in novels set in contemporary times, the sermons in some of John Updike's novels will also be discussed.

The first analysis in the study is Geraldine Brooks' *Year of Wonders*, which offers a minority reading of the history of England's Great Plague in that it tells its story from a peculiarly particular perspective. More generally, the Australian-born author uses her novel to study the interfaces between religion and superstition and among religion, disease, and health. It tells of the plague's effect on the Derbyshire town of Eyam, whose rector William Mompesson is credited with saving neighboring towns from the plague by placing a strict quarantine on Eyam throughout 1665. Incidentally, the town's story also intrigued Arditti in his first novel, largely, as he has said in an interview, because he saw the plague as a useful parallel with AIDS.[9] Not to sully William Mompesson's postmortem reputation, Brooks renames the real-life rector Michael Mompellion in the novel. The credit for saving the neighborhood belongs to the fictional rector and several wise women, chief of whom is the novel's narrator Anna Frith. She is the only woman in Eyam, apart from the rector's wife, who knows the truth of Mompellion's marriage and is perhaps the only woman in Eyam who knows him as a sexual predator. Except for a prologue and two concluding sections, one of which shares its title with the prologue, the novel is a straightforward narrative of the plague town. There are six sermons in the novel, although only one is reported at length. They are the announcement of the closure of the church and the full occupancy of the churchyard (168–70), a sermon in the Delf where the rector likens their situation to both Golgotha and Gethsemane (217), a sermon at John Gordon's funeral, at which point the narrator remarks that the rector is finding it increasingly difficult to raise his spirits sufficiently to continue composing encouraging sermons (227), the instruction to burn all clothes that Mompellion believes is a direct instruction from God (239), a two-line summary of a sermon on enduring life (254), and the sermon reported at greatest length. This comes at the novel's turning point, the event of salvific significance for neighboring parishes. In Mompellion's sermon, he persuades the people of Eyam to set a clear frontier of demarcation around their town (99–107). While Pepys in London was writing in his diary that the plague made us "as cruel as dogs one to another," the people of Eyam were persuaded to self-sacrifice by the suasory powers of Mompellion's rhetoric before he descended from the pulpit and moved among his people like Jesus in Galilee.

The facts that this is fictionalized history and that the preacher is based on an historical figure mean that there is potentially an actual anterior speech position to this fictive sermon, an actual sermon on which Brooks could have based this fictional one. In fact, none of Mompesson's sermons is extant, although two letters, one to his patron when Catherine Mompesson died and the other to his children on their mother's death, are still available to visitors to the Eyam parish church. Brooks, however, consulted seventeenth-century medical texts, books on herbal remedies and midwifery, the journal of a country rector, and numerous sermons of the period for a sense of the linguistic style, theological assumptions, and culture of the period.[10] In the case of the second historical novel discussed in this chapter, Jane Rogers' *Mr Wroe's Virgins*, copies of John Wroe's sermons are still available.[11] These were published as a guide to the "people surnamed Israelite" for their own subsequent preaching. They reveal the real-life

Prophet Wroe as a millenarianist with a preoccupation with the work of Satan, as, for instance, in his sermon on the story of Esther in which he casts Haman as Satan.[12] Set in nineteenth-century England, this novel concerns the founder of a sect known as the Christian Israelites, now debased into a group with racist and fascist tendencies known as British Israelism, claiming two million followers in Britain and the USA. In response to Wroe's request that his congregation provide him with seven virgins by whom God wanted to comfort him, his congregation gave him seven of its daughters who spent nine months in community with him until accusations of indecency and the ensuing trial brought the household to its end. In clearly titled sections, four of these women—Joanna who is most sincerely sympathetic to Wroe, the skeptical Hannah, the besotted Leah, and the particularly vulnerable Martha—narrate these months. Apart from Joanna's brief report of a sermon in response to which people rushed into the river for baptism (25) and her comment that Wroe preached by day and received communication from the Lord by night (57), the skeptical Hannah reports most of the preaching in the novel, as a result of which we read about Wroe's preaching with a strong hermeneutic of suspicion. Although she knows he is a self-conscious performer, she is unable to deny the effect of authority in his preaching, whether it is attributable to God or not (211). Later, Hannah is confused when, after confiding that his ministry is fantasy and charade, Wroe says he simply has to be convincing to convince (226). The author is here raising an important question for readers to consider: Is Wroe a trickster capable of using oratorical skills to manipulate people for his own ends, or is he a wronged and misunderstood religious leader genuine in his intentions?

The sermon reported at greatest length in the novel is preached in Huddersfield marketplace (80–84). The last thing Wroe does before he begins his sermon is to wink to Hannah as an invitation for her to watch what he can do with the crowd. This knowing wink, intended to be seen only by the person to whom the gesture is directed, introduces an element of unreliability to the entire episode. Readers doubt the sincerity of his intentions. At this point he is like Geoffrey Chaucer's disreputable but oratorically gifted Pardoner who invites his listeners to look at what he can do. Nevertheless, Wroe's sole agency is questionable: Is he the only one making things happen? Are there other forces at work? There is a definite air of expectation about his preaching: Hannah has given her account of the journey to Huddersfield a brooding ominous element with her description of the blackness of the night, shooting stars, and low skies hanging over a bleak place. Handbills have announced Wroe's arrival. The reader asks what it is people have come to see—a religious meeting or a freak show? By the time Wroe lifts his arms above his head and, like Moses, lifts a rod over the people to command their attention, readers are expecting quite a performance in which Wroe will play with his audience's emotions with as much manipulative artifice as he uses to control his household.

Both Brooks and Rogers attempt to recreate the preaching styles of former times in these historical novels; indeed, it is likely that they are using these fictional sermons to assist in the cultural and historical setting of the novels. But a word of caution must be sounded; historical novelists too readily labor under a presumption of linear evolution that the historian Herbert Butterfield, writing in the years shortly before World War II, famously called "the whig [sic] interpretation of history,"[13] a complacent view of history as steady progress. When they write in this tradition, historical novelists write of simpler folk living in less complex times and jeopardize the modern reader's acceptance of what their credulous characters do. They also risk giving the impression that such persuasive oratory only works because it is addressed to simpler people who are more ready to kowtow gullibly to preachers quoting Scripture. In fact this is not so. The way Brooks and Rogers employ the Bible in their fictional preaching compares with some of the sermons in John Updike's novels, illustrating that rhetorical manipulation is not restricted to past times but is equally possible in the modern age.

Year of Wonders' Mompellion lets the Bible fall from his hands, and this is significant. Both the prologue and the first section of the epilogue share the title "Leaf-Fall 1666," suggesting that they narrate events occurring in the autumn of the first year since the passing of the plague, yet the title also draws attention to another kind of leaf fall, the dropping of the Bible. At the beginning of the novel, the rector refuses to read the Bible and expresses surprise that Anna Frith has learned to read. At the end of the prologue, Anna once more finds him alone with an unopened Bible. This time without asking his permission, she takes it from him. He takes it from her hands and lets it fall from his. These are the same leaves that fall again in the first section of the novel's epilogue and the same event retold by the narrator; in the second telling, however, letting the Bible slip from his open hand has changed and become a "flinging to the floor" (270). Readers know by now why the rector rejects his sacred text; he is exhausted, bereaved, and challenged in his faith by all that has occurred in Eyam. His strict adherence to and harsh interpretation of the Bible's teaching have guided his life and soured his marriage to the narrator's close friend Elinor.

Although the novel begins and ends with the rector's rejection of the Bible, his preaching is naturally, because of the era in which he lived, infused with biblical allusions. He quotes John 15:13 when encouraging his parishioners to acts of self-sacrifice. Brooks knew that this and the parable of the good Samaritan were probably the texts on which the real-life Mompesson relied in his successful appeal to the villagers in 1665.[14] In the sermon in *Year of Wonders*, the fictional Mompellion describes the plague as a gift like a casket of gold (102). He uses references to the pre-Exodus plagues on Egypt to counter the view that the plague is a curse expressing God's displeasure. Eyam is not like Egypt, and its leaders are not like Pharaoh. Mompellion's imagery of smelting may be an indirect allusion to Peter's teaching in 1 Peter 1:6-7 on suffering as testing for purity. Directly citing Isaiah 30:15-17, indeed repeating three times one phrase, "in quietness and trust," letting his voice descend to a hush, Mompellion adds biblical authority to his warning that loneliness and fear are all that would lie ahead for anyone who faithlessly ignores the proposed course of action (105). Within the scope of the novel, the charisma of his personality, the authority of his role as village rector, and the rhetoric of his oratory seem to be some compensation for his rejection of the Bible.

In *Mr Wroe's Virgins*, Rogers makes comparatively little use of the Bible in the sermons she creates for her preacher. This is remarkable for it is in contrast with the real-life preacher John Wroe, whose published sermons are samples showing how his followers should use the Scriptures when preaching as Christian Israelites; every paragraph makes a direct quotation of at least one proof text, and often more than one, in a manner both Christian and non-Christian readers in the modern age find repetitious, tedious, and unenlightening. Whereas it might appear that Rogers restyles Wroe's preaching to protect modern readers from biblicism or to avoid the trap of alienating them, her real motive for using fewer biblical texts is twofold: first, she wants to portray Wroe as a man of charismatic power who can sway people by the force of his personality, and, second, her real interest is not in Wroe's religion. Recurring themes in Rogers' other novels betray the focus of her interest in this one. These include mother-child relationships, especially when the relationship has been compromised or damaged, as for instance in *The Ice Is Singing*, where the first-person narrator is a mother who has abandoned her children, and in *Island*, where the protagonist is a woman seeking revenge against the mother who abandoned her as a child. Again, in Rogers' more recent novel *The Voyage Home*, the figure from the past foreshadowing the life of the main character is Anne's late father, a missionary in Nigeria in the 1960s, who had returned to England to become a priest. The impact on his faith of his sexual peccadilloes commands less interest to Rogers than the father-daughter relationship and the effect of postmortem discoveries about her father on Anne's life and her eventual realization that what matters most is honesty between parent and child. This recurring theme of child-parent relationships is to be found in *Mr Wroe's Virgins*, too; parents abandon seven children on the strength of John Wroe's request for seven virgins. He becomes a surrogate, but abusive, parent. The novel continues Rogers' interest in the mother-child relationship in that at least one virgin becomes a mother and another becomes a saintly spiritual mother. As a teacher of creative writing, Rogers is also interested in the power of stories and how they are told. This interest finds expression both in the range of stories parents tell their children in *Island*, many of them fables and folk tales concerning parents who abandon their children or, at least, put them at risk and in her employment of several voices to narrate her novels such as in *Promised Lands*, where three narratives are interwoven, and in the four points of view from which Wroe's story is told. Furthermore, there is a recurring interest in the persona of the idiot savant, including Calum in *Island* and Martha in *Mr Wroe's Virgins*. Wroe's religion provides the frame for, but not the center of the thematic interest in, Rogers' story.[15]

Despite his confession to Hannah that his ministry is a façade (225), this most skeptical of the seven virgins is unable to doubt his authority as a preacher, whether or not this can be attributed to God or some other source (211). The Huddersfield marketplace sermon contrasts with the mesmerizing yet forgettable sermons to which the community members are subjected in the sanctuary three times each Sunday. Hannah, however, remembers one of these supposedly "forgettable" sermons. Not long after the marketplace sermon, Wroe preached in the sanctuary on a text from Hosea, "The prophet is a snare to his people" (88), or in the New Revised Standard Version, "A fowler's snare is on all the prophet's ways."[16] Despite the fact that, in its biblical context, Hosea was distinguishing himself, in this self-reflexive oracle, from the ecstatic practices of the court prophets, this is a hazardous text for a self-styled prophet like Wroe to choose. Already readers suspect his intentions and doubt his integrity. Why does he exacerbate this distrust? Is it an act of bravado to preach on this text? Is Wroe playing with the ensnared like a cat playing with a mouse, taunting the virgins to attempt to escape? As there is no evidence to suggest that the real-life Prophet Wroe preached on this text, it appears that Rogers' allusion is preached over the heads of the audience in the marketplace to the novel's readers. It alerts readers to the true, entrapped status of these women and establishes Wroe's status as fowler and fouler.

Hannah, who feels shame and embarrassment and expects a riot, is one of the sermon's hearers. Drawing Hannah into the conspiracy of manipulating the audience by his knowing wink, Wroe knows he is playing a game. Hannah tells us that the language Wroe uses in this sermon is simpler than that used in the sanctuary. Although he alludes to the Revelation of St. John the Divine and the Sodom and Gomorrah narrative, this sermon quotes no Bible verses. Nevertheless there is a sense that Wroe is presenting the Word of God: he begins by saying that he has a message direct from God (83), uses the terminology "according to my prophecy," and claims to know God's order. He confidently foretells that two members of the audience will fall ill (84), and Hannah tells that for some of his hearers Wroe's power was nothing other than the power of God. The woman who interrupts the preaching to ask how she may be saved is reminiscent of the disciple who asked Jesus, "How then can we be saved?" after Jesus had said how hard it was for a camel to pass through the eye of a needle (Mark 10:25-26) and puts Wroe in Christ's place. Despite Hannah's skepticism, she shows that Wroe is bewitching and convincing, which is all he claims he needed to be in order to convince (226).

Spiritual stress becomes palpable: the living tension within Mompellion between his dependence upon the Bible in his exercise of spiritual and community leadership and his rejection of it as a result of what he experiences in the plague year, Rogers' reduction of biblical references in the preaching of the fictional Wroe in marked contrast with the actual Wroe's almost complete reliance on the Bible for the substance of his preaching, and Ted Bishop's contradictory practice in *Easter* of holding the Bible aloft as the Word of God while conflating it with other authoritative literary texts suggest that the novelists' primary concern is other than biblical interpretation. However, all assume that preaching is predicated on an urge to interpret the Bible, so they dare not entirely eschew it as a foundation for preaching. Either novelists are more interested in how a character can control others by oratory, or they include biblical references in sermons because they believe readers will expect some scriptural allusions in preaching to make it authentically representative. These are also the factors at play in John Updike's sermons in *Couples, Of the Farm*, "Lifeguard," *The Witches of Eastwick, Rabbit, Run, A Month of Sundays*, and *In the Beauty of the Lilies*, although with sometimes parodic, sometimes satirical, and other times secularizing results. The last of Updike's sermons was in *In the Beauty of the Lilies* after his character Clarence has lost his faith and turned to selling books. In his sales talk, Clarence tells us that books do for the twentieth century what the Bible was originally intended to do. He points out that his main merchandise is *The Popular Encyclopedia*, which relies on facts and is democratic, or nonrhetorical, in its alphabetical ordering of its contents, although rhetoric would have been a factor in the initial choice of what the encyclopedia contained. The book he sells is authoritative but in a way that is different from the Bible (147). That Clarence actually loses his voice is emblematic of the preacher without faith: he is actually silenced in addition to having nothing left to say. He is as much a failure as a book salesman as he was a preacher.[17]

In his earlier novels, Updike displayed a recurring fascination with preaching, and he combined the literary traditions of both straight and satirical sermons so as to reflect conflicting attitudes toward religion in America.[18] In *Rabbit, Run* Updike places a sermon summary at a turning point in the narrative, and later he recounts a funeral where, instead of a sermon, biblical quotations and formal prayers are recited. The effect of these on the congregation is life changing. The sermon is preached by the Reverend Eccles when the novel's protagonist Harry "Rabbit" Angstrom, who has resolved to turn over a new leaf, is in the congregation. The novelist's use of free indirect discourse enables him to parody sermon rhetoric with the stylized question and answer format taught in seminaries and the hermeneutical leap common in American preaching during and after the Second World War, which somewhat artificially attempts to make the biblical texts relevant. Here is Updike's report of the sermon in full.

> It concerns the forty days in the Wilderness and Christ's conversation with the Devil. Does the story have any relevance to us, here, now? In the Twentieth Century, in the United States of America. Yes. There exists a sense in which all Christians must have conversations with the devil, must learn his ways, must hear his voice. The tradition behind this legend is very ancient, was passed from mouth to mouth among the early Christians. Its larger significance, its greater meaning, Eccles takes to be this: suffering, deprivation, barrenness, hardship, lack are all an indispensable part of the education, initiation, as it were, of any of those who would follow Jesus Christ. (203)

This sermon functions in the narrative of the novel as part of the cause of Angstrom going astray from his new start: he rejects what he hears of the sermon, and he also finds himself sexually aroused by the pastor's wife. The final breakdown for Angstrom, however, comes later in the novel at the sermon-free funeral and burial. The officiant intends to comfort the grieving Angstrom by using images of shepherds and sheep as well as of children and heaven in the quotations and prayers, but their religious sentiments provoke a violent reaction in which he first publicly accuses his wife of killing the baby, then begins to comfort her before pushing her aside and running off. These Scripture passages and prayers have the effect that preaching is supposed to have; preaching can either lead to grace or judgment, and, in this instance, the quoted texts have led to judgment. Updike's use of the Bible in both the sermon and the funeral suggests not only

America's ambivalence to religion but also its ambivalence to Christianity's authoritative text, the Bible, which is a badly read best seller. At the funeral, Updike suggests the Bible's direct and unmediated power to influence his characters; in these circumstances, the Bible alone brings Angstrom to this hard place, whereas in the earlier sermon the authority of the Bible is compromised both by Updike's reference to the oral tradition by which stories of Jesus were initially preserved and by his description of the Gospel accounts of Christ's temptations at the outset of his ministry as legend. The first comment introduces an element of some human involvement in the book's authorship; the second locates the narrative in a genre where historicity is usually absent and where truth is narratival rather than theological. This narratival truth creates a sense of expressive authority.

The sermon fragment in *Couples* is much less subtle, and it is entirely satirical in purpose, effectively establishing the ineffectiveness of the church in the early pages of the novel to leave the way open for the five middle-class couples to create a substitute church out of their erotic games and an alternative liturgy out of their conversations. The preacher is the Reverend Horace Pedrick, introduced as a "skeletal ignorant man of sixty," the occasion is Palm Sunday, and the venue is Tarbox Congregational Church in Massachusetts. Seeing that his parishioners are predominantly businesspeople, Pedrick's decision to use the linguistic repertoire of the financial world results in a risible sermon with inapt imagery in which Jesus is said to ask us not to play a long shot: "He does not come to us and say, 'Here is a stock for speculation. Buy at eight-and-one-eighth, and in the Promised Land you can sell at one hundred.' No, he offers us *present security*, four-and-a-half per cent compounded every quarter!" (26). The absence of any biblical underpinning in this preaching indicates an impotent church, inefficient officers, and rituals that fail to express the spiritual and religious needs of the community, and it may account for the perceived inefficacy of the sermon within the novel.

In contrast, the Lutheran sermon in Updike's fourth novel, *Of the Farm*, as it reaches its denouement, is the novelist's serious attempt to represent an effective, appropriate sermon by a more-than-usually reliable preacher who is predicted to be a bishop by the time he is forty, as long as he keeps a roving eye in check. He is the pastor of a church in rural eastern Pennsylvania to which Joey Robinson has brought his new second wife from Manhattan. Joey's hope is that his mother, who disapproved of his divorce and remarriage, will be more accepting of his circumstances once she has met his wife. The text chosen for the sermon, "And the Lord God said, It is not good that man should be alone; I will make him an help meet for him" (Gen 2:18), is a rather too convenient coincidence, but its aptness allows Updike to offer a straight exposition of Eve's creation that tangentially comments on the three women who have influenced Joey's life, his mother and his two wives. Readers are themselves encouraged to respond to the sermon by Joey's mother's intriguing description of it as "young." In what way was this sermon that Joey called "excellent" young? She does not explain, so readers must consider their own response to an expository sermon that reads a Genesis creation myth as an explanation of God's intentions for male–female relations in the mid-twentieth century. The young pastor interprets this androcentric Adam and Eve legend to teach that women are a subspecies, lower than man in the hierarchy of God's creatures, but to whom man from his lofty position has a responsibility to be kind. This is neither "mildly sexist" nor mildly misogynist but an unacceptable assertion of the supremacy of the male gender claimed with reference to an order that the preacher finds "implicit in the nature of Creation, in the very curves and amplitude of God's fashioning" (148). It bears little relation to the reality of Joey Robinson's disordered life over which he, pulled in all directions by the women in his life, has exercised little mastery. The preacher assumes an inherent authority in the biblical text that makes it applicable to all times and places. For this preacher, interpretation of the Bible entails little more than exegesis of the text; the preacher understood Hebrew terms, and he knew the narrative, but was the resulting sermon flawed because he chose to observe and comment upon inconsequential aspects of the story such as the chronological precedence of dumb animals over Eve? Or was it flawed because in the hermeneutical process he understood only the horizon of the text and failed to account for the horizon of expectations in the context of his congregation in the novel and its readers? Despite its flaws as a twentieth-century sermon on Genesis 2:18, within the scope of the novel it is enlightening inasmuch as it helps bring some resolution to Joey's story and his troubled relationship with his mother.

The earlier short story "Lifeguard," which consists of no more than the interior monologue of a theology student as he works as a lifeguard during the summer vacation, is sermonic in form though it is essentially a parody that culminates in an exhortation both to the crowds at the seaside and to readers to enjoy their sensuality. It, however, makes little use of the Bible beyond a short paragraph in which the lifeguard excuses his voyeurism with the remark that all men are Solomons lusting for Sheba, even if, as in Samson's case, the temple falls. The falsity of the lifeguard's unspoken sermon is reminiscent of an equally perverse sermon in the better-known novel *The Witches of Eastwick*, which depicts the lives of three women in a Rhode Island town who practice witchcraft. Two sermons toward the end of the novel comment on the nature of evil. Brenda Parsley, who has taken over her husband's duties as pastor in the local Unitarian church after he ran off with a teenage girl, gives the first. The second is Darryl Van Horne's secular sermon on evil advertised under the slogan "THIS IS A TERRIBLE CREATION." At the beginning, Van Horne puts the Bible aside and replaces it on the lectern with *Webster's Collegiate Dictionary* from which he cites the definition of a centipede. The sermon that follows is a reading of natural history, "this mess of torture," as he calls it (296). The background to the sermon is that Van Horne's wife is in hospital dying of cancer. His theme, that pain is the state and condition of the universe, is provoked by her suffering and his own anguish. The text he reads from is not the Bible but the natural world. Thus he reaches conclusions that differ markedly from those of the classical Christian tradition where pain, in some theologies, is a crucible through which the sufferer journeys toward holiness. That neither of these Updike sermons is dependent upon biblical hermeneutics further supports the notion that there is more to interest novelists in the effect of sermons on their characters and their novels than there is in the interpretation of the Bible. Nonetheless, few can avoid the question of biblical authority when they touch on the influence and authority of preaching; indeed, they use the Bible to authenticate the preaching in their novels.

What picture of religious authority is created by the sermons in the contemporary fiction discussed in this chapter—the preaching of John Wroe, Michael Mompellion, Reverend Eccles, Horace Pedrick, the Lutheran pastor in *Of the Farm*, Brenda Parsley, and Darryl Van Horne?

What is the force of their concluding amens? Are there any signs that the novelists regard these sermons as in any sense God breathed? Does the presence of Bible texts within the sermons make the preaching more authoritative? How do the novelists communicate to the reader the preachers' belief that their sermons are divinely inspired?

Caution must be exercised when discussing inspiration, for it is a complex and problematic concept, problematic first because it is applied to literary texts as well as to theological texts. When poets appeal to the muses, for instance, people take this to mean something other than when theological writers and speakers claim divine intervention in their writing and speaking. When someone listening to a speech at a political rally describes it as inspired, the listener takes the comment to mean something different from the claim that Billy Graham at an evangelical rally in his heyday in the third quarter of the twentieth century was inspired. The concept is further problematized by the imprecision of the term resulting from the various models used by theorists when discussing biblical inspiration.[19] Of the various theories, the crudest is the dictation theory, which Jerome, Chrysostom, and Augustine were all capable of expressing and which was the dominant Protestant orthodoxy in the first two centuries after the Reformation; in this model it is as if the biblical writer or speaker is a human Dictaphone directly recording the words and voice of God. Instrumental theories regard the author as a passive tool in God's hands, verbal theories suggest that God creates the conditions in which writers can receive and express divine communication, and the theory of plenary inspiration is less concerned with the how of inspiration and more determined to deny any gradations of inspiration in order to argue that all Scripture is equally inspired. All these theories are fraught with questions of authority. Moreover, the lack of sufficient distinction between human skill and divine agency in inspiration theories is problematic for a secularized age such as the present one.[20] For believers, sermons may be an exception, therefore less of a problem. Hearers will often accept that a preacher's technical skill is compatible with his or her sense of being empowered in dispossession of conscious "authorliness" or authorship. Enhanced fluency can be the result of a sense of being taken over by an Author to whom the preacher defers so that human speech is transcended. But this view is often held only in particular ecclesiastical circles and remains a problem in wider society where any form of totalizing narrative is suspect.

In popular understanding, where the term inspiration has entered common parlance, there are at least three levels of inspiration: one claims that the Bible is inspired, a second that sacred texts are inspired, and a third that secular texts may be inspired. All three are present in the strata of contemporary fiction featuring preaching. Some of the novelists may claim to have been inspired as they created their art, their fictional preachers at times are self-consciously presenting themselves as both inspired and inspiring, and they cite inspired—or God-breathed—biblical texts. It is helpful to differentiate these three levels by coining the terms "InSpiration," "inspiration," and "inSpiration," where "InSpiration" indicates the higher inspiration of biblical texts, "inspiration" is the lower secular model, and "inSpiration" is the inspiration of nonbiblical sacred texts popularly, but perhaps confusingly, called "inspirational writing." In each case the claim of inspiration means something different.

Recognizing that sacred texts other than the Christian Bible can also be inspired yet wanting to claim the specialness of the Bible, it has long been widely accepted that the New Testament is not uniquely inspired but that it is both "uniquely informative" and a field where inspiration works.[21] In practice, few are the Christians who believe that the inspirational work of God came to a conclusion when the last word was put to the Bible. Many discern signs of inspiration in other Christian theological and spiritual writings both ancient and modern; for instance, many discern signs of inspiration in hymnody and preaching, again both ancient and modern. Some Christians are prepared to extend this to religious, theological, and spiritual thought outside Christianity. Often this inSpiration is taken to mean that God has in some sense and to some degree "taken over" the writer or preacher, who is both possessed and dispossessed, in that composition seems effortless, enthusiastic, and automatic.[22] This differs from the third, lower level of inspiration only in its source. Some secular writers feel inspired in that they write beyond or outside themselves—they are literally enthused or "a-mused"—and some readers are capable of recognizing inspired writing in both sacred and secular texts, often adjudged on the basis of whether or not it, in turn, inspires them.

The term "double enunciation" usually refers to the belief that a poem, say, comes from both the poet and the divine who is beyond the poet.[23] Double enunciation can be extended to elucidate other aspects of how inspiration relates to the relationship between the writer and the reader around the text. Inspiration is in the reading of texts as well as in their writing; there is an unspoken compact between reader and writer by which the reader understands how to assess and assimilate the text. This understanding, rather than any specific intrinsic feature of the text, determines whether it is inspired.[24] What matters is the reader's involvement with a text. Claims that texts are inspired initiate a complex dialectic of active and passive, objective and subjective, or causative and resultative factors that establishes a definite link between being inspired and inspiring; one cannot inspire others without being inspired oneself. Indeed, if an implied reader is present in all texts, in the case of the Bible this implied reader is an inspired reader.[25] This is a much more dynamic understanding of inspiration than any dictation or instrumental theory; it conceives a divine *ephlatus* breathing in and out between writer and reader, between speaker and hearer. If this is true of the Bible, it is difficult to see how it cannot also be true of all inspired texts, unless one ranks the Bible as an entirely unique and unparalleled text. Moreover, such a dynamic notion of inspiration seems especially appropriate for the dynamic art form of preaching, where the *aptum*, or gap between the preacher and the hearer, is where the sermon exists and meaning resides.

Here the total interiorization expressed in Derrida's notion of "*apprendre par coeur*" is helpful.[26] Texts are inspired if they are taken to heart; texts are inspired because they resonate in our being. John Calvin, in more conventional theological language, called this interaction the "internal testimony of the Holy Spirit." In the sermons discussed, both the fictional Mompellion and Wroe succeed in inspiring their hearers; Mompellion, who claims God has shown him the solution (239), inspires the villagers of Eyam to self-sacrifice for the sake of surrounding parishes by asking them to show greater love for their neighbors, and Wroe, who also claims direct communication from God, succeeds in enthralling—or, in the terminology of the text he cites from Hosea, entrapping or ensnaring—his harem of virgins. Those sermons in Updike's oeuvre that either depend on biblical texts, rely on biblical concepts, or make biblical allusions also succeed in their influence on the novels' characters so that readers tend to perceive them as authentic, whereas those that stand free of biblical referencing are seen as inadequate, inappropriate, ingenuous, or parodic.

In conclusion, these novelists intentionally use texts from the Bible, recognized as Christianity's authorized foundational document, to establish authority for their fictional sermons. But it is important to recognize that the nature of this authority is particular. Although many fictional preachers might argue that the Bible is an authoritative text—and they certainly preach as if it is—it is no longer possible to claim that this biblical authority is inherent, intrinsic, or absolute. Any authority the Bible enjoys is bestowed, or ascribed, authority in that readers give to the text the authority they recognize. It is attributed—or at least the result of an implied contract between the author, the text, and the reader—not intrinsic to the text. So when characters in novels lard their conversation with proof texts, often the citations are received by readers as non sequiturs and the speakers as buffoons, religious maniacs, or putative oppressors. The reader's involvement with the text holds paramount importance, because biblical authority is not coercive but, rather, rhetorically or expressively performed.

This is one of the qualities and strengths of biblical authority that has been described in three ways.[27] The first is epistemic authority, which is the authority of expertise, variously known as cognitive or propositional authority, present in a text when believers accept its propositions. It ranges from "how to" manuals where the explanation is thought to have been written by an expert to books of the Bible where the author is assumed to have theological expertise or some special insight into God. The second is deontic or administrative authority, which is the authority of command.[28] This is present in texts from Scripture when believers hear and obey its commands. The third form is expressive authority. This is a de facto illocutionary and subjective form of authority, which, in the case of the Bible, permits the expression of faith in a particular way, because that is how Scripture expresses it.[29] Such definitions at first may seem unacceptably vague. Closer consideration, however, reveals that this permissive authority liberates the Bible into the vital debating chamber of rhetorical performance, and resurrects biblical citation from the grave of dead quotation into expressive, intonated, confessional speech utterance,[30] which is capable of inspiring faith and creating a sense that the hearer has encountered God. This permissive authority overcomes the jarring conflict that sounds when coercive and manipulative preaching is inserted in fiction. When the fictional sermon is rhetorically negotiated as a compact between speaker and hearer, then it becomes truly authoritative. It is no longer an inserted alien text but a speech where readers are able to discern truth of some sort. When making sermons, preachers are engaged in an interplay with all these forms of authority, sometimes applying a rule to live by, while at other times reinterpreting and updating the application of an outdated rule, sometimes uncovering and learning a propositional "truth" about God from a Bible passage, and sometimes using biblical expressions to express the nature of contemporary faith and experience. Predominantly, in the case of readers and fictional sermons, it is permissive, expressive authority that is at play. Never is the authority absolute if the sermon is effective; it is always confessional, rhetorically performed, and subject to a compact between preacher and the sermon's hearers and readers, an interpersonal relationship. This relationship is inevitably jeopardized when the preacher does not keep faith, and it is to this clamorous dissonance that the next chapter turns.

4

KEEPING FAITH
The Troubled Preacher in Updike and Lodge

The troubled "man of God"[1] struggling with faith issues and wrestling with spiritual, vocational, or intellectual doubt appears in many guises in contemporary novels. He appears as Father Angwin in Hilary Mantel's *Fludd*,[2] Barney Hardstaff in Catherine Fox's *The Benefits of Passion*,[3] Edmond Music in Alan Isler's *Clerical Errors*,[4] Colley in William Golding's *Rites of Passage*,[5] and in other recently published fiction such as Margaret Forster's *Is There Anything You Want?*,[6] Stephanie Johnson's *Belief*,[7] Geraldine Brooks' *March*,[8] and Peter Hobbs' *The Short Day Dying*.[9] So ubiquitous is this character that, in a review of Jonathan Tulloch's *Give Us This Day*, a recent novel about a Roman Catholic priest transferred to a run-down parish in northeast England after falling victim to sexual scandals, the reviewer invented a new genre—"the 'loss of faith' novel [that] despite its unfashionable subject-matter . . . is . . . entirely contemporary."[10] There is little doubt that this is fiction reflecting real life, in that each year clergy leave parish ministry for various reasons, yet the frequent occurrence of the character is also because he is a convenient novelistic invention enabling authors to explore the life/faith dichotomy and the dissonance of faithless men in positions requiring faith. As a result, this character has significantly influenced the imagined world of novelists and readers, where there are two common causes of trouble for preachers. One is the struggle with issues of personal morality or belief. In these cases, the tormented soul, wrestling either with doubts about the Christian faith or with inconsistencies between personal behavior and Christian profession, is tortured on a rack when proclaiming Christianity from the pulpit, and there are likely to be external manifestations of the internal processes. The other challenge to faith is caused by natural or human-made disaster, most notoriously, in the twentieth century, the Jewish Shoah and, in the first few years of the twenty-first, the terrorist attack of 9/11 and the Boxing Day tsunami of 2004. Neither art nor theology should divert their gaze from these or whatever else challenges them, for the enormity of such atrocities demands serious artistic, theological, and philosophical reflection, despite Theodor Adorno's frequently cited and often misquoted comment that "writing poetry after Auschwitz is barbaric."[11] Doing theology is more difficult than it was before 9/11, and preachers certainly have to be more circumspect than they were before 2001, yet the religious undertones of many natural and human-made disasters make theological reflection even more imperative.

Two novels with troubled preachers—one troubled although he makes no pretense of keeping faith, the other wrestling with faith in the face of private and public adversity—arise for discussion. The first is Thomas Marshfield in John Updike's *A Month of Sundays*;[12] the other is Austin Brierley in David Lodge's *How Far Can You Go?*[13] Although Lodge's novel was published in America under the title *Souls and Bodies*, its original British title is preferred in this chapter because it foregrounds the issue of troubled faith.

A Month of Sundays, the journal of a priest forced to take a month's sabbatical in a clinic for reprobate clerics, is in many respects a problem novel. Updike declared it to be his favorite, yet it received a muted reception and has proved to many readers to be objectionable and unlikeable; its interiorized pornography often assumes gratuitousness, and its objectification of women, the gentle readers to whom the book is addressed, becomes all the more difficult by their silence throughout. Updike, or his narrator, if a distinction can indeed be made between them, gives no unmediated voice to the women remembered or lusted after. Jane, with whom Marshfield remembers losing his virginity, is spread naked across the novel's page with her hands tucked behind her head like a centerfold, voicelessly but bodily inviting attention. The novel frequently violates sacred and semisacred texts with immature sexual innuendoes: for instance, when he writes about his mother, Marshfield's memory of the Bunyan verse "he who is down need fear no fall" and the Psalmist's comment that "All they that go down to the dust shall bow before Him" leads to a paragraph in his journal about sexual positions (20). Throughout the novel, Marshfield's typographical errors and playful word games cause readers to feel they are being manipulated, and their distrust of the narrator is hardly ever allayed; for instance, Marshfield congratulates himself for changing the word "love" to "free" in three deft moves via "fove" and "foee," but each move is contrived, even invalid, and if this game was his attempt to prove that free love is "not a scandal but a tautology," most readers remain unconvinced (190). Such linguistic playfulness destabilizes the trustworthiness of Marshfield's journal. It records that an action as innocent as shuffling a pack of playing cards reminds the sexually obsessive Marshfield of orgasm (196). This feels like an unnecessary association, yet Marshfield's association of sex with religion that pervades the entire novel is necessary for Updike's purposes. That Marshfield's obsession with sex and lust for women has replaced the more usual form of religious behavior is made clear when, in a manner likely to offend religious sensibilities, he expresses himself as prepared to stand and ejaculate as he is to stand and recite the Apostles' Creed (159–60). Although Updike guesses that the ideal reader will want to use a blue pencil to censor the work (98), the author of *A Month of Sundays*, as he masquerades as an unreliable journal keeper whose religious faith no longer matters to him, effectively destabilizes our faith in literature and questions literature's capacity to portray religious faith.

Faith—faith in the art and purpose of fiction, faith in the role and intention of the author, and faith in the act of reading as a suspension of either skepticism or belief facilitating the construction of an imagined world that offers a way of understanding the world we live in—remains central to all three activities associated with novels: writing them, reading them, and making a critique of them. When using "faith" in this way, faith is the capacity to imagine an exercise with varying degrees of intensity a state of mind susceptible to crises. The generic fictional character of the troubled person of faith, the troubled amateur theologian, supports evidence for the truth of Paul Tillich's claim that "every theologian is committed *and* alienated; he is always in faith *and* in doubt; he is inside *and* outside the theological circle."[14]

Faith of this kind plays an integral part in the way people make sense of their existence by constructing solipsistic narratives. It becomes a component of the creative urge that is one of the coping mechanisms by which human beings are able to exist in a contingent world by adopting an alternative worldview. Faith is, therefore, characterized by essential "as-ifness," but this does not mean that exercising faith involves perversely and unnaturally choosing to believe something there is no good reason to believe, rather that it involves building on limited understanding of context in order to accept the kind of existence humans have and in order to construct a meaningful worldview. The subjectivity of this understanding opens the way for varieties of faith expressions. No one person will see the world exactly as another does. Marshfield has his view, while his gentle reader will have hers. Marshfield's imagination creates a world he inhabits; his readers create another. This is not self-deception; it is living *as if* something that might be meaningful is indeed so. Perversely akin to Paul Ricoeur's understanding of preaching as a form of mimesis that "opens the kingdom of the *as if*,"[15] Marshfield's journal uncovers the pornographic male mind in a manner that troubles the faithful reader. It also challenges the classical Christian incarnational theology that venerates flesh in the embodiment of Christ as well as the essential bodiliness of human identity enshrined in the doctrine of resurrection.

Causing trouble for the theology of the classical Christian creeds does not seem to bother Marshfield. Belief is not an issue for this minister of religion who claims to "have faith but it does not seem to apply" (172) and for whom a solipsistic harmonization of soul and body is more important than anything else, including the status and well-being of the women whose sole purpose seems to be to arouse and feed his sexual appetite. The religion that finds expression in both Marshfield's behavior and his record of it is far from being a path to purity and holiness. His deformed, or at best stultified, spirituality is "an indicator of a deficiency in the *zeitgeist*."[16] He is a "holy heretic"[17] whose adulterousness, faithlessness, spiritual aridity, and fleshliness are exposed in the four sermons he feels compelled to write for the four Sundays he is in the clinic, only the last of which is said to be a sermon that could be preached (212). His "out-of-season" preaching (192) is in keeping with the state of his soul. Paying attention to five aspects of discourse analysis theory has been particularly illuminating when considering the sermons in preparation for this chapter. These are mainly to do with the preacher's sense of audience, his self-awareness, the performance frames of the discourse, its schemata (or linguistic repertoire), and, using Brown and Levinson's terms from the discipline of discourse theory, the "politeness phenomena" he uses to mitigate the sermon's "face threatening acts."[18]

Denied a congregation by his stay in the supposedly therapeutic desert he prefers not to call a sanatorium, the sermon Marshfield writes in his journal on his first Sunday there begins as a homily on the story of Jesus and the woman caught in the act of adultery, whose placement in the Fourth Gospel is a matter of scholarly debate, and becomes by dint of elaborate rhetorical sophistry a paean of praise for adultery. The sermon shows that the preacher has a strong sense of audience awareness; from the very beginning, when Marshfield comments that his readers will remember the situation in which Jesus spoke the words of the text he has just announced, to the closing paragraphs, in which he seeks a response from his audience with direct appeals, "I beg you" and "I ask you," the preacher lets the novel's readers know that he is aware that he is writing for a certain readership—his parishioners at home. His address to them intensifies as he calls them "my friends," then "dearly beloved." Beyond this, however, readers of the novel are aware that over the heads of this imagined audience there sits an actual audience, the implicitly female-gendered "gentle reader," whom Updike addresses from behind his fictional preacher. This language is so patently the conventional terminology of nineteenth-century fiction that it advertises the rebellious and subversive nature of Marshfield's encouragement of his gentle reader to praise "the sacrament of adultery." This encouragement is given weight by Updike's portrait of Marshfield as a self-consciously scholarly, authoritative preacher capable of drawing on acquired knowledge without recourse to "a copious and insipid encyclopaedia of sermon aids and Aramaic etymologies" (41). He is effortlessly capable of drawing on the Bible, the seventeenth-century English churchman John Lightfoot, and first-century Rabbis Hillel and Akiba, while humbly implying the possibility of misremembering when quoting from Mark's Gospel. This latter implication is part of the politeness phenomena employed by the preacher to keep his congregation on his side: he does not wish to polarize his congregation by persistent use of first- and third-person pronouns by which he would set himself apart; rather, he associates himself with their dilemma. "We *are* an adulterous generation; let us rejoice" (47, emphasis original), the climactic exhortation of the sermon, is but one of many of his usages of the first-person plural pronoun. Although most of the schemata of the discourse are biblical or theological, it is worth noting that by using the schema of shotgun law enforcement by calling the Pharisees a "posse" and the linguistic repertoire of medieval chivalry by referring to adultery as a "tryst" and the male adulterer as a "phallic knight" (46), he not only engages both American and British readers but also implicitly outlaws the Pharisees' behavior and potentially elevates adultery from its banned status. Contrary to conventional Christian morality though this is, the sermon retains the conventional performance frames of preaching, including the announcement of a text, its timing on a Sunday, and its concluding amen and benediction.

The second sermon on Marshfield's second Sunday in the home is similarly addressed to the parishioners he left behind, the very people who had chosen not to sack him but to send him for recuperation and rehabilitation. Unconventional in its import, and more unconventional than the first in its format, the exposition of the announced text at the beginning quickly foregoes any anticipated development in favor of a general discussion of miracles in the New Testament. An even stronger sense of the extratextual audience for this sermon is present in its abrupt and uncompromising attack on American religiosity; the nation that ensures the presence of a Bible in every motel bedroom is unfaithful and exemplifies "the piety of the full belly" while its people's "hands do mischief" and their "heads indict the universe" (102). If this is Updike the satirist ventriloquizing through his fictional preacher, it is brusque and direct satire. Updike, however, later tempers the offense with the reminder that these "people of little faith" are also "dearly beloved" (106). As with the first sermon, the condition and status of the preacher is obvious and important. Marshfield assumes a position of superiority as, in a rather strange expression of awareness of their presence although they are patently absent, he says that he feels his congregation is gathered beneath him as "my docile suburban flock sitting hushed" (106); readers assume that the congregation awaits words of wisdom. Presumptuously adopting the role of prophet, he looks among them for a mustard seed of faith but finds none. Once he recognizes that he and they are therefore damned, Marshfield rounds off his sermon by cursing his hearers, and perhaps Updike's readers, with the vitriol more befitting the Shakespearean stage than the Christian pulpit—that this generation will wither at the root and a better generation be fed by its rot (107). Marshfield has allowed his state of mind to determine the mood of the sermon.

A week later Marshfield's third sermon appears calmer, as he allows his wilderness environment, rather than his feelings, to determine its subject matter and mood. As a meditation on the nature of desert to spread and its capacity nevertheless to sustain life, so the desert of the sanatorium for wayward clergy assumes an analogous relationship. It is the location of Marshfield's temptations, as readers have known from the first page of the novel, but also an environment in which he flourishes. Like the previous sermons, this one employs the conventional performance frames of an announced Bible verse about Jacob in the wilderness, a concluding exhortation "let us be grateful here" and an amen, but, unlike the others, its primary audience within the novel comprises Marshfield's fellow clergy patients rather than his old congregation. He addresses them as "my dear brethren" and uses a tone that is markedly different. By using the first-person plural throughout, the sermon establishes Marshfield's identification with the congregation; they are on common wilderness ground which is both Death Valley and the palm of God's hand. The chapter in which the sermon is written would consist entirely of the sermon if it were not for two short introductory paragraphs, the first being only, "O Lord," which is clearly not intended to be part of the sermon, and the second being, "Another Sunday is upon us," which could conceivably be the sermon's opening words (161). Is "O Lord" a cry of weary desperation or an enthusiastic shout of praise? Probably the former, for in the narrator-preacher of this novel, readers meet one who, though unwilling and in some respects incapable, feels constrained to preach and, on the third Sunday of his hospitalization, he manages to offer a poetic piece which is nearer to being a Christian sermon than the first two were.

Only days before Marshfield is discharged from the unit, he writes another sermon on his fourth Sunday. His primary audience, Mrs. Prynne, judges this sermon to be worth an airing. Like the third sermon, it is addressed to others in the institution, "my brothers" (205), with whom he has both common experiences and shared knowledge that enable him to refer in his preaching to "our capable Mrs. Prynne" (206). The preacher presents himself as a child who used to be terrified lest he pray so well that Jesus walk into the room, as the appalled recipient of pamphlets announcing the imminent end of the world, and as one standing on the edge of a mystery. He is almost Christlike toward the end of the sermon when he reminds his hearers that "soon he must leave them, as they must leave him" (205). Yet, he is aware of the limits of his imagination, which enables him only to imagine paradise in this life, and he demonstrates the limits of his faith when he can speak only of "a Who" who has placed us where we are (212). This is the nearest he can get to an expression of theistic belief, which he has already declared impossible. This is not to say that his preaching is tentative. Indeed, the language of the sermon is in places that of hyperbolic rhetoric, especially in his dismissal of apocalyptic preachers who predict the Parousia; their coarsely printed leaflets "aimed at the puerile" are "a travesty" and "the pornography of faith" (208).

These homiletic passages of *A Month of Sundays* are important; they are four of thirty-one chapters in the novel. If they trace the course of Marshfield's healing and recuperation before his return to parish work, they also show the discontinuity between his life and work, the failure of his sexualized religion, and, in the distorted logic of his written sermons, his weakness as a representative of Christianity. They show a preacher who, rather than genuinely wrestling with the specifics of faith, is in his depravity only trying to get away with being a libidinous church leader preying on women in the parish.

This renders Marshfield less interesting to sincere actual preachers than David Lodge's creation Austin Brierley, whose struggle to sustain faithfulness is described in *How Far Can You Go?*, a novel that discusses both personal and communal challenges to faith. Lodge himself saw the novel as a literary exploration of a crisis of faith and morality, which effected an overall transformation of English Catholicism to the extent that the traditional Catholic metaphysic faded away,[19] one of the post–Vatican II changes being the increasing incidence of sermons in services, an official and liturgical acknowledgement of the necessity of interpretation, teaching, and exhortation to faithfulness. In Lodge's novel, Austin Brierley is the only character who does not exchange one certainty for another,[20] yet there are considerable changes *within* him, echoing those within Catholicism itself. At the beginning, he is narrow-minded and priggish,[21] yet, as Catholicism changes through the sixties and seventies, Brierley embarks upon a lively though uncomfortable priestly career, becoming increasingly radical as he discovers new modes of theology and biblical exegesis. He moves into secular disciplines such as sociology, and by the end of the novel, he has left the priesthood and married, though he remains "a kind of Catholic." At the beginning of the book, Lodge had described the Catholic worldview as a giant Snakes and Ladders board with salvation as the game's goal: heaven at the top, hell below. Complicated rules govern the game in which sacraments, prayers, and good deeds permit the players to climb a ladder while sins send them slithering down a snake. The novel, in company with both English Catholicism, in general, and Austin Brierley, in particular, moves from this metanarrative acceptable to most English Catholics in 1952 to what is strongly suspected to be the present theological perspective of the author. Lodge describes that condition in his introduction to the Penguin reissue of *The Picturegoers* as "demythologised, provisional and in many ways agnostic."[22] The novel's "bitonality"—in which Lodge oscillates between the novel's prevailing frivolous tone and occasional serious passages dealing with fundamental questions of belief, and for which the reader is prepared by the double meaning of the question in the title—enables the author to explore how far one can go in changing the externals of a religion without eroding its substance.[23] The serious passages include several authorial comments, the epilogue, the interpolated authorial essay on *Humanae vitae* in the first eight pages of chapter four, and Austin Brierley's sermons. Passing references to other sermons endorse papal orthodoxy (119), hell-fire sermons in the tradition of Joyce's *A Portrait of the Artist as a Young Man* (286), sermons to maintain the fabric of the church (85), and an allusion to Father McKenzie's unheard sermon in The Beatles' song "Eleanor Rigby" (111). In addition, a parody of a revivalist sermon begins with a lame joke and incongruously uses British European

Airways (BEA) as an acronym for true Christian faith, in which "b" stands for "believes in God," "e" stands for "expects Christ to come," and "a" stands for "will accept him when he comes" (175–76). But the "serious" preaching passages are Austin Brierley's reported sermons, one at Dennis and Angela's wedding (67–68) and the other after what became known in Britain as the Aberfan disaster (106–7). This disaster occurred at a quarter past nine in the morning on the last day before the half-term holiday in October 1966 when, after heavy rains, a waste tip from Merthyr Tydfil Colliery in South Wales slid down the mountainside on to the village of Aberfan. It destroyed a farm cottage and engulfed Pantglas Junior School and about twenty homes before coming to rest. There was little hope of survivors in the sludge that buried so many people. It killed 144 people, of whom 116 were children, and the tragedy profoundly shocked the general public.

Looking more closely at these sermons and their reception, the sermon Brierley preaches at Dennis and Angela's wedding assumes a worldview of Catholicism that had the authority to appoint a world leader and promote the ideal of monogamous heterosexuality, usually expressed, as in this sermon, in male-gendered fashion as "man and wife." Brierley employs the specialized idioms of ecclesiastical language to express marriage as a sacrament for which the relationship between Christ and his church is an appropriate analogy. This hegemonic church is set against opponents such as "rampant materialism," the "teeth of Communist persecution," and "the stormy seas of the Second World War" across which Pius XII sailed a dangerous course. While Lodge gives the sermon in free indirect speech from his point of view, the reader also hears Dennis' father's criticism, Angela's parents' incomprehension, the view held by some of the congregation that the homily was too heavy, and Polly's flirtatious view that it was "beautiful." The irony of this sermon is evident in the nature of its various audiences, which include Dennis and Angela's friends from university days who do not need to be reminded how long it has taken the couple to marry, Angela's parents who are unable to understand the concept of analogy, Dennis' father who fidgets because he feels the sermon is too gloomy, and Polly who, feeling "Magdalenish," desperately wants to marry. Its extratextual audiences, including the "so many young people these days" to whom Brierley refers, are both Catholic and non-Catholic, both those who share a sacramental doctrine of holy matrimony and those who do not, those who believe in Christ's abiding presence and those who have no belief in Christ. Brierley makes allowances for neither his celibacy, which limits his understanding of marriage, his increasing interest in liberal theology and ethics, nor the plurality of his congregation. He merely iterates the conventional official Catholic line on marriage.

On the other hand, his sermon after the Aberfan disaster (106–7) engages more with the problematic questions that flood like mining slurry into the hearers' heads. Brierley's new parish is a dull market town in what is described as a "scandalously flat landscape," scandalous because it is untouched by the mounds and heaps resulting from mining. The term "scandalously flat" prepares the reader to be scandalized by the congregation's impassive response to a challenging and questing sermon. Lodge sets the scene for the sermon with a paragraph that describes the disaster at Aberfan as an eruption of the Industrial Revolution's constipated bowels and points out that, unlike Brierley, few ministers took up the theological challenge of the events. In his sermon, Brierley challenges some conventional responses to the disaster and uses the Job legend, which he reads either as myth or poem, to encourage prayers of protest. In his implied view, the preacher is not God's public relations officer, but a priest. As a priest, he is the people's representative before God, rather than God's representative to the people, so he represents both the people of the parish and the broken suffering people of Aberfan. As in the tensions that exist among the possible responses to suffering represented among Job's comforters, the various theological and philosophical responses to Aberfan are in tension. Given that one might expect outrage, tears, or shock, scandalously the sermon's audience carries a blank expression, as all seem asleep except some mothers who, waking to the link with the mothers of Aberfan, look anxiously at their older children. Readers experience Aberfan as a more profound challenge to religious belief than the issue of contraception ostensibly at the novel's heart. How far can one go in questioning God? In protestations with the divine? With biblical criticism in sermons? And how far can preachers go in criticizing the divine in sermons? The quiescence of the audience suggests one possible, but disturbingly disappointing, answer: the preacher can go quite far without upsetting the assumptions of the faithful if the audience is as disengaged as this one.

Inasmuch as the book chronicles the change from "How It Was" (the title of the first chapter) to "How It Is" (the title of the last chapter), *How Far Can You Go?* is a novel about "fundamental disturbance,"[24] within which Brierley is a troubled preacher struggling to find his place in a church as it moves from preconciliar uniformity to postconciliar pluralism.[25] Post–Vatican II, the Roman Church does not permit a condition of "anything goes," but the plurality of beliefs expressed by the various characters of this novel makes it clear that it *is* a matter of "how far can you go?" The book keeps this question open and presents the dilemmas faced by individual Catholics as they and their church try to take account of living in the plurality and permissiveness of British society in the 1960s and 1970s.

The fictional preaching of troubled preachers thus exposes tensions in three relationships that are critical for actual preachers—those between fiction and faith, between preaching and liturgy, and between preaching and orthodoxy. Each of these deserves attention at this stage. The first deals with the symbiotic relationship between fiction and faith. In his essays on consciousness and the novel, Lodge characterized fiction as "a benign lie because it is known to be untrue yet possesses explanatory powers."[26] This view can be expressed less provocatively; fiction faithfully imagines possible worlds and helps explain the actual world. As a former Catholic believer, Lodge has attained the status of "creative doubt,"[27] in which he is able to see that faith functions in both fiction and religion in similar ways; for the religious believer and the reader of fiction and, by extension, the hearer of sermons, "the life of faith enjoins living on two parallel tracks."[28] Both when reading and in believing, if Ricoeur's "kingdom of the *as if*" notion is developed, being faithful is living on both an as-if and an "as-is" track.

Other characters in *How Far Can You Go?* also feel this tension of faith. One reviewer of the novel atomized the various crises of faith: "Some marry in the course of the story, one becomes a nun, one realizes he is homosexual. One of the married people goes mad, one of the couples has a Mongol baby and then loses another child in a road accident. There are 'affairs,' some damaging, some not . . . and there are similarly varied crises of belief."[29] He also reminded his readers of Lodge's first fiction, published in the Catholic Tell Me Father series, which consisted of four letters from Father Aloysius Brown to an earnest young man on National Service. The third letter urges the recipient to "move on from the land of make-believe to the territory of hard fact!" Although Father Brown expressed this more concretely than is necessary, it is indeed the oscillation made by people of faith—from "as-ifness" (which is not the same as "make-believe") to "as-isness" and back again. These are the twin tracks fiction readers travel; preachers might heed that their hearers also travel these same tracks.

In his earlier sermon at Dennis and Angela's wedding, Brierley had used the homily mainly to endorse papal pronouncements on sexual mores, thus expressing a worldview that sees the Catholic Church as hegemonic, with the preacher, even in the intimacy of a family occasion, conscious of world events as the Conclave of Cardinals met to elect a new pope to follow Pius XII. Even in an untroubled sermon of this sort, there is an as-is world, the family occasion of a wedding, and an as-if world, the higher matters of worldwide church governance. Brierley's later sermon reflecting on the disaster of Aberfan juxtaposes as-is and as-if more challengingly for actual readers and fictional hearers. The Aberfan disaster is a bigger challenge to faith than moral issues of contraception inasmuch as "it strained religious belief of any variety" (106) and it is inescapable. When, for instance, Dennis and Angela set up their new home in a small middle-class estate in rural Warwickshire, there were puddles and mud everywhere leading the narrator to comment, "It seemed impossible to get away from the physical ambience of Aberfan" (109). Brierley's troubled sermon pitted two traditional theological and ecclesiastical responses, either that it was the will of God or that it was punishment for human sin, both of which Brierley finds inadequate, against a response in which believers discover within themselves the Job-like courage to challenge God to justify himself (107). The apocalyptic dystopic scenes of "colossal, obscene evil-smelling mess" and a "thunderous terrifying roar" (106) are answered in the sermon with the reasoning that people would be less than human if they did not protest and complain. The sermon reverses the expected compliance with a hegemonic institution and introduces into worship what people are actually feeling, the as-isness of protest. Readers empathize with Austin Brierley and feel the force of the verses he quotes from the book of Job, while his audience seems unmoved and its members do not use the sacred space he offers to complain to God.

Modern novelists rarely describe things objectively, choosing rather to give the personal points of view of different characters, allowing the writer to test different versions of reality. This "subjective seeing,"[30] coupled with contemporary uncertainty about the means of storytelling itself,[31] puts modern novels into a self-questioning mode that gives readers a choice of textual places to inhabit. So it is with *How Far Can You Go?* Readers may choose to ally themselves with any of the responses of the large cast of characters in the novel as they respond to the challenges of liberalization and permissiveness. Where, and if, readers choose to dwell in a text is an act of imagination, as well as an act of faith in the purposes of fiction, in the intention of the author, in the artifice of the text, and in the act of reading. Paradoxically yet inevitably, acts of faith are prone to entail crises of faith; this is the case both for Brierley as he preaches and for his audiences, both intratextual and extratextual, as they listen or read. The preacher's readers are free to choose how they respond to his verbalized struggle with faith and free to choose where they locate themselves in relation to his dilemma.

This fiction-faith tension is echoed in the second relationship critical to this study—the organic relationship between preaching and the liturgy in which it is set. Potentially, this tension exists in all instances of preaching alluded to in any novel, but it is particularly evident in *How Far Can You Go?* because the reader is made aware of the liturgical changes effected by Vatican II, including an enhanced role for preaching. While the novel appears to be about sexuality, sexual ethics, and the Catholic crises of faith that these matters engendered, the theme of *How Far Can You Go?* is in fact much broader; as Lodge himself said, its subject is "the practical effects . . . of Vatican II on Catholic liturgy, devotional practice and general lifestyles, both clerical and lay."[32] These changes include more frequent, lengthier, and more probing homilies than tended to be typical before Vatican II. So the novel portrays an English Catholicism in whose liturgy "demythologising of the Bible and of traditional doctrine jostles with charismatic prayer, belief in a personal devil [and] 'old-fashioned' belief in the real presence."[33]

This tension between sermon and liturgy can be a creative tension that addresses the contemporary problem of postmodernity in the twenty-first century church. If postmodernity is characterized as "incredulity toward metanarratives,"[34] these are liturgically encapsulated for Christianity both in the creeds and in the preface of the Great Prayer of Thanksgiving at the Eucharist. If another feature of postmodernism is "an insistence that we hear alternative voices,"[35] these may be accommodated in sermons and homilies. When sermons are employed in this way to establish dialogue between the traditional Christian metanarrative and alternative voices or points of view, then forming new theology for the current age becomes possible, thus enabling the church to proclaim afresh in each generation the faith that it believes is uniquely revealed in the Holy Scriptures and set forth in the Catholic creeds.[36] Preaching thus also adopts an appropriate modernizing role of interpretation and development, as it seeks to apply traditional teaching from ancient times to contemporary society. Within novels this may be difficult to achieve because sermons on the page seem to be totalizing narratives and "one-man" performances. They do not appear to have the characteristics of dialogue, the interdependence and interchangeability that permits audiences within novels to inhabit the world of the sermon.[37] This book shows, however, that it is not *impossible* to achieve. Arditti and others succeed. Moreover, readers can enjoy a luxury denied to hearers, who have insufficient time when listening to consider alternatives. Readers can choose how to "hear" the inflection of the sermon's phrasing and can thus hear its polyvocality and discern alternative locations for them to indwell; they can also go back and reread (although this facility is slightly compromised with the emergence of the e-book whose pages are not so easy to flip back through).

Related to, but distinct from, the tension between preaching and liturgy is a third relationship, that which arises between preaching and religious orthodoxy, at times troubled, at other times affirming. David Lodge deals with this particularly well. In his more recent novel, *Thinks . . .*, one of his characters keeps a journal in which she expresses her profound dissatisfaction that the sermons at the University Church are no more than exhortations to obedience, which avoid some obvious questions and problems.[38] In his early novel, *The Picturegoers*, after seeing a film featuring Amber Lush, Father Kipling uses a sermon to express his disapproval of going to the movies.[39] In *How Far Can You Go?*, however, Lodge demonstrates awareness of the creative possibilities of preaching when Austin Brierley, preaching in response to the Aberfan disaster, faces challenges to orthodox belief. The narrator of *How Far Can You Go?* claims that if the waste tip over Aberfan had collapsed a few hours later, after school had closed for half term, it would have been called a miracle in the popular press. As it happened,

> the part, if any, played in it by God [was] passed over in tactful silence. On the following Sunday, prayers were offered throughout the land for the bereaved, the rescue-workers and (in Catholic Churches) for the departed souls of the victims, but few ministers of religion took up the theological challenge of the event itself. (106)

In fact, was this so? In contrast with the outpouring of public expressions of grief whenever a tragedy occurs in the early years of the twenty-first century, public expression over Aberfan in 1966 was strangely muted. Local ministers of religion provided emotional support and spiritual care as, according to a political and sociological study of the disaster, some of the survivors and the bereaved spoke of their faith strengthening them as they came to terms with their losses, while others had their faith destroyed by the tragedy.[40] On the Monday after the tragedy, the local ministers met to make arrangements for the funeral. The local Roman Catholic and Anglican priests nominated the Roman Catholic archbishop and the Anglican bishop of Llandaff to conduct the funeral, but the nonconformists nominated their longest-serving local minister. The funeral, preceding a communal burial, led by all three clergymen, comprised two hymns, three prayers, and four readings, and "hardly took twenty minutes."[41] The *Times* was more precise: according to the South Wales correspondent, it lasted thirteen minutes. The only other official church comments reported in the press were made by the bishop of Llandaff in a television program broadcast the day after the disaster, in which he spoke of both reasonable and unreasonable bitterness and anger in the valley, and by the Archbishop of Canterbury who, in a sermon in a Kent church, said that risks of a similar disaster must be removed.[42]

The main response of the churches was a remarkable example of community development, most notably Tŷ Toronto, a center established as the focus for advocacy, community development, and social welfare funded by the Welsh churches in Canada.[43] Although it was important that the churches should respond in practical ways, this conveniently avoided the crucial and challenging theological questions that Brierley, unlike his real-life equivalents, bravely faces in *How Far Can You Go?* His sermon voices the feelings of those who, like Job, feeling utter despair and alienation from God because their sons and daughters have been killed, are unconvinced by the orthodox arguments of the pious who try to reconcile them to their fate (107). His sermon challenges the orthodox piety of the children's hymn *Loving Shepherd of Thy Sheep* and the Wesley hymn *Jesu, Lover of My Soul*, both sung at the Aberfan funeral, although neither of these is directly referenced in the novel. Brierley acknowledges that words convincing to Job would fail to convince the parents of Aberfan, but the book of Job's point, whether it is read as story, sermon, myth, or poem, is, according to Brierley, that "God only spoke to Job because Job complained to God . . . and let his embittered soul speak out" (108). Brierley's parish priest asks what good it does to make people doubt the goodness of God and suggests Brierley needs a holiday or "a course of some kind," which implies that the priest suspects that Brierley has experienced loss of faith. The novel concludes the conversation at this point, leaving readers to fill in the gap of Austin Brierley's response, because the novel has already alerted readers to the fact that it is Aberfan, not Austin Brierley's response to Aberfan, that causes people to doubt God's goodness. Brierley is facing, not losing, faith; his sermon honestly addresses where people are in their faith and doubt, commitment and alienation.

Those interested in real-life preaching cannot turn away from the positive lessons to be learned from stories of preachers who wrestle with faith. First, preaching, if it is to be capable of responding to the pluralist and postmodern context of the twenty-first century by crafting theology that sustains believers in the current age, needs to respond to the subtle harmonies of our polyphonous world. Second, preachers need to be bifocal, with one field of view fixed on the tradition and the other on the countertradition, minding the gap between the world of the Bible and the world in which they are speaking. Their sights should be set across the tensions that exist between faith and fiction, between preaching and the liturgy in which it is set, and between orthodoxy and new expressions of belief, thus facilitating true interpretative preaching that engages with both sides of the tension. Third, if twenty-first-century pulpit talk is to yield a contemporary word in troubled times, creative doubt at play with the creative tensions between fiction and faith, between imagination and belief, between the world as it is and "God's future fiction,"[44] should be allowed to stimulate people's imaginations so that they can live faithfully in a world that challenges faith. Hence a plea: there is an imperative for continuing and renewing theological, spiritual, and religious exploration in novels, despite any previous nervousness among novelists about theological debate,[45] for, as can be seen in the way Marshfield continues theological exploration in the wilderness, the decline in the influence of institutions that officially encode religious belief in a curious way facilitates the exploration of faith in novels. These are the big, often discordant, issues with which literature is rightly concerned and from which novelists and their readers should not avert their gaze.

5

Heaven in Ordinary
Religious Experience in Fictional Sermons

❦

Commentators sometimes complain about the preachiness of Marilynne Robinson's nonfiction in contrast with her fiction in which "she avoids any kind of preaching in favour of delicately eavesdropping on the spiritual and domestic travails of her characters."[1] Those who make this complaint miss the irony that her two most recently published and closely related novels, *Gilead* and *Home*, are about preachers and that one of the most interesting conjunctions between the novels is their contrapuntal telling of a sermon on the biblical narrative of Hagar and Ishmael. *Gilead*, Robinson's second novel, after a break from publishing fiction that lasted almost a quarter of a century, takes the form of a letter written by an elderly parson to his seven-year-old son with the intention that it be read after he has died and once the boy is old enough to understand. The writer, John Ames, is the son and grandson of preachers, the grandfather having been a firebrand who encouraged young men to take up arms in the Civil War, and the father an antiwar spokesman. Widowed when his wife died in childbirth, Ames had dedicated himself to a faithful, and more or less unremarkable, ministry in a mid-American town. He is so respected that his best friend Boughton, who comes to the fore in *Gilead*'s companion novel *Home*, names his son after Ames. Everything changes for the preacher when Lila comes to his church. They marry and have the child to whom Ames the preacher now writes imparting fatherly advice to read Feuerbach, to cherish the family story, to avoid transgression, to honor his parents, not to be defensive, and to live long enough to outlast all grievances. The letter is also a plea that Ames' son understands and forgives young Jack Boughton, the son who had been given the full name John Ames Boughton after Ames, but who is usually called "Jack." Jack had abandoned his father as he died but, like the Lucan prodigal, he had returned to Gilead where Ames is now like a second father to him. Ames wants his actual son, the unnamed seven-year-old addressee of the letters in the novel, to hear at least one good word about Jack. Otherwise, can there ever be healing, any balm, in Gilead? This "endless letter" (40) gives the novel a long time scale: the letter is written in 1956, it remembers stories of a grandfather from a hundred years previously and a father whose ministry coincided with the time of the Great War, it looks forward to its intended reader growing old and wise, and it looks back on the Bible's fathers and sons—in particular Abraham and his sons Isaac and Ishmael, about whom a sermon central to the book is preached, Isaac and his sons Jacob and Esau, of whom readers are reminded when Ames gives Jack Boughton the balm of a blessing toward the end of the novel, the landowner with two sons in Jesus' parable, and, supremely, God and his only-begotten Jesus. This "spiraling letter with [the] qualities of a sermon" is written with the same zeal that Ames applied to his sermons throughout his career.[2] *Gilead* alludes to several of these.

While Ames' grandfather had been "afire with certainties" (36) and preached men into the Civil War, Robinson indicates that the narrator is a more measured preacher who used a full script when preaching and for whom writing was akin to praying. He avoided taking doctrine and controversies into the pulpit and wrote as if his late wife might walk into his study and look over his shoulder; he would not want to offend. In a brief passage in his letter, Ames reflects on the relationships among his writing, thought, and speech, claiming that, while he does not write as he speaks, he writes as he thinks even though it can sound "pulpitish" (33). Later, when commenting on his failure to achieve the preacherly heights of his predecessors, he tells readers that he understands appropriate preacherly behavior to be formal, deferential, dignified, authoritative, but cordial (137). Dreaming one night that Jesus looked patient, sad, and amazed when he sat in on one of Ames' sermons, Ames is saddened by the realization that his sermons all fell short of the hopes he had for them. Though they contrast with his grandfather's Fourth of July sermon that announced that all that remains in Gilead is dust and ashes (200–201) and his father's sermon in which he expressed his shame for abandoning his father to join the Quakers (220–21), and though he doubts the merit of the estimated 67,500 pages of sermons boxed in the attic because of what he calls the "poverty of [his] remarks" (22), Ames' accounts of his own sermons betray the pride concealed under his humility. He is proudest of an unpreached sermon in response to the Spanish influenza epidemic, burnt the night before he had meant to preach it because his courage failed him. He had thought that his pacifist father would have been pleased with his view that the men who died in the epidemic were spared "the consequences of their own ignorance and courage, [as] the Lord was gathering them in before they could go off and commit murder against their brothers" (48). He interpreted the epidemic as a biblical plague warning that desire for war "in contempt of the will and grace of God" can bring only the consequences of war in the form of the judgment of God.

Other sermons that Ames recalls in his letter are associated with significant moments in the history of either his family or the Gilead community. For instance, Ames recalls a recent Sunday service when Lila brought their son forward after everyone had left, but while the elements remained on the Communion table. She suggests Ames should give their son "some of that" and, though the child is too young, he does. This becomes a marvelous experience that Ames fears he will not live long enough to savor fully (79). The sermon associated with this beautiful moment was, Ames remembers, unusual in that he chose, contrary to his custom at the Eucharist, to preach on the narrative of institution in Mark 14:22. Facing the immanence of his own death, Ames had been preoccupied with thoughts about the human body and both the physicality and temporality of life. The blessedness and brokenness of his physical existence had prompted him to use the narrative of Jacob at Peniel as the Old Testament lesson, then to reflect in his sermon on what he called "the gift of physical particularity," the embodiment that is an essential part of being human and individual, and the way that beauty, goodness, and holiness are mediated through something as tangible as bread and wine. His preaching's rootedness in the life of Gilead is further demonstrated in both a sermon on forgiveness and the Hagar and Ishmael sermon that, since the publication of *Home*, is more clearly to be read as being central to the novel. The sermon on forgiveness is not directly associated with a particular event, although Ames thinks he might have preached it in 1947 when he was thinking about the Marshall Plan. It interprets the clause in the Lord's Prayer "Forgive us our debts" in relation to the Year of Jubilee and argues that "the one sufficient reason for the forgiveness of debt is simply the existence of debt" (183). It also links this with the parable of the prodigal son and his restoration in his father's house. Initially there is little remarkable about this sermon until, only a few pages later in the novel in his letter to his son, Ames writes that he is unable to forgive Boughton, his old friend (187). It is not only that he was an indirect victim of Boughton's lax parenting and wayward way with women, suffering only minor damage in that he has to care for Boughton's son who is given to petty crimes but that he would not know how to begin the process of forgiving him. Herein lies the significance of this sermon to the novel: it demonstrates the disjunction between the preacher and his preaching, his expressed belief and his actual practice, his words and his experience.

The Hagar and Ishmael sermon in *Gilead* merits careful attention because of its contrapuntal retelling in *Home*. Those who read the novels in order of publication first encounter the sermon as recounted by Ames. After a sleepless night, although feeling both weary and anxious, and although surprised by Boughton's unexpected attendance at church, Ames keeps to his intention to preach a sermon pointing out the similarity between the stories of Hagar and Ishmael sent off into the wilderness and Abraham going off with Isaac to sacrifice him, suggesting that Abraham is effectively called upon to sacrifice both his sons. This sermon was planned and written in full in keeping with Ames' usual practice. However, conceding that he was perhaps influenced by seeing Boughton sitting in church as he preached, Ames departs from his prepared text in one section of the sermon and remarks on how many fathers there are who mistreat their children. He initially departs from his script, he says, to make what he thought was a good point—that when a pastor is anxious about his church he is forgetting that Christ is the ever-present pastor of his people through all generations.

Probably because this point reminded some of the women in the congregation of previous much-loved pastors, it upsets them. Seeing them upset and wanting to move on from what caused their tears, he follows another unscripted line of thought that brands Abraham an unkind parent in taking Isaac into the wilderness to sacrifice him. Ames, thus, finds himself in a rhetorical cul-de-sac and, to find his way out and back to his script, he comments on neglectful fathers (146). He then notices Boughton grinning at him. Ames considers it an act of "considerable egotism" that Boughton took the sermon to be directed at him only (149). That Ames made this judgment betrays to the reader that the comment was likely to have been an intentional barbed comment aimed at the grinning erstwhile friend. The inconsistency between this judgment, his concession that he might have been swayed by Boughton's presence, and his insistence elsewhere that he did not intend to use the occasion of preaching in public to take a swipe at Boughton troubles the integrity of Ames as a pastor and lends to his ministry a whiff of hypocrisy.[3]

In the second novel, *Home*, in a conversation with his sister, Glory, Boughton's son, Jack, gives an account of the event with a different inflection, as his father had told it to him. He had described the theme of the sermon as "the disgraceful abandonment of children by their fathers" and had felt himself to have been the living illustration of the sermon that he believed was intended to appall him (215). Boughton had felt that if Ames was extemporizing, as he appeared to be, then he was responding to Boughton's presence. On the other hand, if he was preaching as he had planned, Boughton believed the sermon had been written with him in mind. Boughton claimed that he wore his characteristic defensive smile, not a grin. Whereas Ames, in *Gilead*, thought that Boughton left by the chancel side door as a rebuff and to avoid shaking hands, Boughton's son now claims, in *Home*, that his father in fact left feeling so ashamed that he wanted to pull his jacket over his head (216), and he had sat for hours in the barn to recover his composure. Soon Robinson informs her readers that Boughton's father had later challenged Ames on his "fine sermon" asking whether he believed that, by the accident of birth or the divine determinism of predestination, a father might be punished by the suffering of his child (231). This is a question that lies at the heart of both *Gilead* and *Home*, the products of an author who, in her nonfiction writing, has expressed herself interested in Calvinistic theology.

In an interview, Marilynne Robinson remarked that in her reading of Calvin what has often struck her is his strong sense that "the aesthetic is the signature of the divine."[4] Furthermore, she has written in her collection of essays *The Death of Adam* that her examination of what is plainly before her eyes as she observes, reflects, and writes has led her to conclude that there is more than meets the eye, that "the scene of miracle is here, among us."[5] This prompts an investigation to discover to what extent the signature of the divine is discernible in Robinson's fiction and to what extent its characters' ordinary lives filled with ordinary, normal, unremarkable events are where the supernatural impinges on the natural and heaven meets earth. What makes the experiences associated with the sermons in her fiction religious or spiritual experiences, and what makes the difference? These are difficult questions not only for writers and readers of fiction but also for religious theorists and practitioners: How can claimed religious experience be authenticated? The relatively new science of religious psychology will assist.[6]

The first and most basic point to make about religious experience is its normality; it is normal experience understood at full depth when spiritual or theological interpretation goes to the heart of the experience; it is neither special, unnatural, or abnormal.[7] The normality of religious experience is at the root of several problems about its depiction in fiction, as well as the difficulty of vouching for its veracity in real life where it is widely regarded as the most protean and complex of topics in the psychology of religion. In a critique of religious psychologists from William James on,[8] four main problems about religious or spiritual experience become obvious: diversity, the breadth of the religious experience spectrum from extreme cases to lesser experiences, selectivity in the way experience is reported, and delay in reporting.

The problems associated with the diversity of claimed religious experience were signaled in the foundational work of William James on which most current academic understanding of religious experience among cognitive psychologists is built.[9] James tried to identify and name the notion that a part of ordinary human experience senses an uneasiness that can only be resolved when people are in contact with a higher power. He surveyed the creeds of many world religions as he sought commonality about the human quest for something beyond, reality beyond the quotidian, or "something there"; he suggested the universality of human consciousness having a sense of reality beyond that given by the senses, an experience he called "ontological imagination." Such ontological imagination can be so powerful that it creates experiences that are as strong as hallucinations and totally convincing to those who have them. The authenticity of such religious experiences are demonstrated by the dynamism and zest they give to the experiencer, by the way the experiencer finds significance in the event, and by the enchantment the experience gives to everyday life. He argued that the validity or veracity of the origin of such experiences neither diminishes nor enhances their spiritual significance, for this is recognized by its fruit in people's lives. The quest for inherent common features in religious experiences may never be fulfilled because "varieties" is the key word in the title of James' book. Think only of the range of experiences described in Robinson's novels to see the difficulty. This indefinability or indeterminacy of religious experience presents practical problems. Testing a person's vocation to ministry, assessing the validity of a person's claim to have received a vision or message from God, deciding on the veracity or otherwise of a supernatural experience, discerning God's Word among, within, behind, or over a preacher's many words are all notoriously difficult tasks to fulfill objectively. They become all the more difficult in the naturalness and normality of most religious experience, as unremarkable as listening to music, reading a book, or looking at a picture, as quotidian as sunrise. An almond branch in blossom *is* an almond branch in blossom—or a vision communicating divine truth to the Old Testament prophet Jeremiah. An open book *is* an open book—or a divine invitation for Augustine to pick it up and read there words that changed the direction of his life. And grandfather Ames' amusing story of the stranger's big black horse that sank through the road into a tunnel being dug between the livery stable and a dry goods store is no more than an amusing story from Gilead's folklore—or a moral, even religious, lesson in the importance of correct judgment. This is something of a frustratingly circular and subjective argument, for the acid test of religious experience is only and always retrospective; if the result of the experience is to take either the experiencer, other people, or both deeper into an understanding of ultimacy, then such an experience can be called religious or spiritual, but this cannot be known either in advance of or during the experience. The worth of religious experiences can be known only or, at best, mainly with hindsight. So the discovery of either a single stage-like model of progression that will cover all instances of claimed religious experiences or a classification system that will classify and account for such diverse experiences is unlikely ever to be made. This, of course, suits the indeterminacy of the world of fiction.

The second problem of the breadth of the spectrum of religious experiences raises the question of whether extreme examples of religious experience can be used in any way to comment on less dramatic cases. Although religious experiences differ along many dimensions: "ordinary versus unusual, frequent versus infrequent, prebelief versus postbelief, mystical versus earthly, and so on,"[10] most discussions of religious experience favor the unusual and infrequent. However, the much more common type of religious experience is that which is felt by ordinary people in daily life, the unremarkable in the quotidian. What have these to do with the exceptional cases of, say, Moses at the burning bush or Daniel in the lions' den? Can exceptional figures speak for the masses? Are extreme cases sui generis? Clearly, extreme cases, either dramatic life-changing experiences or experiences felt by people who are either saintly or highly charged spiritually, can mark the upper and outer limits of religious experiences, but most religious experiences are less dramatic and will not result in cognitive restructuring; most people will resume their everyday lives as if little extraordinary has happened. Often the experience will do little more than confirm a pre-existing faith or worldview and not induce new vision. But that makes it no less genuine. This real-life problem carries over into fiction. How is the reader to identify less dramatic spiritual experience as nevertheless authentically spiritual?

This problem is exacerbated by a third problem, the fact that people inevitably use narrative to recount religious experiences. If it is true that narrative requires three components—the selection of experiences for inclusion, a temporal ordering of such experiences, and the imposition of a meaningful theme or moral"[11]—then the telling of the experience is not the experience itself but an interpretation, sometimes a corruption, of the experience. The narration is rarely entirely innocent. The telling of the experience may impose a stage-like structure on the events because the narrator chooses both to omit incongruous aspects and to include all that reinforces his or her interpretation of events. Accounts of religious experiences, which often feature in sermons when the preacher speaks self-referentially, are always "mitigated reality":[12] testimony is an overt narrative of events, interpreted with innuendo, thus, generally, untrustworthy as objective truth. Any account of personal experience, such as Ames' father's explanation of his defection to the Society of Friends in *Gilead* (220–21), is distinct from the "pure" objective experience: in telling of the experience, "what actually happened" becomes "an exploration of the significance of events in my life that made me see things differently." When a character in a novel recounts a spiritual or religious experience, how can readers trust the interpretation the character applies to the events he or she chooses to tell us? In the case of the three Ameses' sermons, is what they recount undermined by the untold countertexts? Is what Ames tells his reader compromised by the limits of language to construct and understand experience? Readers know that, because he is preaching and writing about what he preached, he has selected his warrants and data to suit the rhetorical purpose of both the sermons and the letter he writes to his young son, and they ask: Does this create yet more suspicion about the veracity of his religious experience?

Fourth, what has the passage of time between the experience and its subsequent retelling done to the experience and its account? In short, once a person arrives at a particular outcome or stage in religious experience, both individuals and psychologists—and, by extension, characters within a novel and their authors—have a propensity to look back and identify a particular path that led to the outcome. When people look back on experiences, they tend to schematize and see in them a line of deterministic progression. The tendency among religious psychologists to construct stages as models of religious experience is a phenomenon resulting from the way people create narratives of nature, rather than an essential attribute of the experience itself, and the passage of time between the experience and its telling gives the experiencer, who is also the eventual narrator, time to mold the experience to fit the model. This is not to say that preachers, real or fictional, or others like them who testify to religious experiences are necessarily being dishonest, but it is does highlight the shape-shifting quality of religious or spiritual experience and the indeterminacy of its fictional representation.

Communicating convincing religious and spiritual experience in fiction is difficult to achieve. When novelists choose to use sermons to achieve this, they are consciously or intuitively drawing on features of two specialist novel genres. The first of these is the epistolary novel, a genre that had its heyday in the early years of the development of the novel, but which, as *Gilead* demonstrates, is still vibrant.[13] Sermons and letters in novels enjoy some interesting points of comparison, but, because sermons are often sparsely scattered in modern fiction, the similarities are not always obvious. When novelists use sermons in a more concentrated manner such as in Michael Arditti's *Easter*, when they are set in the context of a letter as in *Gilead*, or when they *are* the story as in Updike's "Lifeguard," then the comparison is clearer.

Several features common to the epistolary novel and the use of sermons in fiction are illuminating and suggest that the inclusion of sermons in novels provides opportunities and creates problems for the novelist similar to those evident in epistolary novels. The first is that the author of an epistolary novel wants readers to read the text of the letters as both fiction and real.[14] That is to say that, in the specific case of one of the best-known and earliest epistolary novels, Samuel Richardson's novel *Clarissa*, readers are expected to have the mental dexterity to switch between reading the letters both as something made up by the author and as an actual correspondence between the characters. This is also true of John Ames' sermons. Readers are expected to read them as something imagined by Marilynne Robinson but also as a record of preaching in Gilead's Congregationalist church in the novel's imagined world. Moreover, the letter to his son is similarly to be read as fictional and true. As a result, readers react not only to what is said in the sermon but also to who is saying it; they react to grandfather, father, and Ames fils as preachers claiming authenticity, as well as to their, and their community's, story.

Second, while there are limits to the epistolary form in that, when the characters do all the writing there is no authorial voice-over, epistolary novels have the advantage of being written to the moment.[15] This means that the letters give the characters' immediate, unmediated response to the action. Like the correspondents in epistolary novels, fictional preachers control both their own story and their commentary on the story around them, perhaps none more so in recent fiction than the rector of Eyam in Brooks' *Year Of Wonders*, who persuades his parishioners to heroic acts during the plague of 1665 and maintains his leadership of the village through the oratory by which he also successfully conceals his own character flaws. In Robinson's *Gilead*, the authorial voice is muted behind that of John Ames corresponding with his son by letter, which gives more immediacy to the reported preaching of the three generations of preachers who represent three degrees of orality: the narrator wrote his sermons out word for word, while his father used notes, and the implication is that his firebrand grandfather preached extemporaneously. Although communicated to the reader in written form, the assumption of orality about sermons in novels remains, whether they began in the fictional preacher's study as the text was written or in the pulpit without written antecedent. If epistolary novels retain a sense of correspondents writing to each other, in a similar way sermons in fiction may retain an immediate sense of orality whether they are reported in direct quotation or mediated to the reader through free indirect speech. The reader's assumption of their original orality beats down any sense of their subsequent literariness.

Third, letters in epistolary novels such as *Clarissa* are supplementary to what they are "about." In *Clarissa* they are about the sexual union of bodies, but this is what is palpably absent from them, so the sexual power between Clarissa and Lovelace is "reduced" to a matter of strategic textual moves.[16] Similarly confessional preaching that narrates the preacher's experience, such as Ames' account of his defection to the Quakers, is secondary to the experience itself, inasmuch as it is a considered, retrospective reordering of events to highlight their greater significance. In this instance, it is a textually constructed narrative in which both the preacher and his son reporting it in his letter are capable of making strategic amendments to the actual text in response to the intratextual audiences of the sermon's intended hearers and the letter's intended reader. Because of the way it is reported to the novel's readers, there can be no certainty that readers have access to the true experience recounted in the sermon.

Fourth, letters in novels are both private and public. They are private in their origins in that they begin as private correspondence between characters, but they become matters of public discourse when published in novels.[17] This is to a lesser extent also true of sermons. Among actual preachers a debate goes on about the extent to which their role is to express personal opinions or toe the party line; they ask to what extent it is the preacher's vocation to proclaim ancient truths and to what extent it is to modify them and forge fresh expressions of them to make them applicable to the contemporary age. In the hundred years of preaching recounted in Robinson's novels, there is a hint of this tension: what grandfather Ames preached during the Civil War would have been inappropriate in the 1950s when his grandson writes his endless letter. The private experience and personal opinions of the preacher, informed by careful study of the Christian tradition, contribute to the continuing development of Christian belief, morality, and praxis. Sermons are both personal and public in that they originate in personal experience and individual beliefs, which preachers may choose to make public when they express what they believe in the métier of public discourse. Preaching includes an element of life writing that has always been and continues to be a vibrant oral and written genre within Christianity. In common with all life writing, religious auto/biography has an inevitable degree of fictionality in that the author reorders scattered ingredients to search for or create an order and meaning to life. Indeed testimony and conversion narratives are subject to processes of intertextuality modeled on narratives of divine calling as well as Old and New Testament redemption narratives—in the case of the Old from slavery through wilderness into a promised land and in the case of the New through death to resurrection.[18] One of the results of people attempting to construct for themselves a Christian identity by locating themselves within what has been pejoratively called a particular "repertoire of emplotted stories"[19] is the sameness heard in the convention of testimony. This genre of spiritual auto/biography, in contradistinction with postmodernity's distrust of both metanarrative and optimistic final resolutions, conventionally includes the elements of a religious childhood lost, a wasteful time in a far country, and a conversionist route to "salvation."[20] On the other hand, there are preachers who override the conventions. In *Easter*, the novel discussed in chapter 3, although Blair Ashley finds it difficult to keep his private life out of the public pulpit, his narrative is unconventional in that, realizing that being a covert homosexual was hardly an option for him, he bares his soul and renders himself vulnerable to rejection.

Furthermore, the first-person intimacy of the letter genre has the curious and paradoxical effect of both intensifying and distancing the "real." It intensifies because of the letter's immediacy, but it distances because all we have are the letters that refer away from themselves to something else.[21] This means that letters in novels are both art form and substance; they are simultaneously nature and artifice.[22] This relationship between nature and artifice is, following the discussion of performativity, problematic for the preacher. Is there an art of preaching that makes preachers actors when they practice it? If so, is there any integrity left in preaching? Can John Ames, disillusioned toward the end of his life, thinking that all his preaching fell short of his high hopes for his sermons and that they all might as well be burnt because at least they would make a good fire, be regarded as a faithful preacher communicating religious truth? Inasmuch as Robinson's readers encounter Ames' inner self or, at least, as much of it as Ames or Robinson allows us to see, the answer can be in the affirmative. The intensity of his experience as a minister in Gilead, of his relationship with neighbors (especially the Boughton family), and of his farewell letter in his final illness is sufficiently strong to convince the novel's readers of Ames' sincerity.

David Lodge also wrote about epistolary novels in his collection of articles *The Art of Fiction*. There he said that the epistolary method creates a pseudodocumentary realism while allowing the same event to be shown from more than one point of view. Moreover, the fact that the anticipated responses of the letters' specific addressees condition the discourse makes them rhetorically more complex and revealing.[23] No doubt Lodge was aware that a similar rhetorical complexity is achieved when sermons are inserted genres within novels, especially where readers can see and hear their intratextual addressees' various responses, for then it becomes apparent that the sermons are intended to be apprehended as both authoritative and suspect, and in some cases both fictive and real. There are skeptical hearers as well as those who are so moved by the preaching that they are caught up in the reality of religious or spiritual experience. This probably compromises the credibility of the religious experience and, as the psychologists of religion have shown, this continues to be a problem common to all accounts of religious experience. It is a particular problem in the Protestant Low Church tradition to which the Ames family belongs where the Word is at the center. The problem is this: If preachers control what they say, how can we trust the Story or their stories? How much credibility does their religious experience carry? How do readers assess how genuine any claimed religious experience is? How can novelists communicate the veracity of religious experiences?

To do so, many novelists deploy the techniques of a second, more recent, but disputed, novel genre known as magical realism, for which alternative terms such as "miraculous," "marvelous," or "supernatural" realism are sometimes more appropriate. For those who read with a Christian preunderstanding, for novelists who want to explore the topic of religious and spiritual experience, and for preachers who want convincingly to communicate the possibility of the spirituality of Self or a sense of Other, the genre of magical realism is an attractive prospect. One of magical realism's distinctive features is the presence in the text of an "irreducible element" that the generally agreed-upon laws of the universe in the light of post-Enlightenment empiricism cannot explain.[24] The concept and genre of magical realism should, therefore, offer some insights into how fiction and other literary art forms, such as preaching, treat religious experience where "there is more than meets the eye." The attractiveness of magical realism lies in its dissonance and oxymoronic nature, capable of suggesting the numinosity of the everyday and the potentiality for reconciling secularized society with its forgotten religiosity and spirituality. The concept of magical realism in literature implies that the disenchanted West can recover enchantment.[25] It becomes for readers what one of its exponents, Isabel Allende, called "a way of seeing in which there is space for the invisible forces that move the world: dreams, legends, myths, emotion, passion, history."[26] However, danger lurks in the genre, in that it can easily imply that the utopian visions it offers can only be imagined.

This real danger appears in the popular tradition of Christian fantasy-writing to which C. S. Lewis, J. R. R. Tolkien, Charles Williams, and George MacDonald have all contributed. They write a theology of what does not exist, a fantasy world parents want their children to know about,[27] a wonderland through the looking glass. This differs from miraculous realism. The miraculous, or magical, realism, whose features contribute so much to an understanding of the form and function of fictional sermons, sends novelists on a continuing search for transcendent experience in a supposedly godless era, a sense of the ground beneath all philosophies and theologies, a conception of the remarkable within the everyday.[28] This promises much for the making of theology that works.

Magical realism is a voguish term, whose tenacity belies its lack of definitional precision among theorists and critics, who have displayed a range of contradictory attitudes toward it. Despite continuing controversy about the genre, because a growing corpus of literary works draws upon the conventions of both realism and fantasy or folktale without allowing either realm to assert a greater claim to truth than the other, magical realism serves nonetheless as a useful tool for understanding specific texts.[29] In the twentieth century, magical realism was first applied as a critical tool to Latin American authors such as Alejo Carpentier and Miguel Angel Asturias, and for some time it was most readily applied to Latino writers, most notably Jorge Luis Borges and Garcia Marquez, before critics transferred it to writers such as Salman Rushdie and Ben Okri. Now the term occurs so frequently in critical reviews that critics are in danger of overusing it to the point of meaninglessness. Clearly, a need exists for precision about the meaning of the term and scope of the concept.[30] Where magical realism is used as a mode of narrative that naturalizes the supernatural, making the "otherworldly" and unseen acceptable and understandable aspects of daily life,[31] it has three essential defining characteristics: the magical realist text must display coherently developed codes of both the natural and supernatural, the antimony between these codes must be resolved, and there must be a measure of authorial reticence in place so that the coexistence and legitimacy of neither code is threatened.

Thus, magical realism differs from its neighboring genres of fantasy, fairy tales, and science fiction, for in these the codes of the "real" have been underprivileged because the narratives have been set in worlds other than the recognizable empirical world. It is also distinct from horror and Gothic because these genres do not resolve the antimony between the natural and supernatural realms. The "inexplicability" of the supernatural must also be maintained in the text; in magical realism the narrator must not wake from a dream, for then the "real" is privileged over the fantastic.

If the accepted coexistence of two realms—natural and supernatural, reality and fantasy[32]—is an essential characteristic of magical realism, then magical realism can be read "from either realm." That is to say that magical realism can be read as both "denaturalizing the real" and "naturalizing the marvelous." Thus magical realism offers novels dealing with theological themes the potential to challenge both religious and secular complacency.[33] When magical realist texts are interrogated with three interpretational questions—what is the source of the supernatural in the text, what sort of dialogue does the supernatural have with the text's more realistic elements, and why does the writer engage this mode at this particular time?[34]—two tendencies within magical realism emerge. One is that the element of the marvelous unmasks the real and shows that the naturalistic world's truth claims are provisional; it reveals that the naturalistic, empiricist, post-Enlightenment worldview is contingent on consensus,[35] which is always vulnerable to collapse. The other tendency is that the supernatural forces its way into the company of the natural, challenges realism's privileged claim to represent and account for the world, and claims an equal right to do so. In magical, or marvelous, realism, the real and unreal exist in a state of contrived equivalence, and this is also a characteristic of sermons in fiction. Magical realism does not of itself preach, although it is the natural milieu for convincingly communicating in novels religious and spiritual experiences by which people come to places of knowing the miraculous, marvelous, and numinous. It also aids the understanding and interpreting of texts such as novels, fictional sermons, and actual sermons that seek to establish convincing and genuine experiences, when characters and actual people feel beside themselves in the ordinariness of their existence.

The robustness of this assertion is tested by considering an unlikely proving ground—the complex literary sermon "Lifeguard" in John

Updike's early short story collection *Pigeon Feathers*.[36] It is in toto the first-person interior monologue of a divinity student who works as a beach lifeguard in the summer months; it thereby has the immediacy of an epistolary narrative, although it is not addressed to a particular recipient. The story has all the hallmarks of a sermon. The lifeguard in his watchtower is the pastor in his pulpit, the red cross on his chair-back his priestly vestment, the Sunday morning beachgoers his congregation. He describes his musings as "my sermon." "Lifeguard" is sermonic in format, with an introduction, a subject that serves as a text, exposition, illustrations, and a concluding exhortation, but the fact that the sermon also serves as the young man's double confession that he is attracted by the flesh as much as by the spirit and that he is studying at seminary without any sense of vocation, complicates it. His situation becomes further complicated by the fact that it is a parody, which becomes irony when he suggests that his work as a lifeguard in which he might be called upon to save people may be compared to saving souls, when he turns his text into an excuse for sexual appetite, and when his final exhortation to enjoy one's sensuality is seen to be hollow in the light of the narcissism of his opening paragraph.[37] However strong this sense of parody and irony is, it does not negate any sense of the sermon striving toward the numinous. The lifeguard-preacher is under the impression that his sermon places an easy burden on the shoulders of any who hear it, yet it reaches toward immensity, beauty, ecstasy, and immortality, all through an invitation to exercise imagination. Referencing, among others, Paul Tillich whose *Theology of Culture*[38] established that anthropological culture provides the raw data both for people's self-interpretation and for the theological task, the lifeguard-preacher surveys from his unequalled vantage point the array of humanity spread out before him. He is aware that he is on "the edge of an immensity" (147), although contra Charles Wesley, of whom Updike's imagery is reminiscent—

> Eager for thee I ask and pant:
> So strong, the principle divine
> Carries me out with sweet constraint
> Till all my hallowed soul is thine,
> Plunged in the Godhead's deepest sea,
> And lost in thine immensity.[39]

—the lifeguard-preacher feels that the ocean can no longer serve as a divine metaphor. Even so, he yearns to lift the mass of humanity into immortality (150), and he declares that what he sees before him is a vision of impossibility, a vision of paradise (151). In short, the matter of this sermon is "ecstasy and buoyance," of which he says swimming is a parable (148). The ecstasy may be more physical than spiritual, yet it is nevertheless the matter of marvelous or miraculous realism in that it takes the young man in his sermon beyond the immediate and mundane. Indeed, the "text" for the lifeguard-preacher's sermon, "there is no discrepancy between my studies. . . . The texts of the flesh complement those of the mind" (147), is one of the abiding concerns throughout Updike's oeuvre as he seeks to reunite body and spirit in Christian thought. The study of beauty, which is the preoccupation of the voyeur on the watch tower, stimulates his imagination so that he is beside or beyond himself in an ecstatic desire to lift the masses into a vision of paradise in which they are conscious of divine presence and the transcendence on whose shore they stand in their day-to-day existence. Because the lifeguard-preacher knows that someday his alertness will bear fruit (152), neither his lack of calling nor the parodic nature of his sermon compromises his more noble aims.

Marilynne Robinson informs her readers in *Gilead* that "A good sermon is one side of a passionate conversation" (51). Far from being the monologue sermons appear to be (and "Lifeguard" appears to be nothing other than monologue), they are but one voice in conversations involving several contributors, among whom are those Robinson's Ames thinks of as the thinking self, the responding self, and God. The apparent monologue by a preacher delivered to hearers—or in the case of fictional sermons to readers—also involves the wider human society in which the sermon is located, individuals within that society, and whatever image of God it carries. The sermon engages readers, addressees, and unintended hearers and is itself a religious or spiritual experience with which its participants can engage. The vividness of the imagination when engaging with sermons found pictorial expression in Paul Gauguin's painting *Vision after the Sermon: Jacob Wrestling with the Angel*, in which a small group of Breton women listen to a sermon on Jacob's story in Genesis. It demonstrates how important are questions about the nature of religious experience to any assessment of the practice of preaching, for either the women in the painting are so devout and suggestible, or the preaching is so vivid and effectual, that the women can imagine the event that is being described, and viewers of the painting can actually see what they imagine. Although the artist is in the painting, for amusingly he has painted himself among the women to the extreme right of the work, the preacher is not there; instead, Gauguin paints Jacob and the wrestling angel in place of the preacher as the object of the women's vision. Thus the invisible is seen in bold outline against a field of crimson, giving visible form to imagined vision. From outside the painting, observers are able to visualize the internal religious experiences of the people in the painting as their imaginations are caught up in the preaching event. Pictorially, Gauguin's painting draws attention to the fact that engaging with a sermon as a listener is potentially an experience that takes people either "beyond themselves" into a spiritual realm or inwardly into the world of creative and spiritual imagination. Listening to a sermon is a potentially religious or spiritual experience, enabling hearers to see what they imagine.[40] The challenge facing the novelist is how to express that potential convincingly on the page.

The exploration of preaching as, and in, fiction ventures into contested ground, for some believe that novels have lost the ability to talk of God in the current age, whether these times are characterized as secular, postmodern, or post-Christian, while others believe that novels are capable of articulating religious matters more forcefully now than people often recognize. The study of fictional sermons has hypothesized, first, that authentic spiritual or religious experience can be communicated in fiction through the pseudodocumentary realism of the epistolary genre, similar to the immediacy of characters' life writing in sermons when they allow their self-narration to intrude in their preaching and, second, that such experience is most convincing for the reader when elements of the genre of magical or marvelous realism are deployed by the novelist in his or her creation of fictional sermons. The world of religious experience is, to use an aptly dissonant phrase, marvelously real.

6

WORDS
Poison in the Ear, a Game with Language, or Naming Truth?

❦

Fictional sermons stand out prominently from their surrounding contexts on the page not only by their presentation within speech marks, in italics, or some other visual cue but also by their use of differentiated language in the form of direct address, specialist vocabulary, or other indications of orality. This examination of the nature of the language employed in fictional sermons, using those in A. S. Byatt's Frederica quartet[1] and later those in an overlooked American novel by William H. Gass, asks whether a clear distinction between the fictional sermons and their contexts is necessary. Must fictional sermons leap out of the novel in such a jarring way?

In debates with others, suggesting that an argument is "playing with semantics" or calling the dispute "mere words" is often taken as a rude dismissal of the argument as being without substance or integrity. Yet, the only one of four clergymen occupying the imagined world of Byatt's Frederica novels to be present throughout the series dismisses preaching as "words, words" (47). Readers encountering this opinion so early in the first book, *The Virgin in the Garden*, take this to be a seriously damning and troubling verdict on preaching, especially when it challenges the high expectations the author assumes of preaching within the rest of the books and especially when the speaker is the only clergyman never to preach in them. The Frederica novels, written and published over a period of twenty-five years, compose a sustained meditation on metaphor, in which Byatt's principal concerns are the nature of language and truth. The clergyman concerned is Daniel Orton, whose vocation to the priesthood had been aroused by the skillful oratory of an unnamed member of a High Anglican religious community preaching to schoolboys at a Civics Week in Sheffield. Daniel's career path in the novels takes him out of conventional parochial ministry into practical ministry as a Listener in a fictionalized version of the Samaritans, the telephone hotline for the suicidal and desperate staffed by volunteers throughout Britain. His sustained presence, throughout the decades chronicled in the novels, means that his unconventional ministry is conducted across several eras of theological and ecclesiastical trends. Mainly because Byatt uses the preaching of the other clerics in the series to locate them theologically, spiritually, or ecclesiastically within these trends, both the absence from the novels of any record of Orton's preaching and his low opinion of sermons are highly significant. He resists classification, and his views on preaching expressed within the novel trouble the way Byatt uses the others' sermons to classify them. The other clerics in the novels are Mr. Ellenby, Daniel's first vicar when he is a curate, whose appointment is taken up by Gideon Farrar in the second volume of the quartet, *Still Life*; Canon Adelbert Holly, who participates with a religious community that Gideon Farrar establishes; and Joshua Lamb, known also as Joshua Ramsden, a religious leader who emerges within the community exercising a priestly role though not ordained. As a lay member with a charismatic personality, he rivals Gideon Farrar for effective leadership of the Joyful Companions, a religious community with sect-like characteristics that emerges as the focus of the last book in the series.

Although Byatt resists this reductive description of her work, the Frederica novels do chronicle the 1950s and 1960s, which in political, sociological and religious terms were turbulent times of great change.[2] Clashing convictions and sociological upheaval made these decades times of interesting and heated debates. Not least among these debates were theological discussions about radical understandings of God, ways of reading the Bible that opened its pages to fresh insights, and the nature of religious language. These clashes troubled some religious believers; academic theologians did not support the people in the pews in their beliefs as they wanted. Dissonances heard in the language of these debates are the context for the sermons in Byatt's novels.³ Giving primary emphasis to the nature of the language in the fictional sermons in Byatt's Frederica novels sheds light on this problem and leads toward an understanding of the nature of religious language as a possible subset of ordinary human language.

The Virgin in the Garden includes three sermons, preceded by an earlier allusion (39) to a sermon written in anger by the young Bill Potter when a Congregational minister burnt his copy of *Jude the Obscure.* The first sermon persuades Daniel Orton by its "mesmeric incantation" to pursue vocation to priesthood (68). A silent, lonely child, fat, ponderous, and a burden to his widowed mother, Daniel's inarticulacy and outsider status render him susceptible to a response of admiration for a powerful orator. In the absence of his deceased birth father, the unnamed spiritual Father who preaches promises Daniel, who feels somewhat excluded, that he can be an effective contributor to the society of which he longs to be part. Ellenby preaches the second sermon in *The Virgin in the Garden*. In its choice of subject, "decomposition . . . reversed" (202), and its accent on the barbarity and blood of Easter, there is clashing dissonance between the sermon and the schemata of "English" Easters, with their association with the arrival of spring—a dissonance that disturbs Stephanie, around whom this first novel revolves, who finds herself repelled by their particular unpleasantness (200). Her extreme reaction comes because she is conflicted emotionally; she realizes too late that she ought not to have gone to church that day and that her true motive for going was to watch Daniel at prayer. Readers with a mischievous mind, aware that sermons are composed by writers, will find themselves asking what a discourse on "decomposition reversed" composes or constructs. The answer is that all texts construct or attract a textual community around them, but the mischievous reader's question also plays with words and their meanings, in this case decomposition and composition. The fictional sermon and its original author, Byatt, make the same implied puns. Ellenby preaches the third sermon in the novel at Daniel and Stephanie's wedding and attempts to accommodate the varied interests of both; he weaves into the sermon allusions to Spenser and Milton for the benefit of the English student, Stephanie, and an allusion to Genesis and ordination for Daniel. That these allusions are only partially successful makes the sermon gently, but unintentionally, humorous, and implies that Ellenby is forcing the allusions.

In two of the later Frederica novels, the more natural contextualization of religious language appropriate to a novel's era, and idiom appropriate to the preacher's particular theology, is more effective. The second volume of the quartet, *Still Life*, includes two sermons. Bill Potter's antisermon on the folly of belief in the virgin birth comes first with an argument against the reality of supernatural elements in the four Gospels.[4] Bill's intimidating style robs all potential color, light, and warmth from his potentially liberating theological stance. Byatt follows her reference to Bill's antisermon with a description of the Church nativity play as "a believed fairy tale" (50) in which Herod occupies the pulpit. No less appropriate person could be placed there. This incongruous juxtaposition of antisermon and nativity play makes both Bill Potter and Herod disturbers of the peace and usurpers of the pulpit. Gideon Farrar's treatise on personhood, which he preaches when he first arrives in the parish, is the next sermon, reported in direct speech but with elisions shown by ellipses (158–59). With the convention of a three-part discourse on distinct aspects of the concept of person, it treats the Trinity as three persons, then the parson as person, and finally, personal relationships in which he expresses the impertinent hope that he will be invited into the homes of his parishioners for meals. This sermon refers to Dietrich Bonhoeffer, whose execution in 1945 led to his theology and ministry being used as captivating sermon illustrations in the following decades. It also depicts emergent new understandings of the parson's role, in which the parson represents church in society rather than representing the people as *persona exemplaris* before God. Combined, these reflect something of Byatt's perception of the changing role of parsons in postwar Britain, when the influence of the Church was in decline, and the rise of a sense in society that "it can do without God, in science, in politics, even in morals" (159).

No sermons are featured in *Babel Tower*, although its continued exploration of religious language as metaphor contributes to understanding the nature of language in preaching. In *A Whistling Woman*, however, as many as six sermons occur, more than in any of the earlier novels of the tetralogy. Seemingly incidental to the novel, they are in fact neither incidental nor accidental. After all, one of Byatt's own characters, Stephanie Orton, was prompted by Gideon Farrar's first sermon in *Still Life* to reflect that everything in a novel is there because it signifies something, not because it actually was there (SL, 161). Sermons are no exception to this general rule. Indeed, in *A Whistling Woman* each sermon contributes to Byatt's fictive building of the Joyful Companions, the religious community at the heart of the book.

One of the sermons in *A Whistling Woman* is Gideon Farrar's final sermon in the quartet. Since he last preached in *Still Life*, readers have learned that Farrar has been accused of child molestation and sexual malpractice: few women escaped the attention of his wandering eye and roving hand. This contrasts sharply with his sustained eye contact when preaching his first sermon in *Still Life* (158). Indeed, the last thought Stephanie had before her fatal accident reminded her that Gideon Farrar was a dangerous sexual predator. In *A Whistling Woman*, Farrar still uses the charge of sexual energy to manipulate those who belong to the community he has established. In the view of Brenda Pincher, who observes the community for research purposes, Gideon's sexual manipulation makes people feel special because of the thrill of his attention (193). Brenda gives a disturbing account of Gideon's sermon within the Community. The secretly recorded tape that she sends to her correspondent begins with strange shufflings and snufflings, recording the touching and feeling that are required at the beginning of all meetings of the Community. Brenda's description of Gideon Farrar's overtight jeans that accentuate his ample buttocks and a straining fly zip make these snufflings particularly disturbing. The sermon about fellowship, one of Gideon's favorite words, ends when he approaches Lucy Nighby and puts his hands heavily on her shoulders. She writhes under the pressure for some time, before he lets go, and she shakes herself like a dog shaking off mud or water and crossly walks out of the room. In effect, Brenda has witnessed ritual abuse. "Laying on of hands" for ordination or healing has become, in Gideon Farrar's manipulative and predatory community, the more threatening "laying hands on." This is symptomatic of a problem with the realist novel form; realist novels depend on making things materially present, so they often have difficulty representing spirituality without reductionism.

Joshua Lamb gives three sermon-like discourses in this novel. In the first, the presentation of a paper on Kierkegaard, he speaks so eloquently that it provokes trembling among his hearers (122), an ironically appropriate reaction, given that Kierkegaard's best-known work, about which Lamb's mentor had been speaking on the previous page, is entitled *Fear and Trembling*. The second occurs in the course of a discussion about the merits and demerits of television. Joshua expresses his views on the matter in an impressive and ludicrously pompous speech that Elvet Gander reports in a letter to Kieran Quarrell. He concludes that Joshua sounded like a preacher (197). Later Brenda Pincher reports that Joshua gave talks and sermons on Manichean belief to members of the community to whom he refers as "Hearers" (223), implying that the chief characteristic of belonging to a community is little more than passively hearing edifying words, although in a scriptural or liturgical context hearing also implies "listening to with favor and granting a request."[5]

Canon Adelbert Holly also preaches in *A Whistling Woman*. His themes—the death of God, Deus absconditus, and the impossibility of the church—are radical yet appropriate to the 1960s. He gives an impromptu sermon on St. Lucy's Day around a campfire, about which Brenda Pincher speaks in a letter to Avram Snitkin. Readers cannot rely on this report, for, because she was high on acid, her memory of the night is unclear. She does recall, however, that the "half after-dinner speech, half pagan paean" (233) hailed Lucy Nighby as blessed among women for providing the Hall for the religious community and declared that, by virtue of her name, she was Lux, Lucis, the Maiden of Light. Brenda also recalls that she was impressed by Holly's brilliance in interweaving John Donne's "St. Lucie's Day," as she spells the poem's title, with a prayer to an absentee God. She reflects that perhaps Holly was so adept in this sermon because "religious men always twist" (232). Readers can trust neither Brenda's report nor the preacher. Holly's second sermon, heard by the entire Potter family and the Hearers of Dun Vale Hall, responds to the local vicar's invitation for Holly to preach at Freyasgarth Church at Christmas. The vicar had given Holly a few days' notice, so it has been prepared. As Canon Holly makes his way to the pulpit, readers realize that there is a sense of occasion about this preaching; he has, unusually for him, put on his clerical collar, and his white hair is described as "patriarchal, even angelic" (241). He begins self-importantly, leans over the pulpit as he speaks, and smiles "beatifically" as he concludes. He asks where God can be found when theologians have so often sought to distance God from the earth. He then links his Death of God theology with kenoticism, a doctrine of incarnation closely associated with Philippians 2:5-11, to argue against the notion that people are to live in this world with no sense of God, no sense of heaven, and no fear of hell. Instead, people can live with God's daily incarnation, or, to use Holly's terms, God's self-shrinking of infinity into finite flesh, God's shrinking of timelessness into historical time. Holly clearly believes he has said something profound, even innovative and groundbreaking, but Frederica gives a less than fulsome verdict on the sermon, judging that it was "*almost* meaningful, but . . . in the end a game with language" (242).

Many will justifiably assume that a novelist's use of specifically theological language in sermons within fiction will distance, decenter, or dislocate the reader who is likely to be unfamiliar with its terms.[6] Moreover, because the presence of specifically theological language allows additional voices to the narrating voice to speak, namely those of the institutional church and of the academic discipline of theology, many will also assume that specialist theological language tends to render anachronistic or inapposite any theological and philosophical comment in novels.

But of course religious language is not essentially strange, distancing, or anachronizing, even though much academic interest in the nature of religious language asserts its peculiarity.[7] Language cannot avoid being value laden; it is never innocent of at least some "angle of telling," for it unavoidably bears the cultural assumptions, political beliefs, and institutional practices of its speaker.[8] People, therefore, often distrust words. The slick sales executive is a menace. Words can lead people astray, tempting them to taste forbidden fruit or take wrong directions in life; they can poison minds; they can speak lies when seeming to speak truth, and, even when they speak truth, they can be twisted so that they mislead or be misunderstood when heard. But people also rely heavily upon words, as humankind's chief means of communication. Moreover, words constitute the building blocks of speeches. Words are the tesserae of the linguistic mosaic of assumptions, beliefs, and practices that compose a preacher's sermon. In the sermons in Byatt's novels, words encode theological, religious, or spiritual worldviews; they communicate ideologies derived from "taken-for-granted assumptions" and shared value systems within the institution of the church.[9] In most, but not all, cases, these givens include the presumption of God's existence and a shared "theory of how the world is arranged."[10] This textual ideology forms a linguistic construct rather than an objective reality, and this means that theology is preeminently verbal. In the 1960s this observation led the academic discipline of linguistic philosophy to understand its business to be a study of both words-about-words and words-about-the-Word. The unattractive, tautological term "logology," literally "words about words," thus came into newly minted academic usage. The relationship between the study of language (words about words) and theology (etymologically "words about God"), could not be closer.

Logology led to some general observations about the paradigmatic function of theological language. As language serves as a human means of communication, so theological language functions as a human attempt to communicate first-order religious claims, rather than a divine dispensation revealed to humans from on high. Nevertheless, using language theologically transforms it. Indeed, when language is employed for theological purposes, it tends to develop new, ultimate connotations that then migrate back into nontheological uses of the same language.[11] For example, the meanings of the terms "grace" and "create" have been augmented during their migration in and out of ordinary usage and theological application. This augmenting migration occurs because all language, and most obviously religious language, is essentially metaphorical, so much so that "everything we say is metaphorically said."[12] The "magic" or plasticity of metaphor achieves this linguistic transformation of words. Because religious language is a "complex web of metaphors and symbols pointing towards an imperfectly understood reality" and because these metaphors stretch human communication beyond literal sense to talk of God,[13] the loss of the elasticity of the symbolic is a risk that needs to be averted. Otherwise, the symbols themselves become idolatrous, demonized, or elevated to ultimate reality,[14] and the language itself usurps its subject. People live by metaphors, and God-talk is essentially metaphorical.

When people employ language theologically, the literal and the figurative become locked in a signifying relationship of double-voiced discourse that results in indeterminate interpretation.[15] The meaning a term conveys and the meaning it was intended to convey can differ;[16] surface and latent meaning can differ;[17] literal and metaphorical signification can differ. But the louder voice is always metaphor. Christians do not always find this easy to grasp when they want to talk about God. Recently, for instance, a tutor introduced a new class to his way of doing theology. He asked whether a theologian can be a poet. In their answers, some struggled to see how theologians, whom they assumed aimed for precision, the smoothing out of inconsistencies, and systematic reasoning, could live with what they perceived as the imprecision of poetry, whereas others saw that theologians are necessarily poets working with figurative language in attempts to express the inexpressible and ineffable. While some novelists write their fictional sermons with the same assumption as that held by the former group of students, they write their novels as if they belong in the latter group. Study of fictional sermons leads toward the conclusion that theologians and preachers are poets as much as novelists and other literary artists are.

A distinction between metaphor and analogy should be maintained. Analogy is an unknown understood in terms of a known, whereas metaphor is two knowns forced into equivalency by establishing common fields of meaning.[18] In other words, analogy is argumentative and explanatory, whereas metaphor (like its big sister, poetry) works on senses and emotions as well as minds, providing "a moving and human framework for ideas, partly because they are full of contradictions and may even be illogic [sic]."[19] Because metaphor does more than make comparisons[20]—rather it makes accessible what would otherwise lie beyond our linguistic grasp—metaphors cannot be replaced by literal equivalents.[21] The language of preaching uses metaphor, not analogy: contra Alan Bennett's parody of a sermon in which a ludicrous vicar compares life with a tin of sardines, preachers do not argue "this is like that"; rather, in the metaphorical language of preaching, they say in a faithfully persuasive way that "this is that by which we live as if it is so." The essence of metaphor is "understanding *and experiencing* one kind of thing in terms of another."[22]

Since philosophers tend to regard metaphors as "out of the ordinary imaginative or poetic linguistic expressions,"[23] for some Christians the problem with regarding theological language as metaphor is that it compromises the "truth" of their faith. But, as Pilate implied in his challenging question to Jesus, it depends what one means by "truth." It is a slippery concept. While people of power seek to impose their brand of truth to control other people by fabricating a notion of objective truth, real truth is much more amorphous. The institutional church participates in this power play in the way it distinguishes between orthodoxy and heterodoxy. Nonetheless, truth remains an important aspect of daily lives, in that all human actions are based on what people take to be true, from something as simple as where shoppers can buy a loaf of bread to something as complex as the way human beings can express their sense of the numinous. People then ritualize their actions, from where they shop to how they engage with God, on the basis of their perception of truth. "Truth," thus, becomes culturally embedded. Furthermore, the concepts enabling people to categorize and grasp the meaning and truth of statements are carried in metaphors;[24] people understand the world, think, and function in metaphorical terms.[25] In the absence of objective reality—a problematic concept for anyone working in either faith or fiction (and doubly problematic for anyone working in both, as here)—metaphor carries truth. Once again, literal translation cannot replace metaphor.[26] The contingency of truth combines with the tensional quality of metaphor, derived from its stereoscopic, split-referential, or bifocal vision,[27] to give language the dynamism to generate new meaning in theology as well as in literature, in speech as well as in writing, in academic as well as in confessional theology. In *A Whistling Woman*, Hedder Pinsky refers to this inability of human beings to think without metaphors (353), a major preoccupation of Byatt's work.

This preoccupation in her work comes from a sustained academic interest in metaphor since the 1950s, when she worked at Oxford on a (never finished) doctoral dissertation about religious metaphor in Renaissance poetry. The thesis remained in her mind almost fifty years later, when she referred to it in a newspaper review of a National Gallery exhibition in 2005.[28] That Byatt gives Ellenby, Farrar, and Holly distinctive speech idioms in a determined intention to differentiate among these preachers bears significance for this study even though the sermons in the Frederica tetralogy have little effect on the characters and have small roles in the novels' plots. The sermons in these novels appear as incidental texts-within-texts, but, inasmuch as nothing in novels is meaningless, Byatt includes them as a contribution to her continued exploration of the dilemma that the language of humankind is unable to speak adequately of God.

The language of the King James Version of the Bible characterizes both an Easter sermon and a wedding address the local vicar Ellenby preaches in *The Virgin in the Garden*. The Easter sermon about "decomposition . . . reversed" (202) composes a resurrection narrative intentionally recomposing the body of Christ as the church and enabling the congregation to celebrate its composition as the beating heart of Christ (202). Ellenby's composition of resurrection narrative is more *re*composition in that it comprises a repertoire of Pauline biblical allusions, such as "condemned to eternal death," alluding to 1 Corinthians 11:32, "if after the manner of men . . . I have fought with beasts at Ephesus, what advantageth it me, if the dead rise not? Let us eat and drink; for tomorrow we die," quoting 1 Corinthians 15:32, and, "we too live forever," taking up the theme of Romans 8:12-13 (201). The language of the King James Bible similarly informs his address at Stephanie and Daniel's wedding, as he refers to Genesis 2:24 and some verses in Ephesians 5, especially 28 and 32, in which the letter writer, in the tradition of Paul, sees the relationship between a man and his wife as analogous to that between Christ and the church (343). But the success of his attempt to communicate is limited. Ellenby is unable to read Daniel's blunt "yes" in response to Ellenby's private comment about the marital status of St. Peter, and he suspects Daniel is "half pagan" (343). At the back of the church, Marcus distractedly only "partly heard" the sermon, and Stephanie "harboured briefly savage thoughts about the essential shiftiness of argument by analogy" (344). The author reveals Stephanie's thoughts; both analogy and metaphor are unavoidably "shifty" in that they depend upon shifting meanings of signifiers. Stephanie, in this revealed thought, thus challenges the very basis of all preaching as well as the possibility of all talk about God.

The interpretative repertoires employed in Gideon Farrar's preaching, in both *Still Life* and *A Whistling Woman*, move away from biblical discourse to use other forms of discourse. Nevertheless, in the sermon he preaches when he first arrives in the parish, he (mis)applies to Christ a Pauline phrase, "all things to all men" (SL, 158). The sermon is more theological than biblical and also uses the linguistic repertoire of the social sciences. This casts suspicion in the reader's mind and causes readers of this early novel to distrust Farrar as a modernizer of religion who is maverick enough eventually to distort Christianity in the final Frederica novel. After reminding his audience of the many parts Shakespeare expected people to play in their lifetimes, Farrar uses sociological jargon and the interpretative repertoire of the theater to warn that the roles people play should not be "confining cells" but "masks," and he speaks of "the relations of men in groups" and "primordial groups" (SL, 159). He announces his subject as "the Second Person of the Trinity," "Jesus Christ the divine man," and the way people behave in personal relationships. He draws a theological distinction among the real, the sacramental, and the symbolic, distinctions also present in fiction.

When readers next encounter one of Gideon Farrar's sermons, several years have passed, he has founded a breakaway religious community, and he is addressing its members at a communal love feast for the Children of Joy. Because Byatt uses a letter in which Brenda Pincher analyses Farrar's leadership style to communicate this sermon to readers, discourse analysis of Farrar's preaching, in this case, cannot be pure. Language governs all negotiated human relationships, but readers cannot be confident that they have access to Farrar's own words; Pincher chooses how she will convey the sense of Farrar's preaching to her correspondent. Readers do not know how or whether she has inflected them in any way. Nevertheless, readers are aware that Farrar has not entirely eschewed biblical quotation; he cites "come unto me all ye who are heavy laden and I will give you rest" (although Pincher says it is unclear whether "me" refers to Christ or Farrar), and he quotes John 8:32, "The truth will make you free," before claiming that *he* will cast out fear and shadow so that community members may live "in the clear" (WW, 203). Byatt, through Pincher, thus shows readers that Farrar has appropriated the Word. The lexis or linguistic repertoire of traditional ecclesiastical language populates the sermon; for instance, Farrar talks a lot about the openness of fellowship, but he also prefers to use circumlocutions such as "'grievous faults', 'errors', 'mistakes' and even 'misfortunes'" (WW, 203) rather than require "a full public confession of . . . sins." He also interprets Jesus casting out demons in terms of "painful birthing" (WW, 203).

Canon Adelbert Holly preaches twice in *A Whistling Woman*: once giving an impromptu sermon on St. Lucy's Day and on the other occasion giving a Christmas Day sermon at the invitation of the vicar of Freyasgarth. The first plays on variations on the theme of the interpretative repertoire of enlightenment, as Holly quotes John Donne's "St. Lucy's Day" and, according to Brenda Pincher, twists his quotation into a desperate prayer to the Deus absconditus who is "reborn in the Particles of Light in all of us" (WW, 232). In his "half after-dinner speech, half pagan paean," Holly's riff on Lucy's name and its mythical and religious associations elevates her to the inappropriate level of being on par with Mary, mother of Jesus, who alone is conventionally hailed as "blessed among women" (WW, 233). Holly's Christmas sermon uses the lexis of kenotic theology, which systemizes the image of God's self-emptying in Christ. Intending to say something "real, rather than a few nice platitudes," he speaks of "a steady distancing of God from the earth" in the history of the development of theological thought, culminating in Nietzsche's eventual declaration of the death of God (WW, 241). Holly equates Nietzsche's "death of God" with the moment of incarnation when God "emptied himself out" into "finite flesh" and "entered History [in such a way that] . . . His birth is repeated daily in historical time" (WW, 242). In a phrase reminiscent of Daniel Orton's dismissal of preaching near the beginning of the first novel in Byatt's quartet, Frederica, in real time almost twenty-five years later, expressed her irritation that the sermon was "*almost* meaningful but not quite, [merely] in the end a game with language" (WW, 242). Without Frederica's literary appreciation and analysis of the poetry of "In the Bleak Midwinter" that follows Holly's sermon, this remark merely reiterates her sister's earlier unexpressed criticism that Ellenby's wedding sermon displayed the shiftiness of argument by analogy (VG, 344). Remarkably, the unmusical Stephanie finds that the carol's music enables her to "make sense" of Donne's words. This confuses readers, but it enables Byatt to imply the ease with which language can slip from sense to senselessness. This fluidity of language fascinates

Byatt, who has therefore been dubbed "a very 'wordy' writer,"[29] and gives her fictional sermons—and those of other novelists—their efficacy and power.

An essay on reality in the first Frederica novel described *The Virgin in the Garden* as "experimental and realist, about images and about real people,"[30] a clash of the real and imagined which Frederica herself embodies. For instance, in Alexander Wedderburn's play about Elizabeth I, whose first performance is planned to take place in the grounds of an Elizabethan mansion at the time of Elizabeth II's coronation, Frederica plays the young queen, and Byatt informs readers that she, "as the embodied real form of his imagined heroine," fascinates Alexander.[31] The observation that "Alexander's imagined Elizabeth was a real temporal figure, while Frederica, who is to realize her in the play, is herself a figment of Byatt's imagination" exacerbates the complexity of the real and the imagined and demonstrates the potential for them to be coterminous.[32] Writing is a form of reality, although "the realities . . . characters perceive [are] artifices which exist only in the mind."[33] Byatt parodies the writer's passion for the imaginary in Alexander's preference for "imagined contact with real women," found in a salacious correspondence with Jennifer Parry, and "real contact with imaginary women," found in his proxy passion for his Virgin Queen. In this way, Alexander demonstrates "the incapacity of the image to encompass what is real."[34] Thus, as a verbal artifact, the novel defines itself as a form of reality: "the real exists through the mediation of the unreal verbal form."[35] This, the ineffable finding true expression in the verbal artifact of the sermon, is also the problem of theology and preaching, especially for literalists.

Still Life, a novel that asks how accurately language can represent actual phenomena, takes up the problem again. This time Byatt chooses to exemplify the problem through the alternative medium of painting. She retains an immediate link between the painter's vision and the writer's art by centering the problem on Alexander Wedderburn again, as, this time, he works on a play entitled *The Yellow Chair* based on Van Gogh's final years.[36] This novel confirms that for Byatt the most powerful feature of language is metaphor; indeed, her fascination with its creative and educational capacity leads her to comment directly and extensively within *Still Life* on the metaphorical basis of language in general and names in particular.[37] For instance, in one episode in the book, Alexander considers how he might accurately describe a damson plum, and he realizes that the terms he might employ—"oval," "purple-black," "hazed with bloom," and "marked with a pronounced cleft"—would lead readers to infer "flower-bloom, skin bloom, bloom of ripe youth . . . human clefts, declivities, cleavages" (199). By some process in his brain, these *become* metaphors. Surplus meaning, or superfluity of signification, fills the language to overflowing so that the metaphor—and indeed the entire fiction in which the metaphor is set—transforms and transfigures reality.[38] This is an important idea not only in relation to metaphor but also for the way sermons work on their hearers. In her essay "Still Life / Nature morte," Byatt herself points to Ricoeur's work on metaphor as one of the intellectual influences on the discussion of metaphor within *Still Life*.[39] In particular, she pays credit to the last of Ricoeur's three stages of mimesis, the *new* configuration that may be either refiguration or transfiguration or both. Here, fiction represents reality and attains transfiguring or transformative capability.[40]

A helpful by-product of Byatt's extended exploration of metaphorical language in these novels is that she establishes an analogy between writing and preaching, between novels and sermons, between literary language and religious language. At least twice in *Still Life*, the author steps into the action to explain her attitude when writing the novel. Once, the author intrudes (131) and says:

> I had the idea that this novel could be written innocently . . . without, as far as possible, recourse to simile or metaphor. This turned out to be impossible: one cannot think at all without a recognition and realignment of ways of thinking and seeing we have learned over time.

Again, toward the end of *Still Life* when Marcus Potter is compiling a list of grasses, she intrudes (364) and says:

> I had the idea, when I began this novel, that it would be a novel of naming and accuracy. I wanted to write a novel as Williams said a poem should be; no ideas but in things. I even thought of trying to write without figures of speech, but had to give up that plan, quite early.

She has repeated these observations on at least two further occasions. According to her essay on *Still Life*, she intended this to be her "bare book" in that, in a very down-to-earth way it would attempt "to give the 'thing itself' without the infinitely extensive cross-referencing" of its prequel, but, twenty years later, in an article reviewing an exhibition of still life pictures at the National Gallery, she admitted that she could not achieve her aim.[42] Like one of the characters in the novel, Raphael Faber, Byatt discovered the necessity of metaphor when writing *Still Life*. Faber's lecture on "Names and Nouns" comments on the way language was once regarded as "Adamic naming" in that words were somehow part of the thing they named. Now, however, people tend to see that human language has become "unfitted," torn loose from the world, and metaphor is the way people perceive likeness, in "a network of our attempted sense-making" (245). At this stage of the book, readers also remember that the narrator had earlier disparaged Daniel Orton as a preacher when *Still Life*'s prologue stated that, although Daniel

> knew about the light shining in the darkness [he] had come, for reasons completely different from Alexander's desire for exactness, specificity, to mistrust figurative language. He never now made a sermon from a metaphor, nor drew analogies: he preached examples, cases, lessons. (11)

When, after Stephanie has been electrocuted, he does think metaphorically of God, the image he uses either shows that he is blaming God for Stephanie's death or suggests his inability to select appropriate images. He goes to the church to pray to "the old, thick, undifferentiated God who held together the stones of that place, who *lived like electricity* in its heavier air, whose presence he had sensed only rarely" (423, emphasis in original). As this seems an unlikely image for the prosaic and terse Daniel to employ, this is either a lapse on Byatt's part or intentional. There is nothing in the passage to alert the reader to an intended metaphor. Even Daniel cannot help but revert to the language of imagery and analogy.

In these ways, *Still Life* shows that writing, speaking, or preaching without recourse to metaphor simply cannot be done. Byatt, for instance, imagines two futures for Frederica:

> There were two hypothetical future Fredericas—one closed in the University Library writing something elegant and subtle on the use of metaphor in seventeenth-century religious poetry, and one in London, more nebulous,

writing quite different things, witty critical journalism, maybe even a new urban novel like those of Iris Murdoch. (343)

Quite apart from the fact that Byatt suggests that these two hypothetical Fredericas were in fact one, and quite apart from the obvious temptation for readers to identify both as Byatt herself, significantly both futures mapped out for the character engage with metaphor. One involves studying it; the other involves using it, for, as Raphael Faber argues, metaphor is inescapable. Furthermore, when deliberately attempting to avoid metaphor, Byatt includes classified "lists of simple denominated things,"[42] where, for instance, Marcus Potter derives pleasure from nothing other than the taxonomic exercise of listing grasses, and where the author shows inexhaustible attention to detail when naming colors. Both lists engage with one of the main concerns of the novel: "the relation between visual perception . . . and its representation in language."[43] The last novel of the tetralogy reaches a climax in this style of listing when her concern for naming and accuracy is obsessively and strangely directed to the life cycle and taxonomy of snails. Some readers find this superfluity of information wearisome and excessively showy.

But this sustained concern for naming and accuracy arises from the author's interest in the precision of language. Superabundance of image and superfluity of signification are incomparably important—in writing as well as preaching, in novels as well as sermons, in literature as well as theology. Moreover, Byatt claims, in a conversation with Iris Murdoch, that *Still Life* is about "the hard idea of truth."[44] Naming truth, which is language's major challenge, is the hard idea both for fiction and for preaching. Byatt's novels present preachers as people who seek meaningful convergence between faith and experience that enables people to live faithfully. Meanwhile, real-life preachers seek the accuracy and density, opacity and polyphonality, wealth and superfluity of meaning in language that empowers believers to imagine, "name," and realize their faith. Charles Wesley longed for a single voice to call the world to Christ's feet in one of his well-known hymns:

> O for a trumpet voice
> On all the world to call,
> To bid their hearts rejoice
> In him who died for all! (*Hymns and Psalms* 226)

But to be effective with their diverse audiences, real-life preachers ought to have more than a trumpet voice; they need to be multivoiced or polyphonous.

Because language gives people their sense of reality and because people live only in the confines of that language, language used theologically and homiletically should be multidimensional and display "metaphorical aliveness."[45] In *Cadences of Home*, a provocative book referring to and questioning the conventions of preaching, a similar point of the inadequacy of language to provide truth without the contribution of multiple voices is expressed differently. Because reality is scripted, that is, shaped and authorized by text, postmodern preaching must have density. Hegemonic communities with accepted assumptions that are unspoken and unquestioned may be content with thin, minimalist, and superficial preaching, but such preaching serves neither the contemporary church nor contemporary society.[46] Moreover, the inadequacy of thin preaching is plain to see when inserted in contemporary novels. "Density," here, follows from the literary theory of intertextuality which establishes the unavoidable interrelationship of texts, but *Cadences of Home* develops it further. Because neither the biblical texts nor the gathered community nor the preaching is anything other than intertextually "thick," three "densities" converge in sermons: intertextually dense texts, hearers with multidimensional memory both as humans and as church community, and a God beyond simple definition, who is quixotically and enigmatically filled with contradictions. Preaching supplies the mutually understood "coded winks" that bring these densities together in meaningful harmony, thus "reconvening the web of significance."[47] The term "polyphony" might be preferable to that of density when discussing sermons, because they are oral and aural. Because of the essentially polyphonous nature of human culture, preaching functions as an ongoing argument between the polyphonic voice of God and the polyphonic voice of the world, an argument that is centered on the preacher and in which engaged hearers are caught up.[48]

Comparing theological discourse to an interrupted conversation in a parlor, truths in sermons, likewise, do not start off anew but always build on what has been heard before. Speaking wisdom in the pulpit involves connecting the gospel to human life in all its current and future facets.[49] Furthermore, a reader engaging with a fictional sermon builds on supposed unheard previous sermons and his or her actual experience of preaching to bestow meaning on what is read. Preaching names the world, and this, of course, requires the right use of words to describe the world truthfully.[50] If sermons are like metaphorical language—both in metaphor's steady balance between the two "knowns" in the metaphorical equivalence and in metaphor's ability to go either way across the comparative tension—then successful sermons go both ways: back and forth, from life to Word to life.[51]

Central, then, both to reading fiction and listening to sermons is the use of imagination—not flights of fancy but the readerly ability to invoke mental images, move them, and move around within them. This imaginative identification in preaching[52] lies at the heart of any discussion of fictional sermons, the study of which supports the twin hypotheses that metaphorical language invites readers to use imagination and that imagination's refusal "to play in one key or on a single instrument, but [to] experiment with the whole range"[53] energizes, invigorates, and "thickens" the texts. However, neither this polyphony nor the transformability of these key changes denies or detracts from the thought expressed by Daniel Orton, the preacher who never preaches in Byatt's chronicle, that the building blocks of religious language, sufficiently versatile to speak God to people, are nothing more than just "words, words."

The sermons within William H. Gass' *Omensetter's Luck* provide a fine example of differentiated language in American fiction.[54] In this neglected novel by a novelist-philosopher with a sustained philosophical interest in the making of fictional worlds and the part played by language therein, speech defines the Reverend Jethro Furber and, in his section of the novel, speech is everything. His preaching demonstrates a further, but troubling, capacity for differentiating language to name truth, for his words construct the reader's perception of him, they tell lies about an innocent man he has set out to destroy, and they mark his "change of heart."

The story of Gass' novel can be quickly told. Brackett Omensetter moves his family into Gilean in Ohio, where his prelapsarian harmony with nature impresses his new neighbors. His "luck," evident from the day he moved into town on the only dry day in the rainy season through a continued series of incidents, including the correct prediction of the gender of his wife's third child and the misdirected hammer blow that knocked a splinter from an infected finger, causes admiration. While most envy this luck, his landlord, Henry Pimber, sees in Omensetter's carefree happiness the lost opportunity of his own life, and he hangs himself. Feeling threatened by Omensetter, Jethro Furber sets out to destroy his reputation not only suggesting that his luck is really knowledge, sinister and magic, but also casting aspersions on him about Pimber's death. Eventually townsfolk drive Omensetter out of town, but not before Furber has a change of heart and not before it is too late for Furber's residence in Gilean also to have become untenable. Speech, poison in the ear, achieves all of this.

The novel comprises three unequal parts, the first set about fifty years after the main action and told by a local historian, the second giving the main story from Pimber's perspective beginning with Omensetter as a "wide and happy man" (31) and ending with Pimber seeking a tall tree to hang from, and the third, more than two-thirds of the novel, giving Jethro Furber's intense monologue, variously muttered and bawled as he paces the parish garden like a caged animal. The monologue alternates between first- and third-person narratives. As a stream of consciousness, cascading like a torrent of words and thoughts,[55] it is a sermon in all respects except for the fact that there is no audience within the text of the novel. The section contains Furber's report of two sermons, one being a fiery sermon on Jeremiah, the other being what can be regarded as the heart at the heart of the matter in that it relates to the preacher's change of heart (210–21).

Earlier in his monologue, Furber had toyed with names, exploring their significance, musing what difference it would make if Romeo had been Bob and if God's name were Simpson, yet this is only part of his fascination with words. While Furber chooses to destroy Omensetter by telling lies about him, thus using his skill as a wordsmith, storyteller, and mythmaker,[56] Gass self-consciously deploys language as the principal tool of perception. Both Gass and Furber construct worlds distanced from, yet related to, reality: Gass makes as little effort to contextualize his narrative as Furber does to root his depiction of

Omensetter in truth. The book tells readers nothing about small-town Ohio in the last decade of the nineteenth century and nothing at all about late nineteenth-century sermons. The reader can easily forget where and when the book is set. As a result of such detachment from time and place, both the action of the novel and Furber's fabrication of a disreputable Omensetter exist primarily in Furber's head or, more accurately, his speech. His facility with speech is such that he can, virtually and linguistically, make love with the women of his congregation through his preaching, tickling them so they laugh, spanking them so they howl, caressing them so they sigh, "touching them without touching" (113). Yet, while he fears above all else the loss of command of language, for the greater part of the novel he mispronounces Omensetter's first name. He gets it right for the first time[57] when he discovers Omensetter's true nature for the first time—at an eye-opening moment when "like the slowest worm, we sense . . . but like the mightiest god, we *know*," terms Furber uses to describe Adam and Eve's revelatory moment of knowing good and evil (220). The moment becomes as astonishing as that when Omensetter naively comes to him as a friend after discovering Pimber's body hanging from the tree. The encounter would have rendered him speechless were he not so loquacious. Furber's heart begins to change: "My god. My god. A friend. I've spent my life spreading lies about you. A friend, eh? a friend, a friend—" (240). And the change of heart is marked by his confession: "What a godforsaken soul I have. Ba–Brackett–what a shit I am" (242). Pronouncing his name correctly at this moment of self-perception suggests that he now recognizes Omensetter's innocence and perceives his true nature; such is the power of words that Furber feels the full effect of grace when Omensetter offers unconditional love.[58] The novel shows this power of preaching, yet the problem for Furber and his readers persists—he preaches one thing aloud and another silently to himself.

Embedded in this interior monologue, two sermons show Jethro Furber's public face. In his first sermon, upon taking up his appointment in Gilean at the close of a hot summer, he likens himself to a drying wind and delivers judgment on his sinful hearers (97–99). Criticized for addressing people he did not know in this manner, Furber often justified this sermon by referring to the evidence around him: the land would not be so parched if they were not so wicked. Three aspects of his preaching trouble the sermon's integrity. First, Gass tells readers that Furber justifies the theme of his preaching in as automatic and formulaic a manner as he found the rituals of worship. Second, the stream-of-consciousness style of the narration of the event makes it plain that the audience—and what he will later discover about its members' pasts and future experiences—distract Furber from his task. He tries to avoid these distractions by reminding himself that he should think of their yellowing gnarled toe nails when he is preaching. Third, his domination of his hearers by staring "as one did over dogs" betrays a disregard and disrespect for his hearers that ill befits a local pastor. That these are known to the reader, and probably involuntarily communicated to Furber's congregation, compromises what he preaches.

The other sermon, in which Furber makes partial confession of his duplicity, is similarly compromised for the reader (210–21). First, the theatricality of the beginning of his sermon, fueled by his inner excitement, a sleepless night rehearsing the sermon, and the eager expectation of the gathering congregation, leads readers to question whether this is an insincere performance, indeed a "sideshow" in which he feels "moved to poetry" (220). This suspicion is corroborated when Furber expresses his intention to fill his hearers' ears with fire and lift up these creatures from their misdirected lives. Eventually, total corroboration comes when he considers cushioning his head on the Bible as a desperate gesture to impress the congregation. In exaggerated and improper self-assessment, he likens his role as a preacher speaking into the space before him to that of God speaking chaos into order (211). The main body of the sermon comes in two parts, the first inviting the members of the congregation to consider why, if they lead such futile lives, they were born into "one long stream of piss" (214), and the second using Genesis chapters 1 and 2 to suggest that God had labored long before creating humanity. Although this section disturbingly drifts into the metaphor of seduction and rape when it speaks of God stealing upon Adam "while [he] lay asleep" (217), Furber has more innocent intentions for the sermon. Furber means to imply but does not state that human existence has a purpose that is contrary to the Gileans' experience of futility. Gass' interest as an author, however, lies in neither this theological point nor its homiletical appeal but in Furber's self-awareness as a preacher. Interspersed through the sermon, the preacher makes a running critique of his own sermon: he feels he has made a fine beginning, he recognizes he is on tiptoe straining with effort, he notices people leaving, he urges himself to take control, and, toward the end, he knows that he is losing the thread of his argument. All this happens despite the fact that this sermon serves as the pivot of the novel when it is read from Furber's point of view. Furber publicly confesses that he holds few convictions (214), by which he means, though it remains unspoken, that "he cared nothing for what they believed" (215). This preacher "[has] nothing to tell [them]" (215). Words came easily to Jethro Furber, but they are "just lies upon lies" (215). Thus Gass distinguishes Furber's public persona from his true inner self.

Lies upon lies; words upon words. Words can cover that there is nothing to say, or they are the substance of what people say. Words matter; they cannot be dismissed as "mere words." Analysis of the language of the fictional sermons in Gass' and Byatt's books gives some useful pointers to guide readers as they encounter sermons in novels and also to guide actual preachers as they draft their sermons. First is the base on which all discussion about language is built: all language is essentially metaphorical. Second, any survey of published sermons—not only fictional sermons but also those published by actual preachers—will reveal that sermonic language is not the peculiar beast people expect it to be. Indeed, almost all vocabulary can be used, though there are specialisms, conventions, and pieties and there is little doubt that some language, while shocking in print, would cause even greater offense uttered from a pulpit in the context of an act or worship. A published Ash Wednesday sermon, for instance, attempted to communicate the offense of the traditional Ash Wednesday words "You are dust and to dust you will return" by beginning "You are shit." In defamiliarizing liturgical language, the preacher was seeking to address the problem of linguistic conventions in liturgy rendering some phrases cliché, but the attempt, if she had used it in the pulpit, would surely have misfired. However, and as a third point, study of fictional sermons shows that cliché can be an important tool in the writer's toolbox not to be relegated to the writer's dustbin, for cliché can serve to suggest the redundancy of some preaching. An important fourth point should be borne in the minds of all who write sermons: as cross-cultural discourses speaking in the world of the Bible and the audience's world, sermons need to be double-voiced. Both fictional preachers and their readers—and actual preachers and their hearers—need to be bifocal, with one eye on the text of the Bible and the other on the text of the contemporary world. They need to be stereophonic, with one ear attuned to the voice of tradition and Scripture, and the other attuned to contemporary voices, steering a steady course through the dissonances. In the pulpit, preachers stand astride the gulf between these worlds, and their language helps them negotiate the divide. A fifth point for preachers to learn from this discussion is that the superfluity of meaning inherent in metaphorical language gives sermons the capacity to transfigure and to transform. The many layers of figurative language provide valuable sustenance to feed the imaginations of those who listen to sermons. They make the Christian imagination. What is more, readers always know that writers are playing with words to conjure up a story. Sometimes, as in Furber's interior commentary on his own sermon, they specifically tell readers what they are doing, and this implicitly warns them of the need to mind their language (to use the phrase of parental guidance to outspoken children). Words are the building blocks of utterances and, as every cent counts for the saver, so every word counts for the speaker who seeks to name truth.

7

Shaping Paradise through Preaching

The various communities that gather around fictional sermons are conflicting in their expectations, diverse in their form, and imprecisely defined. Above all else, they are imagined. That in itself is not a problem. Despite the apparently gloomy sociological prognosis that the only viable communities in contemporary society are imagined communities, this pessimism is more apparent than real. Imagined is not the same as imaginary, and the potential of imagined community, as opposed to imaginary, was demonstrated in Benedict Anderson's famous study of nationhood. It finds that nations are before all else imagined communities in that, although their members do not know each other, "the image of their communion" and "deep horizontal comradeship"[1] are active realities in their minds. This imagined communion exists in church politics in the notion of the Anglican Communion, the Methodist Connexion, and other denominational groupings and in ecclesiology, in the doctrine of "one holy, catholic and apostolic church" as well as in the doctrine of the communion of saints. Homileticians in the continuing development of homiletical theory have recently adopted the concept, too. Before discussing the sermons in the novels of A. S. Byatt and Toni Morrison, two writers who have little in common with each other, besides shared gender and appreciation of the community-shaping role of sermons in church, a discussion of views from selected homileticians about real-life preachers and the communities shaped by their preaching will inform an analysis of fictitious preachers and their communities.

Because language constitutes a world whenever a speaker speaks, preachers' words are the building blocks of symbolic worlds that enable congregations "to view the 'real' world in some new way, perhaps as a realm of God."[2] In effect, the use of imagination in preaching is capable of "forming faith-consciousness"[3] and shapes a new world for congregations to inhabit.[4] The same assumption lies behind most of the essays recently collected in *The Blackwell Companion to Christian Ethics*, affirming the notion that worship forms a believing community that is taught, trained, or encouraged to behave in a particular way. For instance, "Listening: Authority and Obedience," by Scott Bader-Saye argues that in a world of competing convictions the conflict between authority and freedom often reflects the conflict between community and individual. How can the individual be free when the community wants to exert some degree of legal or moral control? This tension is potentially reconciled ritualistically in liturgy, through which a community gathers around authoritative texts, namely the Bible, the sermon, and the creeds.[5] Indeed, any healthy community requires collaborative, negotiated, and mutually agreed-upon authority of this sort;[6] freedom is found in the individual's choice whether to belong and participate.

The notion that the human capacity to imagine enables people to "envision new realities"[7] underpins this book. Walter Brueggemann, one of the greatest exponents of this highly creative potential in the fields of both biblical scholarship and homiletics, describes the art of preaching as "the reimagination of reality."[8] For Brueggemann, this view is informed both by his exposition on the Old Testament as a document for an exilic community and the partial dissolution of the church in the postmodern age. Because of the diversity of congregations, the old monologic model and Enlightenment script of church absolutes can no longer be trusted.[9] The tradition of dominating, authoritarian preaching had prevailed from the time of the Constantinian establishment, which made Christianity an ally of power through the Catholic system and focused power on the church, to both the Reformation and Counter-Reformation, which continued absolutist claims. But it can be sustained no longer. Some fictional sermons in contemporary novels fit the pattern of hegemonic authoritarian preaching, partly because many novelists are using a remembered genre but also because they are using sermons as a shorthand way of expressing a dominant voice of faith to which their characters are reacting. Such preaching had two facets. One is that it was propositional: it claimed universal credence stemming from unquestioning certitude. The other is that sermons tended to adopt a three-fold structure; first describing a universal problem, then defining a clear solution that is universally applicable, before finally stressing that the new possibility is everywhere available.[10] Such preaching, or "thin discourse,"[11] is now impossible in a decentered church. As an exiled community, it has lost its mother-speech.[12] With the decline of form criticism, thinkers have argued for rhetorical criticism as the next stage in biblical interpretation because in originally oral texts speech cadences determine intention.[13] In addition, feminist rereadings of the Bible have successfully destabilized male authority over Scripture.[14] Brueggemann argues for preaching that has been "thickened" by the intertextuality of the sermon, the multidimensional memory of the hearers, and the text's pointing beyond itself to what he calls the "Primal Character."[15] This bears particular interest in relation to sermons set within novels in that their setting "thickens" them further. Brueggemann's argument posits that authentic preaching for the postmodern age is more dialogic than what was once practiced in Christian pulpits. Contemporary preaching "is an act of imagination . . . through which perception, experience and faith can be reorganised in alternative ways."[16] This reorganized faith results in faith communities constructed to honor people's individuality and acknowledge diversity; these are, indeed, imagined, possible, or reimagined communities.

Such rejection of dominating monologue as improper for the contemporary age in favor of a more dialogical model of preaching prompts a question: Is authentic preaching for today's pluralist society a site of "unlimited conversation," by which is meant the capacity for all people to participate in the speech situation?[17] Of importance is that the widest possible range of input be heard in the thematic content of sermons. Such experience will involve gaining access to voices submerged under the dominant tradition and establishing vibrant communication within and across congregations and other groups, including heterodox and minority perspectives.[18] Such unlimited conversation in which many voices are heard becomes possible because "people inhabit *multiple worlds simultaneously*,"[19] and effective preaching becomes conversation grounded in "relational solidarity"[20] or, more straightforwardly, community. This unlimited conversation is properly located in the church, which stands as a potentially unique community, in that it is capable of both re-membering past alternative "lifeworlds" and imagining future ones.[21] Such community is no less realized for being imagined than is the actual discourse community, or lifeworld, where humankind daily negotiates and shares common meanings and values.[22]

When people speak of the church as a community, some will rejoice and take the view that community is a term that "plays a major legitimising role in our talk about institutions."[23] Others will despair and fret that community has become such a buzzword in church circles, used with alarming frequency to refer often interchangeably and confusingly to wider society, local neighborhood, congregation, fellowship, and even small interest group meetings, that it risks losing significance as a term. However, in recent years, *Religion and Community*, an important study in comparative religion, included a rigorous theological analysis of the church as community. The church looks like a sectarian community of disciples inasmuch as it believes that God has called it into being, and it exists in tension with wider human society,[24] but its true nature is that of an organic community known as the body of Christ, presenting Christ through preaching and sacrament. Michael Arditti satirically and troublingly explores this ascription in fictional form in *Easter*.

The study also suggests that the church is primarily a teaching, charismatic, sacramental, and moral community. The church serves as a teaching community because it does not "present itself as a defender of unchanging truths which resist new knowledge and critical enquiry." Rather, the church presents itself as the bearer of a gospel that needs to find fresh expression in each new age. This Christian Gospel has the characteristics of greater understanding, of freedom of inquiry, and of creative interpretations of tradition.[25] As a teaching community, the church must also be a learning community. At a time when some in the church express a concern about a loss of the sense of being teachers and learners together, the church should be encouraged to regain Origen's sense of the learning process being for all and for the whole of life to be heeded in its expression of spirituality and understanding of theology.[26] The church is also a charismatic community, because it seeks to live by "egalitarian, participatory, pluralistic and disclosive" principles rather than exert hierarchical, patriarchal or authoritarian influence;[27] although diverse, the church is a believing and sanctifying community in which shared beliefs provide "a sense of mutual significance."[28] Third, the study sees the church as a sacramental community primarily because sacramental ritual lies at the heart of the community and participation in these rites defines community membership. Moreover, it also exists as a sacramental community because, in catechetical words, it "outwardly expresses an inward reality." The church is a visible sign of invisible irreality, an alternative term for the opposite of reality that does not imply nonexistence or insubstantiality but rather suggests intangible existence. When this sacred community meets, its plurality becomes submerged but not concealed under its historical continuity and shared tradition. Finally, the study sees the church as a moral community. Many people regret that, as such, it tends toward authoritarian moral conservatism, because its true calling and intended purpose is to be a body that gives innovative, often countercultural moral leadership, a community that collaborates with all within it and those around it to achieve ethical reform.[29]

This theological appraisal of the church as community has found implicit support from the perspective of the academic discipline of communication studies. "Interpretive Community," an essay in the *Journal of Media and Religion*, identifies four main characteristics of community: first, communities are based on a unity of shared circumstances, interests, customs, or purposes leading to a strong drive toward the establishment of solidarity; second, members of communities share common moral obligations expressed in social rules, etiquette, or ethical codes; third, over time communities achieve some status of stability, usually cemented by the use of canonical texts, rituals, or myths so that unity and moral obligations can be formed; fourth, social networks develop communicative occasions and codes by which it becomes apparent who is inside and who is outside community membership.[30]

These characteristics can be observed in the three types of community—sects, churches, and the readership—gathered around the fictional sermons in the last novel in Byatt's Frederica quartet. This, *A Whistling Woman*, has its primary focus on the formation of a sect— the Children of Joy, otherwise known as Joyful Companions, a religious community developed by Gideon Farrar—but it also discusses the communities of church and readership. Members of the community known as "academia" infiltrate the Joyful Companions to research it. A psychologist, Elvet Gander, observes the community at work and communicates from within it by letter to his psychiatrist colleague on the outside, Kieran Quarrell. Two specialist sociologists, Brenda Pincher and Avram Snitkin, also write letters to each other, discussing their findings and opinions about the sect-like community Brenda observes. As a more conventional, less extremist form of religious community than sects that are both implicitly and overtly present at various times in the novel and that, in the real world, easily spill over into violence, the church, as an organization that nevertheless expects committed participation, exists in tension and in contrast with the absolute claims of sectarian commitment. Members of the readership, as a discourse or interpretive community, also become associate or virtual members of the communities imagined or fictively constructed within the texts they read.

A Whistling Woman features several communities. When one reviewer read it as a satire of the sixties' romantic ideal of communal living, she suggested that Byatt represented it in three ways: "a Quakerish cult," "the joyless Joyful Companions," and the Anti-University,[31] but there are many more groups or communities in the novel than these three. The television community, the academic community among whose members Frederica moves, and the local parish church whose services the reader visits from time to time also feature. Furthermore, the Frederica quartet is set in the context of the theological debates of the third quarter of the twentieth century, most notably the "Death of God" theology and the "Honest to God" debate, each of which spilled over into the remainder of the century. These theological movements attracted adherents, and, in the context of the novel, they have their followers among the ordained characters. In the early stages of the formation of the Joyful Companions, three of the clergymen choose symbols or "spiritual images" for themselves that tend to associate them with certain theological trends: Adelbert Holly chooses a cross with a man-shaped hole, Daniel Orton selects a leafless tree with deep roots, and Gideon Farrar takes an angel wielding a flaming sword, each choice justified within the text by comments such as that of Elvet Gander: "Does [Daniel Orton] have a deep, quiet faith or is he a Priest of No God like [Holly]?" (65). Of the five characters who exercise a priestly role in the Frederica quartet, these are three of the four associated in some way with the sect-like religious community of Joyful Companions. The fourth is Joshua Lamb, also known as Joshua Ramsden, a lay member of the community with a charismatic personality. He places himself as a rival of Gideon Farrar to be its leader. Byatt intentionally makes readers conscious that the narrative of the Joyful Companions is, in the world of the text, contemporaneous with the well-known Charles Manson story. The clandestine researcher Brenda Pincher, starved of news from the outside world, asks who Manson is and what he has done, in one of her letters to Avram Snitkin (387). Byatt's choice of name for Lamb's charismatic and influential schoolteacher, Miss Manson, also references those events (103). Real-life cults such as this taint the book's depiction of religious community.

The account of the sermons within *A Whistling Woman* in the previous chapter ended with the observation that the final comment about these sermons was made by Federica herself. Commenting on Adelbert Holly's Christmas sermon, she said it was "*almost* meaningful, but . . . [it was] . . . in the end a game with language" (242). That it was the last comment and made by Federica means it cannot be overlooked. What is the nature of this game with language? When analyzing these and other fictional sermons with the tools of rhetorical narratology, the game involves Byatt's use of four techniques of narrative and rhetoric: the point of view from which the sermons are reported, their settings and their effect on the sermon, the intended effect of the utterances and speech acts within the sermons, and the preachers' awareness of audience.

Taking each of these techniques in turn, first, Byatt's use of perspective or point of view contributes to a significant extent to the reader's reception of these fictional sermons. The fact that many of the sermons are recounted from the point of view of letter writers reporting the activities of the Joyful Companions to absent but interested addressees distances readers from Gideon Farrar's sermon, most of Joshua Lamb's preaching, and some of Adelbert Holly's preaching. Byatt "permits" readers to read these letters, too. This multilayered reading and focalization enlivens quoted sermons that otherwise, like quotations of other purported externally authoritative texts, would risk being dead quotations. The variety of points of view achieved by this filtering—in which one of the characters present in the text controls what readers learn of the story—may skew the narrative, but it also enriches the sermons because readers view them through varifocal lenses or, to use alternative terminology, the variety "thickens" the sermons. In other words, the letters allow Byatt to enrich her narrative by telling it from various perspectives.

For instance, many of Brenda Pincher's letters are written to her fellow academic Avram Snitkin, who is dilatory in his replies. The letters accompany tape recordings of community activities that she has surreptitiously made, but she also reveals that her longing to hear a fellow sociologist's views of her findings prompts her to write. In one of these letters, Byatt effectively tells readers what to think about Gideon Farrar's preaching. Byatt foregrounds the preacher's problematic use of Jesus' invitation, "Come unto me all ye who are heavy-laden and I will give you rest." Pincher, identifying the manipulative nature of Farrar's preaching, says she does not understand whether it is Farrar or Jesus who issues the invitation (202). She also expresses the view that, because Farrar feels that Joshua Lamb threatens his leadership of the community, his preaching has become more intense and flamboyant. However, earlier in the letter, she remarks that Farrar has not really learned "not to deliver sermons" (201). This is less a comment on how he preaches than a comment on his persistently preacherly manner reminiscent of Charles Dickens' Chadband in *Bleak House* who confronts poor, illiterate Joe with elevated preacher talk that simply puzzles him. The preacher persona has taken over this self-aggrandizing former priest. Through Brenda's critique of the sermon, Byatt draws readers' attention to the discrepancy between Farrar's appeal for truth, by which he means full public confession of sin, and his consistent preference for locutions such as "'grievous faults', 'errors', 'mistakes' and even 'misfortunes'" (203) in avoidance of such a blunt term as "sin." When, at the end of his preaching, Farrar accosts Lucy Nighby, supposedly to free her of her torment, by laying his hands on her shoulders with the result that she jerks, writhes, and almost collapses, before she stands up and shakes herself free of his attentions, Brenda, in parentheses, calls him a "twister" (203); this uncompromising colloquialism causes readers to reflect both that members of the community can observe that he is literally a twister in that in his hands Lucy writhes, and that, from Brenda's point of view as an outsider pretending to be an insider, she can see through his pretense to his nefarious, manipulative motives. At this stage in her letter reporting the event, Brenda's understanding exceeds what she can in fact know. In her letter, she is like an author who knows the inner thoughts, feelings, and motives of her characters when she claims to know what Farrar was thinking when he tussled with Lucy, although she does so tentatively: twice Brenda says, "I think he thought . . . " (203), causing readers to speculate whether she, as one who listens to the subtext, is hearer, listener, or observer; in other words, how insightful is Brenda capable of being? Can she reach beyond the superficial to deeper truths? Can she discern inner meaning in the words she hears? Of course, readers do not know unequivocally whether other hearers make the same judgments as Brenda. Sermons like this manipulate, craft, or shape those present into a community that hears and, hopefully, obeys. At this early stage in the life of the community, readers assume that only Brenda notices the bulging fly zip in his tight jeans when he speaks about members of the community laying themselves open to each other, and they assume a shared privileged judgment because they know more than the community.

Brenda also focalizes, or filters, Joshua Lamb's preaching in the novel. Once again she is writing to Avram Snitkin and reports that the community at Dun Vale Hall is emerging as an embryonic religious cult welded together by hard work and community-shaping ceremonies (224). These include Lamb's talks on the "'gentle Manichees,'" which she calls "sermons" (223). Another correspondent, Elvet Gander, writing about another occasion when Joshua Lamb addressed the Hearers, said that he sounded like a preacher (197), but Brenda makes no such claim, so why does she use the term "sermon" for what were in effect teaching sessions on the principles of Manichaeism applied to the practices of the Dun Vale Hall community? Indeed, she reports some of the "curriculum" matter-of-factly. Is it because as a sociologist she recognizes that the latent function of these lessons is to form community, a function they share with sermons? Is it because Byatt wants her readership to appreciate that, as it is a community gathered around a common text—her text—so the Hearers are a community gathering to listen to Lamb's lessons? Or is it, conversely, that she wants readers to recognize that, as her readers are disparate individuals with only this one shared experience, that of reading her novel, so Lamb's Hearers are disparate?

Earlier in *A Whistling Woman*, Byatt directly tells readers her view of Lamb's early preaching; unlike other reports of preaching in the novel, this is not reported in a letter. As a young man in Durham, Joshua was under the tutelage of Father Burgess, who encouraged him to read Kierkegaard. As a result of this study, Joshua gave a paper that cautiously expressed Kierkegaard's understanding of the difference between tragic heroes and knights of faith such as Abraham (121). Both in her casual drift between free indirect speech and direct speech and in her (or Lamb's) quotation of Kierkegaard and Lamb's commentary on it, Byatt enables herself, as an intrusive narrator, to convince the reader that the young Lamb is capable of stirring those who listen to him. He has become "suddenly eloquent" (122), by which, through Byatt's intrusive parenthesis in which she gives the etymology of "eloquent,"[32] readers are told she means he was speaking "out of himself" (122). He was inspired. This reminds readers that only a short while earlier Byatt had said that Lamb always possessed the capacity, or charismatic ability, "to see himself from outside" (120). Later, he, like other members of the community, becomes the subject of the letters exchanged by the academics secretly studying it.

The other occasion on which one of Lamb's talks is reported to the reader is when there is a heated debate in the community about whether the television, a potential distraction from the purity of committed participation in community life, should remain. During the course of the meeting, Elvet Gander mischievously asks Lamb's opinion, because he wants to hear him speak. Gander later reports Lamb's contribution to the debate in a letter he sends to his psychiatrist colleague Kieran Quarrell apparently verbatim, although he acknowledges the fallibility of his power of recall. Readers are persuaded by Gander to regard this speech as being "on a knife-edge between the ludicrous and the impressive" (197), and, in telling his correspondent that Gideon Farrar murmured approval of the point Lamb was making, they are also able to surmise Gideon's view of the speech. Gander opines that he believes Gideon can imagine himself using the medium of television to extend his congregation to the wider community of the entire

English-speaking world. Gander's report of this meeting includes both the assertion that Lamb sounds like a preacher and the implication that, in their intriguing eloquence, Lamb's silences are forms of preaching, too. At the end of his letter Gander says, "Lamb . . . returned to his normal courteous silence," and his audience looked at him, "like an unexploded bomb that might go off. What will he say next? What is he preaching?" (197).

The same letter writer, Elvet Gander, suggests how readers should respond to Adelbert Holly's first sermon, which, although he calls it both impromptu and little, he admires (232). He understands Holly's achievement in the sermon to be a masterly use of John Donne's poem "St. Lucy's Day," turning it from an expression of dark, erotic despair into a prayer to the God in which he finds it difficult to believe, an achievement made possible because, as Gander suggests in recognition of the ineffability of truth and the necessarily metaphorical nature of religious language, "religious men always twist" (232). The novelist herself recounts Holly's other reported sermon, on Christmas Day, another festival of lights, from her point of view unfiltered by any of her characters, although the local vicar introduces it as a sermon "on the meaning of the Incarnation in a time of doubt and trouble" (241) from "one of the most lively and up-to-date of our new dispensation of theologians" (240). This effectively colors how both the characters in the audience and the novel's readership hear the sermon so that, when Byatt herself resumes reporting the sermon, she can be relatively neutral in its telling, using direct speech for much of the time. As a result, readers are almost as close to the sermon as the hearers in the novel, less directed in their responses, and more open to being caught up in the act of imagination and to being convinced by the preacher's presence and argument. This directness is tempered both by the novelist's free indirect speech at the beginning, when she says Holly began the sermon with a degree of self-importance, and her return to free indirect speech in the later stages of the sermon, when she suggests his amiability by referring to his beatific and blithe smiles. Readers must choose whether to belong to the camp repelled by the overbearing manner with which he began his sermon or the camp appealed to by his winsome smiles.

The second technique of narrative and rhetoric that Byatt employs in her fictional sermons is to use their settings to inflect their readers' reception. The sermons' settings and the effect these have on the dynamics of the occasions contribute to their community-shaping capacity, sometimes clarifying and, other times, blurring the boundary between preacher and congregation as well as the boundary around the community. In the case of Holly's Christmas sermon, for instance, the space used for the occasion is the conventional arrangement of pulpit and pews in Freyasgarth parish church. Above the congregation seated in formal rows, Frederica notices that small stone angels looking down on her adorn the roof space; the preacher also looks down on her as he leans over the pulpit to address the formally ranked congregation. This formality and implied hierarchy, however, do not prevent the convergence of two congregations; indeed, the enforced formal seating arrangement conceals from the casual onlooker that the congregation includes both parishioners and visitors from the community at Dun Vale Hall. Paradoxically, the formality of church blurs the two communities' edges so that sect and church merge. In a similar way the final sermon in Arditti's *Easter*, Blair Ashley's sermon preached from a tombstone outside the burnt-out church, brings together two disparate communities, the regular congregation gathered for worship on Easter Day and the pack of journalists eager to report a scandalous story about the curate's sexuality.

When Holly preached earlier in *A Whistling Woman*, however, the setting more clearly defined the community he addressed. Gathered around a bonfire, the Joyful Companions—wrapped against the cold in leather coats fringed with fleece and Tibetan goatskin hats—look like priests; their self-conscious shuffling and occasional prancing as they chant hymns whose words they do not know prompt their observer, Gander, to draw attention to the absurdity of the ritual (233), although his account of the event cannot be entirely reliable because of his acid-induced forgetfulness. The effect of a group of priest-like people, similarly attired, circling a bonfire in chant and dance is community defining; the warmth of the fire draws people into a community gathered around a central focus as its heat and light rival the speaker for hearers' attention, but it also leaves outsiders in the dark. The circle looking inward excludes others.

The setting on the occasions Joshua Lamb addresses the Joyful Companions operates in a similar way. In the letter in which Brenda

Pincher remarks that any sociologist could see that the Joyful Companions were being forged into an embryonic religious cult (223), she tells of Lamb's talks on the "gentle Manichees" whose community boundaries were clearly defined as divided into the Elect and the Hearers, the latter group being those who accrued merit by serving the Elect. Moreover, in choosing to call the Joyful Companions "Hearers," Lamb is setting the community's parameters in a manner reminiscent of Jesus, who concluded many of his parables with the injunction that effectively excluded some: "Let those who have ears to hear, hear."

The setting of Gideon Farrar's sermon to the Joyful Companions effectively breaks down the barrier between the preacher and his congregation and also obfuscates the borders of the community. Brenda Pincher ruminates on Farrar's oppressive presence. Whereas he was once "the robed untouchable beyond the altar rails," and raised a symbolic wafer before a sacred altar (202), he has now, by a process of demystification and demythologization, removed the distance between preacher and congregation so that there remains no space, only oppressive and invasive touch that "overstep[s Lucy Nighby's] boundary" (203). The hands-on "therapy" intended to identify Lucy as a member of the community or perhaps initiate her into an inner grouping succeeds only in repelling her, and Brenda Pincher regrets the loss of "mystery and distance and ceremony" on which she feels religion thrives (202). As a result Farrar has to work much harder at his rhetoric to achieve the effects he desires and to win the enthusiasm of his followers.

At this point in her treatment of fictional preaching, Byatt makes crucial and overt use of a third tool of narrative and rhetoric—performative speech acts. Farrar does not conceal his facility with powerful speech utterances and is much more coercive as a preacher than others in the Frederica series. The intensity of the performative speech act when Farrar accosts Lucy seemingly terrifies and certainly angers her and, at this stage in the sermon, the assertive speech act may also be seen as a directive speech act ordering whatever he thinks is possessing her to depart in "painful birthing" (203). On the other hand, some of the immediacy of the earlier speech acts within Farrar's sermon is dissipated by the way Byatt reports them through indirect speech within a letter between an observer and her correspondent. In a prelude to Farrar's approach to Lucy, he says, "No matter what you have done, no matter what has been done to you, . . . sharing it will start up the healing process, confession will set you free" (203). This is an example of a speech act that is covert about its performativity;[33] it does not need to be communicated or identified as either a commissive or a predictive speech act to perform as such. It will perform as intended, nonetheless. Whether Farrar intended it as such and whether Lucy heard it as such, Farrar's utterance offers both promise and prediction for the reader and observer.

The account of Joshua Lamb's preaching comes in the same letter from Brenda Pincher to Snitkin as the account of another community member's ritual pronouncement, that of Clemency Farrar, as she ceremoniously frees the farm animals. Clemency is Gideon Farrar's "endlessly patient helpmate" (206). Joshua's talks on the Manichees draw attention to their division between the Elect and the Hearers who serve the Elect: "Joshua rather charmingly said that he felt that all of us were Hearers, and none of us were, or should behave as if we were, Elect" (223). Byatt's placing of both Clemency and Joshua's declarations within the same letter brings into question the nature of both these utterances. In what way is Clemency Farrar's dismissal and commission to the animals, "Go free, bless you," akin to Joshua Lamb's reported description of his audience as "Hearers"? Clemency's ritual pronouncement functions as a declarative speech act; the words accompany the actual unlocking of the gates and the shooing of the animals. Joshua's utterance is also a declarative speech act inasmuch as those who listen accept the thought within it as a description of an actual state of affairs; from there on they are, indeed, known as Hearers. In this way, Joshua's preaching helps to define the community and establishes its borders.

But not all preaching in the novel achieves the same effect. In Adelbert Holly's St. Lucy's Day sermon, for instance, his utterances associating Lucy with the theme of light and calling Lucy the most blessed among women for providing the Hall for the Hearers is not performatively effective in the same way. Its failure lies in the fact that Gander's report of the sermon, in which Holly rhapsodizes, "Lucy . . . was Lux, Lucis, the Maiden of Light and was blessed among women" (233), influences readers' thinking in such a way that they interpret his ascription as hyperbolic. Brenda's report that Clemency immediately pointed out that Lucy was not a maiden, although Brenda immediately questions her accuracy, reinforces the sense that Holly exaggerates Lucy's status. Although Joshua Ramsden pronounces that, from the moment of the solstice, by which all things are made new, Lucy is a maiden, readers cannot be certain of Lucy's standing: Is she blessed among women or still a maiden? If she is not one, she might not, or cannot, be the other.

If, on the one hand, calling people Hearers makes them Hearers, and if, on the other hand, calling Lucy blessed among women does not make her so, what about Canon Holly's words about God? Do his words about God, spoken in the context of a nihilistic ritual in which participants are encouraged to burn their treasured possessions so that they become "things that are not," resurrect a dead God and realize an absent God, Deus absconditus? These are important questions for the practice of preaching. To what extent can preachers be said to realize God? To what extent can they be said to speak God into being? Do utterances image the existence of God? Does the imagining community image God? Does the theological subject matter of sermons contribute to the creation of a believing community? Holly fictively addresses these questions in his Christmas Day sermon. In saying that he intends to "say something real" when he preaches, he implies that what is commonly heard from many pulpits is "a few nice platitudes" (241), the existence of which is almost a denial of speech-act theory; the uttering of a platitude *is* just saying something. On the contrary, Holly believes he is *doing* something when he preaches, yet readers are left to consider for themselves what he achieves. Does he make real God's entry into History?[34] Does he enflesh supernatural concepts of God in incarnational terms? Does he make the finite infinite and the incomprehensible comprehensible? Or does he, as Frederica feels, simply play with words (242)?

The answer to these questions relates to the way audiences respond to the discourse, either in their compliance with or their resistance to what the discourse says and what is done in the saying. Put bluntly, does a hearer have to be a believer for the literary game of faith to work? Here, Byatt engages a fourth tool of narrative and rhetorical technique to make her fictional sermons work in the novels: her sense of audience for the sermons. At this point, another type of community present (or, more accurately, *implicitly* present) in the novel—its primary interpretive community, its readers—enters the discussion.

Readers are not isolated readers but a virtual community, a body of people called the readership.

Contrary to Byatt's repeated insistence that she writes for a general readership, critics have often expressed the view that her actual audience is an educated literary readership. For instance, the *Christian Science Monitor*'s reviewer of *A Whistling Woman* rather cruelly divided Byatt's fans into two groups—those who cannot understand her novels and those who lie[35]—while the *Daily Telegraph*'s reviewer called the world of *A Whistling Woman* a "vast, erudite world" in which she implies what is first and foremost on display is the author's erudition.[36] Furthermore, the *Independent*'s reviewer and fellow novelist Stevie Davies, fatigued by Byatt's "virtuoso cleverness," presumes that she writes for "the cognoscenti."[37] Full appreciation of her novels certainly requires a readiness to enjoy, or at least tolerate, Byatt's ventures into literary and philosophical side streets tangential to her books' main concerns. The heavy demands she makes on her readers are also evident in Farrar's, Lamb's, and Holly's sermons, for their readers require a developed theological, literary, and rhetorical awareness beyond that of many nonchurchgoers.

The intended audience of Farrar's sermon within the novel comprises the Joyful Companions, particularly Lucy, who is singled out as the recipient of Farrar's unsolicited attention. Its actual audience within the book includes Brenda Pincher, the skeptical letter writer, and her correspondent, Avram Snitkin, as well as Elvet Gander and his correspondent Kieran Quarrell. These, other characters and Byatt herself encourage its actual extratextual audience, the novel's readership, to adopt an attitude of suspicion about both the integrity of Farrar's leadership and the quality of the rhetoric by which he tries to establish his authority. Similarly, in the case of Joshua Lamb's preaching, the audience comprises on the page both the Hearers and the academic researchers who are more sympathetic to him than they are to Farrar, but his preaching appeals particularly to an extratextual audience, whose members are more questioning than accepting. Readers who, like both Kierkegaard and his fictional interpreter, are troubled by the terror of Abraham's near-sacrifice of Isaac in Genesis 22 are incorporated into a common audience wrestling with what Lamb calls the text's mystery, to which the only appropriate response is silence.

The paradox, Lamb suggests, is that silence is both the "demon's lure" and "divinity's communion with the individual" (122). In sharing this response with those in the novel who listen to Lamb, members of his wider audience, Byatt's readership, become Hearers, too. When Adelbert Holly preaches, he appears to be conscious that his audience is also a medley of characters: the atheist Bill Potter is there to hear his granddaughter sing; three clerics—the local vicar, Daniel Orton, and Gideon Farrar—are collared, implying (conventionally, at least) both a state of committed belief and theological expertise; the usual congregation is swollen both by people from the parish who attend only on high feast days and the Joyful Companions from Dun Vale Hall, whose religious faith and practices differ from those of the local congregation; and Frederica, who, impatient with preachers who play games with words, although physically present, absents herself from the purpose of the occasion. And the subject matter of the sermon implies that Holly expected that his intended audience would include people who wrestle with their sense of God's absence as well as people who agree with the philosophy of Nietzsche. Holly uses his Christmas Day sermon, in which he proclaims "the mystery of His Birth . . . repeated daily in historical time" (242), to attempt to shape a community of religious nihilism in which God, the irreal God, is incorporated, enfleshed, embodied with humanity in divine community. Byatt extends this community with the divine to include in its embrace any of her readership willing to suspend disbelief to grapple with God-as-human-construct, God of fiction, God of preaching, God—as Holly says—"infinitely finite" (242). Holly, despite his Death of God theology, is speaking of a realized God; Byatt speaks directly to the readership here, too. If all addressors and addressees, both actual and fictional, are spread along a spectrum with the author of the novel at one end and its readership at the opposite pole, then the sermon within the fiction functions as a mechanism by which the author can address the readership directly without facing the charge of being preacherly.

In this respect, Byatt follows the example of her mentor, Iris Murdoch.[38] Murdoch uses sermons given by rival community leaders in *The Bell* to encapsulate their alternative approaches to the spiritual life and leadership of religious communities. Their sermons provide the frame for the novel's debate between taking the saint's course, attempting to do the best you know, and the artist's course, choosing the more achievable alternative, the second-best in which you are confident of acquitting yourself. James' eloquent sermon to the members of the lay community on the outskirts of Imber Abbey, on the theme "Be ye therefore perfect," charges Michael with having ideals but no principles. A week later Michael's sermon impishly begins exactly as James' had: "The chief requirement of the good life is . . . ,"[39] yet the sermons are at variance with each other, for Michael's commends what James' had decried. Which of these two ways wins the hearts and minds of the sermons' intratextual listeners will determine the eventual shape of the Imber Abbey lay community; furthermore, which of these ways proves persuasive to the novel's readership will determine how successfully Murdoch has argued that it might be better for the well-being of humanity to seek slight improvement rather than neurotically pursue perfection. Murdoch directly uses these two sermons to foreground the debate between the saint and the artist that will occupy much of her writing. From this Byatt derives her technique of employing the rival preaching of Joshua Lamb and Gideon Farrar, both to express conflict within the Joyful Companions and to determine the community's shape. Incidentally, Byatt owes another debt to Murdoch: Byatt has Bill Potter give an atheistic antisermon for Christmas in *Still Life* (44); Murdoch introduced this concept in *The Time of the Angels*, where Carel Fisher expresses his longing to be able to step into a pulpit and announce that there is no God.[40] A type of atheistic sermon follows, delivered conversationally to his brother Marcus, parodying Murdoch's own religio-philosophical, a/theistic views.[41] This, however, does not detract from Byatt's achievement of using sermons to shape, form, or forge *A Whistling Woman*'s communities of sect, church, and readership.

Another outstanding instance of sermons shaping community occurs in Toni Morrison's *Paradise*, which curiously, given Morrison's radical streak, highlights the persistence of preaching as a male-gendered role in the modern novel; the masculine voice is heard more often than not in the fictional pulpit.[42] Baby Suggs in *Beloved* is, of course, a notable exception and it is significant, rather than a point of omission, that in *Paradise* the town of Ruby, next to a convent, has no women preachers. Although the novel takes the form of a collective of women, with each chapter bearing a woman's name, the preachers there are the Reverends

Simon Cary, Senior Pulliam, and Richard Misner. Two of these preachers collude with Ruby's self-perception, while the other tries to get the people of Ruby to imagine an alternative. Ruby is a dream town "deafened by the roar of its own history" (306), where only the blackest of blacks are regarded as true inhabitants. The people of Ruby, formerly known as Haven, intend to protect themselves at all costs and seem to prefer segregation to any form of accommodation to the outside world. They attempt to create an exclusive paradisiacal community, which includes no unsaved or unworthy strangers and comprises only people with "unadulterated and unadulteried 8-rock blood" (217). This is further represented in the novel by the absence of a cemetery in the town and the citizens' refusal to admit death, which reminds the reader of the picture of heaven offered by The Revelation of St. John as a place where "death shall be no more." Ruby excludes the unsaved, whereas the adjacent Convent permits complete freedom to come and go and has already admitted sin, sex, and death.

The fact that there are only two occasions in the novel when Morrison moves away from her calm and sympathetic narrator—the extract from Patricia Best's history book and the sermons of Cary, Pulliam, and Misner—draws attention to the significance Morrison gives the sermons. Like Pat's history book and the strange enculturated nativity play with seven holy families (211) that strongly affirm Ruby's self-perception, Morrison uses the preaching of Cary and Pulliam to shape the town of Ruby as it is. The story they tell in their preaching is Ruby's story. Morrison demonstrates in two ways the fact that, over the years of their ministry in Ruby, these two preachers have "formulated a credible, sermonizable account" of the town (297). First, Cary's iteration of a theme, which was so popular he included a version of it in each Sunday's sermon, weekly reminds the people what they have given up in order to live in Ruby. He counts the sacrifices off on the fingers of his left hand, and each item in the list reinforces the notions of segregation, privilege, and superiority. The spoken response from his hearers and their laughter show that his preaching is well received. Each reiteration of this sermon underscores the boundaries and strengthens the walls around the town of Ruby. Second, Pulliam's wedding sermon in the section entitled "Divine" comes as a blasting, stinging, and burning diatribe, proving that he has earned the right to carry the nickname

Senior "Take No Prisoners" Pulliam (143). A sermon like this, which tells those who listen to it that God is not interested in them, does not contain much gospel.

This bullying, manipulative sermon angers the third preacher featured in the novel, the newcomer Richard Misner, who always acknowledges that he is an outsider but lives in the hope that the people of Ruby are able to distinguish outsiders from enemies. The local historian, Pat Best, gives him little reassurance when she tells him that in Ruby the words "outsider" and "enemy" are synonymous (212). When Morrison first introduces Richard Misner to the reader, she remarks that he is very close to being too handsome for a preacher (58). This arouses the reader's suspicions about how genuine he is and they come to distrust Misner for other reasons, too. His self-understanding as God's instrument (87) and his preachy tone when in conversation with Pat Best also make him suspect. However, the one-to-one "sermon," that is this preachy conversation with Pat Best, enables the narrator to introduce the reader to one of the themes of Misner's preaching, the concept of heaven as an open home. Misner challenges the idea that a fortress like Ruby may be "a true home . . . a real home . . . (one's) own home" (213), and he believes that his vocation on coming to Ruby is somehow to free the community from the shackles of the past so that its people will engage with the world around them and move toward a much more open and inclusive paradise than that envisaged by Ruby's townsfolk. He images an alternative paradise for Ruby. In his anger at Pulliam's wedding sermon, Misner begins to trouble Ruby with this image, and he responds to Pulliam's biting sermon with a silent sermon in which he simply stands before the congregation and holds the cross before their eyes. This unspoken sermon replaces both the words he had planned and the words that come to his mind but that he dares not trust himself to utter in the immediacy of his reaction to Pulliam's sermon. The narrator, who speaks of what Misner can't, speaks of the necessity of this primitive sign or "original mark":

> Remove [this mark], as Pulliam had done, and Christianity was like any and every religion in the world: a population of supplicants begging respite from a begrudging authority; harried believers ducking fate or dodging everyday evil; the weak negotiating a doomed trek through the wilderness; the sighted ripped of light and thrown in the perpetual dark of choicelessness. (146)

The narrator then interprets the sign and, at length, describes what Misner hopes the congregation will see in it:

> See? The execution of this one solitary black man propped up on these two intersecting lines to which he was attached in a parody of human embrace, fastened to two big sticks that were so convenient.... See? His woolly head alternately rising on his neck and falling toward his chest, the glow of his midnight skin dimmed by dust, streaked by gall, fouled by spit and urine, gone pewter in the hot, dry wind and, finally, as the sun dimmed in shame, as his flesh matched the odd lessening of afternoon light as though it were evening, always sudden in that climate, swallowing him and the other death row felons, and the silhouette of this original sign merged with a false night sky.... The cross he held was abstract; the absent body was real, but both combined to pull humans from backstage to the spotlight, from muttering in the wings to the principal role in the story of their lives. This execution made it possible to respect—freely, not in fear—one's self and one another.... God loved the way humans loved one another; loved the way humans loved themselves; loved the genius on the cross who managed to do both and die knowing it. (146)

The narrator shows readers that Misner urges "the crossed oak in his hands ... to say what he could not, that not only is God interested in you, He *is* you" (147). However, remembered images of crosses hanging from the rear view mirrors of cars full of white men arriving to insult the young girls of Ruby, tattooed on the arms of dedicated killers, and spread for miles across military cemeteries, prevent Steward from seeing the image Misner desires. He determines to collaborate with the equally ironically named Deacon to put a stop to Misner who must be "wrong" (154). This suggests that, as readers might have expected, Misner's unspoken words have indeed gone unheard.

The narrator's observation that the minutes ticked by as he stood before them anticipates the novel's final sermon about "tick-tock" time. This sermon, preached at the child Save-Marie's funeral in place of the customary eulogy, notes the brevity of Save-Marie's life and suggests that her life was probably more blessed than theirs because she lived her life in the light of the visions and dreams she had (307). Still, even though he officiates at this important and poignant community rite, Misner has not won over the people of Ruby, for, as he speaks, they are so engrossed in the chit-chat of their daily lives and their own musings that he fails to hold his audience's attention. All is not lost, however, for Morrison implies Misner's eventual success with Ruby in Consolata's vision of paradise, with which the novel closes. This vision, open to a range of possible readings, pictures a seashore littered with bottle tops, a radio, and a sandal. Although the passage speaks of solace and "the unambivalent bliss of going home to be at home" (318), this is not an idyll but a scene from the real world. The surf quietly laps the shore, and the ocean heaves rhythmically against the land. Yet work remains to be done, the endless work "they were created to do . . . in Paradise." Morrison thus leaves her characters with a task, that of constructing P/paradise that is not ethereal, but "down here." The paradise Misner has tried to show the people of Ruby is comforting, earthy, and welcoming to all. It is also open to the present and the future.

When hearers are caught up in a speech event (as Misner's hearers may or may not have been), there is not only the potential for change within the hearer but also the potential to change social structure.[43] One of the aims of Christian preaching, in that preachers present in their preaching pictures of what Christ called the kingdom of God, is to try to shape an alternative society, an alternative way of living, and an alternative future for the audience; Toni Morrison reflects this in her sermons in *Paradise*. Cary's and Pulliam's sermons have shaped the town of Ruby with its dysfunctional collective memory; sadly, they have shaped a community unable to engage with the present and the future. Misner's preaching, on the other hand, shapes an alternative and tells a different narrative. He tries to reshape Ruby into paradise. Readers can only hope the people of Ruby will eventually take up the alternative he proposes, but, even if they don't, Morrison has appealed to her readership to engage with it.

Michael Arditti is doing something similar in the last sermon he records in *Easter*. In Ashley Blair's sermon in the graveyard outside the burnt out church, Arditti invites his readers to live in a morally untidy world that has been graced by God incarnate in its messiness, to see the love for God in human relationships, including those people in former ages regarded as unworthy, and to celebrate the essential goodness of humanity that is the image of Go(o)d (to employ a neat, but unpronounceable neologism of Iris Murdoch's). The invitation extends beyond the curate's hearers; the sermon also works as a mechanism by which Arditti invites those who read his book to join this theological, religious, and spiritual responding community.

The central question remains unanswered. What is the nature of the communities constructed by these sermons in fiction? Are there any common characteristics of the communities shaped by fictional sermons such as these? There are at least four.

First, these communities are incomplete. This distinguishes them from sects that derive their cohesive power from the threat of alienation. In sects, the rhetoric of the defining text exercises repressive power, asserting truth for its worldview and keeping people in its grip for fear of being ostracized. Farrar and (to a lesser extent) Lamb in Byatt's work, and Cary and Pulliam in Morrison's, aspire toward the establishment of such communities, in which the sermons they preach are common self-defining texts designed to build the group and enthrall its members. But they fail, for the dominating preachers and their oppressing texts are unable to stand untroubled in the novels. In *A Whistling Woman,* interlopers such as Brenda Pincher problematize Farrar's preaching, and abused Children of Joy such as Lucy Nighby overcome anxiety about being alienated. In *Paradise*, the troubling presence of Misner potentially disarms the power of the others' controlling rhetoric. The authorial intentions are both to construct and take apart the community.

These incomplete communities are "groups-in-formation," and these are very loose models of community. In groups-in-formation, each member of the community subsists in a state of mediation with other members and negotiates understandings of the group's purpose as expressed in any foundational documents it may have. In such groups, members are at liberty to respond variously to the group's self-identifying texts; indeed, such communities not only tolerate but welcome critical appraisal of their constitutive texts because the activity of mutual reflection and self-reflection strengthens community.[44] Such a group-in-formation can be associated with the Pauline metaphor of the body of Christ in that both are "unified yet many-membered organism[s] in which each member has its function and the whole could not remain alive without each."[45] This is an important theme in Arditti's *Easter*, where the novelist chose to set his satire in a church because, as he said in interview, only under a church roof can one find such a wide cross section of people;[46] ironically, however, *Easter*'s congregation is a body of people fearful of touch. The Pauline ideal, of which Arditti's congregation of St. Mary-in-the-Vale falls short, is a community in which "each individual in his or her uniqueness becomes a context for the necessary reflection upon the common project, so the group is not bound by the threat of alienation, but by a vital adhesion to a common task of mutual regard which both defines and ensures the well-being of the whole."[47] Misner in Morrison's novel strives for this paradisiacal ideal.

Second, communities that these fictional sermons construct are communities of response, a term long associated with Robert Detweiler's theory of religious reading that suggests that a reader's absorption into a fictive world should not be denigrated as escapism, because when people read realistic fiction they are enticed into a role-playing game by which they are affirmed or challenged in their identities. Furthermore, the relationship between reader and author is akin to that between lovers, inasmuch as the most positive and productive result of the narrative experience provokes a compassionate reaction of mutual care and concern.[48] This is the reaction that creates a "community of response." "Religious reading" of a novel is neither about readers being persuaded to accept a particular interpretation of the text nor about readers being overpowered with a superior reading but about their empathetic response. Applying this argument more particularly to the reading of sermons in novels, reading a sermon within a novel does not expose readers to the threat of being either persuaded or overpowered by a superior rhetor. Despite the rhetorical intention of the preacher to persuade, readers have control of their reception of the text and allow themselves to be admitted into and included in the sermon's community of response. Readers retain the freedom to respond as they choose.

The third characteristic of the communities gathered around fictional sermons is that they are interpretive. Stanley Fish's concept of "interpretive community," which followed his identification of texts as events rather than entities on the basis of the joint responsibility of reader and writing in the making of meaning, has become attractive to both Christian literary critics and Christian biblical interpreters, partly because he uses religious language for his literary ideas. Fish understood an interpretive community to be one in which fellowship is an indicator of shared interpretive strategies, evident in "the nod of recognition" among readers.[49] Fish's argument becomes important in that the interpretive strategies, the sharing of which creates interpretive communities, are learned rather than inherent strategies and are based on assumptions held before the act of reading;[50] they do not result from the author's powers of persuasion, nor, in the case of sermons within fiction, do they result from the preacher's rhetorical power to convince. They are prevenient. Novels, therefore, do not have a single interpretive community, but several interpretive communities, as groups of readers bring to the text shared assumptions and interpretive strategies based on many factors, perhaps including race, gender, religious creed, life experience, societal status, and so on. Some interpretive communities are public, more or less stable, and self-consciously named, while others are less intentional and less open to public scrutiny.[51] To which of these two categories of interpretive community Christian believers belong is a matter of debate. Shared belief is likely to include variety of belief, and Fish did not intend to deny the possibility of either disparity or dissent. The communities gathered around Byatt's, Morrison's, and Arditti's invented sermons are permitted to respond as they will and interpret them as they may. Inevitably, within all the communities around the sermons, dissenting voices are present, and this offers readers a variety of interpretative and responsive sites to choose from. They can inhabit any of these sites.

Finally, these communities are virtual. Here, current homiletical theory about the actual practice of preaching converges with this study of preaching within fiction. Many contemporary homileticians implicitly sympathize with the view that the only viable communities are imagined communities, and, although they express themselves variously, they often claim that preaching constructs alternative worlds, or communities, for their hearers to inhabit. In the way that actual preaching potentially constructs virtual worlds, the preaching examined in the books studied herein forms virtual communities. In the early years of the twenty-first century, with the growth of social networking websites, people have become increasingly familiar with the notion of virtual communities established when people remotely exchange messages and forge relationships with others across the globe with similar interests—making friends with people they have never met. People have become familiar with, and are perhaps increasingly disturbed by, the psychological and social implications of these virtual communities where "disembodied relationships are carried out *as if* they were a community in the usual sense,"[52] as a result of which these as-if communities compose a parallel world. To suggest that the communities around fictional sermons are virtual communities does not, of course, imply that their native sphere is cyberspace. It does, however, assert that, as with social internet communities, their members' sense of belonging is often tenuous and that the community's borders are simultaneously porous and elastic. Moreover, like the notion of a nation as imagined community, the community only exists in that a number of people, with a sense of mutual significance, consider it to exist.[53] This is the character of all the communities in and around contemporary novels containing sermons, including the sects, because ultimately, by their dissonant presence in the open texts of a novel, they are bound to fail to achieve the closed status to which they aspire.

Incomplete, responsive, interpretive, and virtual, the imagined communities shaped by fictional sermons, above all else, exist as religious communities. In creating these sermons, the fictional preachers and actual authors facilitate the possibility that around these sermons there may gather believing, learning, sanctifying, yet diverse communities through which new realities may be envisaged and from which alternative futures may emerge. Indeed, it may be that fictional sermons are more enabling than actual ones in that they are open to greater discussion by more people over more time than most spoken sermons. This is in keeping with the theme of embodiment that recurs in many of these novels, but it brings closure of this discussion at the discordant, uncomfortable, but optimistic point that readers and hearers of fictional sermons constitute a fascinating paradox—a disembodied Body.

8

Memory and Imagination

With such potential for dissonant chords—clashing authorities, jarring linguistic repertoires, the conflict between realism and spiritual experiences, the gathering of diverse communities with different expectations around a text, and the tense balancing act of keeping faith in a complex world—why do British and American authors continue to write fictional sermons for their novels? Why is the voice of fictional preaching still heard? And when it is, are novelists who include sermons in their books merely using a remembered genre? Do they succeed in avoiding the perfunctoriness resulting from the literary representation of a primarily spoken genre? Do they avoid what Bakhtin warned against—inserting dead quotations in the text? Do they use sermons as a crafty means of directly addressing their readers? Do they commit what some critics think is the worst sin a writer can commit, that of preaching to the readership? Moreover, in the sermons they write, do they toe the conventional Christian party line, do they use sermons to show that the preacher wrestles with faith, or do they use sermons creatively to forge new theology, describe a new Christian ethic, or express fresh ways of being Christian?

Conservative or defensive answers to these questions would disappoint. More is going on when preaching features in fiction than either that the novelist wants to preserve a traditional genre or that the novelist wants to locate a character within a particular tradition. This chapter shows how sermons in fiction shape the readers' perception of Christianity through cultural memory and faithful imagination. An analysis of preaching in Jeanette Winterson's *Oranges Are Not the Only Fruit*, by a writer who has avowedly eschewed religion but who seems incapable of avoiding religious themes in either her fiction, her journalism, or her philosophy of her art, follows.

Rhetoricians and homileticians have for centuries widely acknowledged the role of memory in preaching. At the very least, it was the penultimate of Cicero's five steps in the preparation and performance of a speech that he described in *On the Orator I*. The orator's theoretical and practical task begins with "invention" when the orator thinks of what to say. The second step is "arrangement" in which the orator organizes and sequences the material so that the various elements of the speech have due weight, and the "right order" is established. In the third step, known as "style," the orator devises "suitably embellished language to clothe the results of his [*sic*] thinking."[1] In the penultimate stage, called "memory," the orator commits the form of the speech to memory before its eventual final stage of "delivery." Good speakers, Cicero claimed, instinctively employ these procedures: they are rules derived from the example of other orators' eloquence, for eloquence cannot be achieved simply by following maxims. However, Cicero's treatise betrays his concern for oratorical reputation and notes that only one error in performance is sufficient to ruin a reputation.[2] Orators are rare, he said, because few are the people who possess the necessary combination of qualifications for this demanding five-fold task. He does not burden them with the expectation of superhuman omniscience, but, astonishingly, he does expect them to possess a memory "capable of retaining a host of precedents, indeed the complete history of past times."[3] Memory is "a universal treasure house."[4] This is a high expectation, but it is only one aspect of the relationship between memory and preaching. Cultural memory, as a shaping tool in preaching, is greater than memorizing.

In the late twentieth century, renewed academic interest in cultural or collective memory was prompted by study of the Holocaust and other twentieth-century atrocities and by the emergence, with the dissolution of the communist bloc, of new and rediscovered nationalist identities. Interest in cultural memory found expression in the development of collective acts of memorial such as national observation of silence in the wake of tragic events, flowers placed at crime scenes, and, in Britain, the political pressure to observe both Armistice Day and Remembrance Sunday. The rapid development of such practices, and their continued intensification in the twenty-first century, is in direct contrast with the more muted official response, less than fifty years ago, to the tragedy of Aberfan discussed in relation to the preaching in *How Far Can You Go?* Concurrent with this academic interest and this cultural change, people have rediscovered that preaching is itself "a stream of social memory,"[5] or a living practice of memory, in at least four ways.[6]

First, preaching functions as a living practice of memory in terms of the self-reflexivity of preachers in their sermons. In the last decade of the seventeenth century, John Locke recognized a relationship between identity and memory and worried about whether amnesia altered personhood:[7]

> Suppose I wholly lose the memory of some parts of my Life, beyond a possibility of retrieving them, so that perhaps I shall never be conscious of them again; yet am I not the same Person, that did those actions, had those Thoughts, that I was once conscious of, though I have now forgot them?

Continuity between past and present is as much an essential ingredient of cultural and collective identity as it is for the individual, for the cultural memory that occurs in the present continuously interprets and modifies the past and shapes the future.[8] Memorial presence of the past in the present moment may take several forms, including nostalgia, conscious recall, involuntary re-emergence, and polemic use of the past to reshape the present. Often this results in a tension between the here-and-now and the there-and-then.[9] Memory is always subject to active social manipulation and revision,[10] so much so that no one can rely on it for faithful recovery of an actual past. Indeed, any culture's collective memory is located in many places and shaped by many factors. Architecture, including memorials and ruins, deserted and utilized buildings; literature, both ancient and modern; and art from both the memorialized past and the memory-filled present are sites bearing cultural memory. Ritual, dress, and language carry cultural memory. A person's nostalgic yearning for a lost past, the camaraderie and fellowship of an existing community, and the longing for a renewed, restored, or discovered future are also bearers of a culture's memory. And cultural memory is also located in a culture's narrative, of which preaching is a type. Preaching, of course, also has associations with architecture, the performance of ritual, nostalgia for a lost past, and yearning for a promised future.

Each telling of a self-narrative changes the story, and this challenges the conceptual possibility of both an individual's autobiography and a community's self-narrative. The narrative of memory has three stages—the event, the memory of the event, and the writing of the memory of the event—and the third stage constructs the only version of the first two that we can know.[11] That "memory of the past is continuously modified by experiences of the present and the 'self' who is doing the remembering"[12] is an unavoidable adulteration of the original events. What is written is a version of the past, not the past itself. The autobiographical elements in the fictional sermons contained in many of the novels in this study support this view. All too often the formulaic pattern of testimony in sermons leads readers to suspect that preachers are reordering events and modifying their own history for polemic effect. Even when sermons are less obviously autobiographical, they are related to the genre of life writing because no speaker can avoid putting something of the self into speeches. In the self-doubt of Blair Ashley in *Easter* and Austin Brierley in *How Far Can You Go?*, in the strength of conviction expressed in the sermons of both Wroe in *Mr Wroe's Virgins* and Mompellion in *Year of Wonders* (but not always in the way they live their lives), and in the manner in which Byatt's preachers pin their theological colors to the mast, the preacher's persona cannot be kept out of the sermon. In each case, the preacher's life writing as presented in the sermon, whether partial or complete, is subject to readers' doubts. They ask, is the preacher merely, consciously or unintentionally, giving his version of the past, and how trustworthy is it?

Furthermore, preaching is a stream of social or cultural memory because hearers listen with remembrance of previous sermons. First-time readers of novels build up an understanding of the plot partly through the continuous action of memory, and when they reread novels they engage in a process of reconstruction and interpretation facilitated by the knowledge of what happens next.[13] The act of reading involves the use of memory, as words build into sentences, sentences into paragraphs, and paragraphs into narratives in which the reader can think back and anticipate forward. The Freudian analogy of memory as an archaeological site, while attractive for many reasons, is less helpful here than the Derridean metaphor of footnotes and codicils, where he suggests that the text can be deciphered only in footnotes or endnotes.[14] Seemingly, memory functions not only to enable readers to remember earlier pages of the novel they are reading so that they can grasp the plot and identify recurring themes but also to remember previous readings of the novel as well as previous novels read. Such memory teaches the rules of reading novels and locates the novel being read within a particular genre. These observations about reading books also apply to listening to sermons, even though keeping the thread of memory is more challenging when listening than it is when holding a book whose pages one can flick back over to refresh failing memory. Memory floods into the minds of congregation members as they listen to the preacher. These are memories not only of what has already been said in this sermon but also of previous sermons this preacher has preached. They are also memories of sermons they themselves have heard in other churches and, though they are out of earshot, sermons by other preachers in the history and breadth of the Christian tradition. This is so even of the very first Christian sermons. Peter's at Pentecost references Joel and the Psalms to find a place for the strange Pentecostal occurrences within a tradition, while Stephen's before his martyrdom draws on memories of Jewish preaching to give a concise history of the Jewish people.

Any current instance of Christian preaching has a location relative to the tradition of preaching. As a fictional example, the last sermon in *Easter* is Blair Ashley's Easter morning sermon outside the burnt-out church. Arditti can be confident that his readers remember something of preceding sermons in the novel, including Blair's address at Alice and Dee's lesbian union behind locked doors in the side chapel. Arditti's expressed motivation to write *Easter* as a retelling of the narrative of Christ's passion suggests that he is conscious of the reading public's increasing unfamiliarity with institutional Christianity, yet he can also expect that at least some of his readers will read Blair's sermon with echoes and memories of Easter sermons from services they themselves have attended. Some might also read it with memories prompted by the allusions Arditti makes, including the Wesleyan reference discussed earlier. Moreover, Blair's habitual appeal to Christian tradition all the more encourages readers to consider this sermon in the light of remembered others.

Third, preaching serves as a living practice of memory in that preachers select and employ mnemonic markers around which sacred memory proclaiming the revealed activity of God, known as kerygmatic memory, may be formed. These markers, or *topoi*, are the words by which "this" is named "this" and "that" is named "that."[15] This is reminiscent of the concern for preaching's proper naming of the world prompted by A. S. Byatt's *A Whistling Woman*, where accuracy of naming is an obsessive worry. Key sacred words and images, serving as markers for kerygmatic memory, come usually from the authoritative texts of Scripture, ritual, or liturgy and require neither translation nor elaboration, for their embeddedness in the believing community's collective memory triggers imaginative recreation of the original past.[16] This can be either a deliberate technique or involuntary aspect of preaching, and it is employed by all except the most exceptional and contrary preachers to associate their preaching with the "great tradition" of preaching. Among fictional sermons, it is best seen in two groups of preachers: those featured in historical novels and "conventional" preachers. The latter group includes the religious convention speaker who uses forced acronyms in *How Far Can You Go?* and Ted Bishop in *Easter*, who "trot out" citations of biblical texts and follow formulaic sermon structures. Around the time Lodge wrote his novel, many Christian bookshops stocked many books of preaching aids in which sermon outlines based on handy acrostics and alliterative section titles were peddled. Similarly, the creaking conventional sermon structure of three points framed by an introduction and conclusion is still adopted by many preachers; the sermon Ted Bishop preached at the healing service in *Easter* has remnants of this structure in that its main body is an attack on humanists, atheists, and liberals in turn. This comes between an introduction that includes the proclamation of a biblical text and a conclusion in which the bishop seems to get so carried away with his theme of the power of Christ that he declares that Jesus never caught so much as a cold (268). In each case, formulaic conventionality has the capacity to trigger a lazy "nod of recognition"[17] and either a yawn or smile. Seemingly, writers of historical fiction find this particularly helpful in that the conventional sermon form may be employed as schema for cultural or historical contextualization of the narrative. Many such writers can be said to use the sermons of their central characters in this way so that readers accept their novels' imagined pasts.

This sacred kerygmatic memory is not the only form of memory at work in preaching. Mimetic or imitative memory is also present. In this case there is no kerygmatic selection or emphasis, only the repetition of original words from the sacred past in such a way that it is evident that this is an original to be copied. Mimetic memory is a more significant way of remembering the past that at first appears because it forces the preacher to make use of some form of dynamic equivalence between the biblical text and contemporary life in sermons.[18] Furthermore, if sermons in fiction are to translate into the reader's world or to have persuasive influence on the reader's way of thinking, the author must also establish some analogy or equivalence between the fictional world—the world of the sermon—and the actual world. If it is true that "the past is made not found,"[19] then the past is a fictive realm,[20] and, like these fictive pasts, the worlds of novels are similarly constructed through acts of the imagination building on the words of the text. These constructed and imagined worlds proposed by the text are, according to Ricoeur in *Time and Narrative*, dependent upon three degrees of mimesis—prefigurative, configurative, and refigurative. Detailed critique of Ricoeur is beyond the scope of this study, yet it holds great importance to the science of homiletics. The chief characteristic of Ricoeur's prefigurative mimesis, or mimesis$_1$, is *memoria* or simply remembering.[21] In preaching, this prefigurative mimesis enables the church to recognize its imagined past as an original, and its imagined future as an ultimate. Both of these are worthy of imitation by organizing analogous acts and combining them into a coherent faith narrative involving both the actual stuff of everyday life and spiritual matter.[22] In this way, preachers gain access to lost memory, correct faulty memory, and establish true memory for the Christian community.[23] Ricoeur's second form of mimesis, configurative mimesis or mimesis$_2$, is akin to preaching sermons "in the shape of scripture," that is, configured in the shape of the texts they are mimicking.[24] This opens to the hearer the as-ifness of the kingdom, from which humanity has been estranged and toward which Christian believers aim. Ricoeur's third degree of mimesis, refigurative mimesis or mimesis$_3$, is capable of refiguring reality in preaching; indeed, this moves beyond imitation—it *is* imagination.

Relating this information to historical fiction will be enlightening. Historical novels deal primarily with the divergence between *res gestae* and *historia rerum gestarum*, that is, events in the past and narrative discourse about them between which there is always a degree of discontinuity.[25] Historical novels often articulate a struggle over "point of view," or the power to select what may be accepted as legitimate testimony and the authority to narrate. Especially when there are issues of class, gender, or race, the legitimacy of the narrators of historical novels may be questioned in terms of their control over the narrative, mainly because marginalized groups have difficulty recovering suppressed history, keeping it alive, legitimizing the testimony, and living in the present while constituting a future consistent with the legacy of the remembered past. Readers having access to a variety of narratives, historical perspectives, and versions of common sense proves to be better.[26] The "jarring witnesses" of the four narrators of *Mr Wroe's Virgins* supply "a plenitude of historiographic testimony,"[27] whereas the young woman who narrates Brooks' *Year of Wonders* herself contributes various points of view. As a privileged observer of intimate moments in the lives of the people with influence in the village, she enjoys the privileged vantage point of a servant who observes much. Thus, readers can assess for themselves the relative veracity of the narratives. Historical novels often reveal a radical discontinuity with the past as well as a discrepancy between what happened and how history records what happened. When historical continuity with a desired past has been severed like this, idealization of the past is a powerful recurrent urge. Religious belief, which is often expressed in inherited memory, contributes to this urge and is also a significant factor in repairing discontinuity with the past. Such religious belief should be carefully distinguished from the ontological existence of God or any existential sense of providential design.[28] Even if it is no more than a human or social construct, religious belief salvifically repairs severance from the past. Religious belief—or religious memory, rehearsed, for instance, in the Eucharist as "a foretaste of the heavenly banquet prepared for all people"[29] as well as in prophetic preaching—is also capable of repairing fractured continuity with a desired future. Thus, if it is conventional to see recurring memory, or anamnesis, as making the past available for the creation or development of the self's future in creative collaboration between past, present, and future, then preaching has the same anamnetical, or nonforgetting, role perpetuating the tradition's memory. This may be compared to what happens in Anne Michaels' novel *Fugitive Pieces*. In the years after a Greek archaeologist, Athos, rescues a child from his fate in Auschwitz, Athos insists on the boy learning Hebrew because it is his future he is remembering.[30] This is the remembering of effective preaching.

Finally, and subversively, preaching is a living practice of memory in that it allows the presence and voicing of what the philosopher Michel Foucault called countermemory, speaking across or contradicting memory. In a complex argument, Foucault suggested that, on any given originary event, there takes place a collective hesitation signaling a confrontation in which forces that not wholly benign struggle. There follows "the hazardous play of domination,"[31] through which one representation of the originary event is asserted as orthodox and others are designated as heretical. Countermemory aims at liberating "effective history" from "traditional history" by focusing on the inscription of history on the marginalized body and reading backwards to the countless unremembered events that never became part of collective memory.[32] Thus, countermemory moves behind and beyond historicist, mimetic, and kerygmatic memory to encounter otherness, alterity, and difference.[33]

In fictional preaching, the way in which Blair Ashley, the curate in *Easter*, is able to "preach sense out of" both his experiences in Holy Week, when he disrupts the Maundy service at St Paul's Cathedral and the revelation of his sexuality, which pushes him to the margins of the church, demonstrates the presence of countermemory. Counterculturally, Blair recovers ancient submerged texts that wrote what is now known as "gay theology," as well as liturgical texts for the authorization of same-sex partnerships. The voice of countermemory is also heard in the interior struggle by which Austin Brierley, the curate in *How Far Can You Go?*, is able to continue to preach with integrity even though he is up against the dominant tradition that wants to suppress the questions that challenge religious faith in the aftermath of disasters, such as Aberfan. This tradition is represented when Austin's parish priest, appallingly, asks what good can come of making people doubt the goodness of God (108). Experiences of preaching like Blair's and Austin's mean that homiletical countermemory is rather like "a prolonged moment of erasure" in which the preacher's own well-formed memory and the collective memory of the sermon's hearers dissolve into "things unremembered" and contradict the patterns and processes of the past on which Christians have traditionally relied.[34] And if so, contemporary preachers must learn the double-consciousness that dislocates their positions within the field of kerygmatic memory and releases an awareness of memory positions that are, or could be, otherwise. An alternative term used earlier was "bifocality." This conveys the notion that one field of the preacher's view is fixed on the tradition, while another is on the countertradition. This locates the church both culturally and counterculturally. Although this is an uncomfortable place to be, preachers such as some of Arditti's, Byatt's, and Lodge's are able to inhabit it. The bifocality of less domineering preachers, which pays attention to the matter—or bodies—around them as well as to the bodies inscribed with the kerygmatic and mimetic, often painful and submerged, memories of the dominant church tradition, funds hearers' imaginations so that they are able to exit what has been called "the house of tradition" and enter the strange land of the eschatological community of "unlimited conversation."[35] This is one important reason why novelists continue to use sermons; they are capable of a creative and illuminating bifocality, or double-consciousness, by which readers' perceptions of Christianity are formed and through which they can find their place in the cultural memory and imagine alternative worlds.

Although Walter Brueggemann has most consistently championed imagination as the crux of the homiletical enterprise in a postmodern age, theologians have also recovered imagination from the world of "make-believe."[36] Thus, imagination is recognized as the locus or "anthropological point of contact for divine revelation" not so much a way of doing theology but simply the place where it happens.[37] The term "imagination" once flourished in theology only among practitioners of the academic discipline of "religion and literature," but it is now receiving wider theological attention.[38] Nevertheless, for a long while, imagination has been regarded with suspicion theologically, because those who fail to distinguish between what is imagined and the imaginary think it tends toward a reductionist direction in theology. One of Samuel Taylor Coleridge's outstanding contributions to literary criticism and theological thought was his theory of imagination and its implications for religion in which he effectively "desynonymiz[ed] Fancy and Imagination."[39] Coleridge established a distinction between primary and secondary imagination. Primary imagination, which is necessarily shared by everyone, mixes together ideas or images that are already present into a mere "mechanical juxtaposition of parts," whereas secondary imagination, a higher and more creative faculty, fuses ideas and images in a mark of genius into the creative unity of a "living whole or organism." The combined effect of this "esemplastic power," as Coleridge called it, can be observed in one of the ways metaphor works; the primary imagination supplies the images that are then forged into creative unity by the secondary imagination.[40] So, arguing against a long tradition that regarded "imagination" as equivalent to "fancy," Coleridge saw imagination as "the mind in its highest state of creative insight and awareness";[41] it is the creative faculty with the highest expression of truth.[42]

Later, in response to what was popularly received as a challenge to the value and objective reality of religion, in that Feuerbach called it "the dream of the human mind" and Marx described it as "the illusory happiness of the people," a distinction between realistic and illusory imagination was established. This distinction helps humankind to cope philosophically with a problem common to both religion and literature, that of nonpresent temporal and spatial reality. In the case of temporal nonpresent reality, imagination facilitates memory of a past that is no longer present.[43] Further to this, imagination also facilitates anticipation of a future not yet present. In the case of spatial nonpresent reality, imagination lets people in one room accept the existence of a table in the next, an unseen Taj Mahal, microcosmic subatomic structures, and macrocosmic astrophysics, to use the examples Garrett Green cites in a discussion of the relationship between imagination and theology.[44] It also lets readers accept the existence of characters in a novel, enabling them to write and read about the preachers in this study as if they were present, as well as the existence of the gods of their religion, enabling them to write and read about the "substance" of these preachers' beliefs. In theology, paradigmatic imagination, through which people look for a pattern by which they can explore objects in a larger world, assists us in our interpretation of experience and language and makes accessible something that would otherwise be beyond our linguistic grasp.[45] This is the problem of the nature of the language used in fictional sermons discussed in chapter 7. In a phrase reminiscent of David Cunningham's definition of the rhetoric of preaching as "faithful persuasion"—and coincidentally making a neat link between the delivery and reception of a sermon—the *locus* of revelation is "faithful imagination."[46]

That such faithful imagination is the essence of reading is a concept with origins in the theology of Augustine, for whom desire is the prime motivator of intention. The desire to understand is much more than an intellectual desire in that it engrosses and affects readers' appetites, metabolisms, sleep patterns, and physicality. It circulates around the reader and the text in such a way that, in Augustine's theology of reading, reading affects both what people do and what they become. Indeed, reading is a spiritual exercise: "When we read we engage with dynamics more powerful than we are aware, enter and extend the rich store-houses of our *imagination*, open ourselves to an exterior, an other which can injure as well as heal us."[47]

This creative and spiritual understanding of faithful imagination is related in some way to John Ruskin's concept of "Imagination Penetrative." Like Coleridge, Ruskin distinguishes fancy from imagination, and he regards imagination as "the highest intellectual power of man [*sic*],"[48] but, unlike Coleridge, Ruskin believes imagination to be more interpretative than creative. Imagination, for Ruskin, is the mind's tongue capable of piercing through whatever substantial or spiritual subject is submitted to it. Like a pholas, a sea mollusk that makes holes in stones, imagination penetrates the text with pathetic and interpretative consequences.

Schema theory has informed this study of sermons in fiction, and the convergence of schema theory with these religio-literary theories of imagination suggests a crucial role for imagination in actual preaching. Brueggemann sees this role not as describing a coherent thought system but as the voicing of pieces out of which people can put their lives together in fresh configurations; it is the provision of materials and resources that fund the imaginative shaping of a new world.[49] Schema theory builds on the notion that "little pieces" of incomplete schemata may be adequate to fund readers' imaginations. It suggests that imagination functions as a tool in the way readers use pre-existing mental expectations to fill in gaps between key linguistic terms so that they can make sense of a discourse and imagine its world. Key linguistic terms act as triggers in the text enabling readers to retrieve from their memories organized packages of connected pieces of information that are stored either sequentially as a script or nonsequentially as a frame.[50] The mental typification of schemata is established and tested by schema reinforcing, preserving, and refreshing, each of which is necessarily preceded by schema disruption.[51] Take, for instance, the schema script for preaching a sermon in a typical English parish church. The culturally remembered script will include situational aspects such as the gathering of a congregation, the use of a pulpit, and the sermon's setting within a liturgy; personal aspects such as the preacher's self-presentation as a bold interpreter of culture, Scripture, and faith; and instrumental aspects such as wearing a preaching stole. Schema disruption, which can never be total because schema recognition would be prevented by the resulting loss of key linguistic triggers, involves changes to one or more of these aspects. The preacher might, for instance, deliver the sermon from the floor of the church instead of the pulpit or wear a woolen scarf instead of a stole. The schema refreshment that follows may be the result of the destruction of old schemata (for example, the readers' recognition that old forms of preaching are outdated and ineffective in the current age), the construction of new schemata (which might include the realization of new styles or patterns of preaching), or the establishment of new connections between existing schemata (perhaps finding a new connection between the schemata of lecturing and preaching). In all these schematic games, both memory and imagination have vital roles. Without one or the other, schemata would be a jumble of senseless pieces rather than the building blocks for new worlds for preachers, hearers, and readers to inhabit.

These comments about the roles of memory and imagination in the reception of fictional sermons can be tested against the sermons in Jeanette Winterson's *Oranges Are Not the Only Fruit*. These are remarkable for their playfulness despite their serious intent.

In the twenty-five years since *Oranges* was awarded the Whitbread Prize, Winterson has established herself as a literary critic, novelist, and journalist of high repute. *Oranges* is a spiraling study in intertextuality, and this has established a pattern for most of Winterson's art, almost all of which is conscious of the literary, gender, and religious traditions in which she writes. For instance, *Lighthousekeeping*,[52] chosen at random from among her novels for this purpose, references in bold, general, and obvious ways Robert Louis Stevenson's *Treasure Island*, Virginia Woolf's *To the Lighthouse*, and the Bible's Tower of Babel. *Oranges* appears to tell Winterson's own story, although when she wrote an introduction to a later edition of the novel, she wrote that it is "No not at all and yes of course" autobiographical (xiv).[53] Like Edmund Gosse's *Father and Son*, literary and religious echoes of which can be heard in *Oranges*, its true genre lies somewhere between autobiography, biography, and fiction.[54] Winterson herself described *Oranges* as an antilinear experimental novel with a complicated spiral structure. The plot, within this complex structure, is the story of Jess, a girl brought up by a strict fundamentalist Christian foster-mother in a small industrial town in northern England. At sixteen she falls in love with Melanie, a girl of about her own age. The evangelical community, led by its pastor and Jess' mother, destroys their relationship, publicly humiliating the girls and forcibly subjecting Jess to violent exorcism. Following a second, less traumatic lesbian relationship, Jess refuses to renounce her sexuality and leaves church and home, eventually to go to university. A textual complexity that denies categorization weaves around this core narrative. *Oranges* cuts across so many cultural and critical categories that it refuses to be pigeonholed into one sort of text or another.[55] It attracts a wide diversity of readers who can read it variously as lesbian text, feminist text, *bildungsroman* tracing the growth of a character finding her identity, or *kunstleroman* tracing the development of the central character as an artist; it is also, by virtue of the novel's sermons, its depiction of the environment Jess grows away from and its chapter headings by which Winterson establishes a relationship with the first eight books of the Hebrew Scriptures, a religious text. The book is a portrait of a writer's textual and sexual development, whether or not we take that writer to be Winterson herself—which, despite Winterson's prevarication, seems the obvious conclusion to reach—and the story of this development is complicated by the insertion of four narrative types, often running concurrently, which can be identified as fable, ontological tale, hermeneutical tale, and conversion story.[56]

The most obvious of these inserted genres are the fables, "collages of fairy tale, folklore, biblical symbols and Arthurian romance which interrupt the 'straight' or mainly chronological narrative in every chapter and grow in length from the brief fragment in 'Genesis' to the extended tale of Winnet Stonejar and the sorcerer in 'Ruth.'"[57] These fabulous interludes rehearse and develop the readers' understanding of the anxieties that drive the plot. They are typical of feminist uses of extrabiblical narratives and retellings of biblical narratives to trouble the assumed patriarchal authority of the biblical narrative. They also have the positive effect of recovering the malleability of the biblical text. Less obvious in the novel are the ontological tales that recur, usually with the intention of establishing identity. The novel begins with the story of Jess' origins, returns to it at key junctures, and complicates it with other stories of begetting, and, because these stories are to do with issues of sexuality and creativity, they establish her dual identity as a lesbian and as a writer. The presence of a third inserted genre, the hermeneutical tale or stories about language and story-making, assists this development. Episodes throughout the book return to the question of how to interpret signs and wonders not only in the religious world of the supernatural but also in the signs and wonders encountered in the material world, including the indications and joys of her own sexual being (17). The fourth story genre inserted into *Oranges* is the conversion story, which also contains the structure on which the larger plot turns. The miniature stories of the converted sweep and the Hallelujah Giant, whose conversion involved miraculous shrinkage from abnormal gigantism to the height of a conventionally tall man (7–8), introduce the formulaic structure of conversion stories, and it is soon apparent to the reader that almost everyone in the novel has one. The notable exception is Jess: dedicated at birth to the Lord, Jess has no need of one, though through her preaching she is the agent of others' conversions. Jess' trajectory is, from the perspective of conventional Christianity, a reverse conversion: she is liberated from legalistic religion into the freedom of the deeper virtues of love and loyalty between women. In the way *Oranges* functions as a subversive feminist text critical of closed and repressive religion, these four genres are vital tools for Winterson. No less important are the sermons embraced within her novel.

There are many, although none of them is reported with the same detail and at the same length, as those in some of the novels discussed in this book. Only three occur at turning points in the narrative, effecting changes in the narrative's direction. Each is set against or alongside other texts. The last is a reference to Jess' success as a preacher, because of which services at the mission church are well attended, set against her mother's "antisermon," which results in women being barred from their pulpit. Near the beginning of the section entitled "Judges," Jess' affair with Melanie has become known. Following private conversations between Mrs. Winterson and the pastor, the matter is referred to their denominational council, who advise that the congregation is in error inasmuch as, contrary to the teachings of St. Paul, it allowed women power in the church. They should not be allowed to preach. When this advice is reported to the congregation there is uproar:

> [T]hen a curious thing happened. My mother stood up and said she believed this was right: that women had specific circumstances for their ministry, that the Sunday School was one of them, the Sisterhood another, but the message belonged to the men.... My mother droned on about the importance of missionary work for a woman, that I was clearly such a woman, but had spurned my call in order to wield power on the home front, where it was inappropriate. She ended by saying that having taken on a man's world in other ways I had flouted God's law and tried to do it sexually. This was no spontaneous speech. She and the pastor had talked about it already. (131)

In that Mrs. Winterson's speech offers an interpretation of Scripture, is delivered in a church setting to a gathered congregation, and is planned, it is to all intents and purposes a sermon, but it is a sermon to stop sermons in that it effectively silences women's voices in that congregation. Her antisermon bars all women from the pulpit, not only her daughter who she believes had chosen to allow herself to fall to the Devil (126).

Earlier in the novel, the author reports an example of Pastor Finch's preaching, which coincides with Melanie's first time at the church. He is on a regional tour and arrives in an old van customized with evangelistic designs. One side portrays the eternal damned while the other depicts the heavenly host, and the back and front of the van pose the question "Heaven or Hell?" and the challenge "The choice is yours." He has a collapsible portable cross which he sets up outside the van before preaching. After a self-written temperance song, Pastor Finch begins his sermon with an account of how many souls have been saved on his tour and an account of the epidemic of demons spreading throughout the northwest of England. This develops into a sermon on unnatural desires, and all who hear it agree it was a "very fine sermon" (83). It ends with an altar call, to which Melanie responds. This sermon sets the tone for the conventional, official response of this religious community to the lesbian relationship that develops between Melanie and Jess during the period in which Jess counsels the new convert. It is set against the novel's critique of fundamentalism, with the novel, taken as a whole, directly challenging the pastor's assumptions.

The first sermon in the book occurs during a special Society conference hosted in their town after Jess has been delivering evangelistic tracts. The sermon is on perfection, and it comes at the crucial moment of Jess' first theological disagreement. It is reported very concisely:

> Perfection, the man said, was a thing to aspire to. It was the condition of the Godhead, it was the condition of the man before the Fall. It could only be truly realized in the next world, but we had a sense of it, a maddening, impossible sense, which was both a blessing and a curse.
>
> "Perfection," he announced, "is flawlessness." (58)

Jess' feelings that the preacher's definition of perfection as flawlessness unattainable in the mortal realm is itself flawed are explored in the Fable of the Perfect Wisewoman who is first courted, then beheaded, by a prince in search of a flawless woman. The fable immediately follows the report of the sermon and constitutes the remaining half of the chapter. It troubles the assumed orthodoxy of the sermon's theology. In the fable, when he is disappointed in his quest for a perfect woman, the prince chooses instead to write a book entitled *The Holy Mystery of Perfection*, and, when, at last, the perfect woman appears but refuses to marry him, he says she must because he has written all about her (62), as if in his mind the text is supreme. For three days and nights, the woman tries to disabuse the prince of his conviction that perfection is flawlessness, using her own perfect balance of qualities to show that perfection is a search for balance or harmony. The prince is advised that he cannot retract his book's thesis without loss of authorial authority, for what is written is written. The only solution his advisors can suggest is to kill the woman, but they all drown in her blood. At the end, the prince encounters an old man who offers him another book about "this geezer who gets a bolt though the neck" (65), thus drawing a threefold comparison of the story to Frankenstein, the prince's fantasy of a flawless creation, and the preacher's definition of perfection. Juxtaposing this sermon and the fable establishes for the reader a sense that Winterson's novel is a quest for balance and symmetry, harmony and integrity, before legalistic flawlessness. Juxtaposing the sermon and fable challenges the notion that the biblical narrative has supreme authority and challenges the assumption that the church is the sole interpreter of these ancient texts. Juxtaposing the sermon and fable offers a critique of clerical authority, and it denies the existence and destabilizes the universal acceptability of any totalizing explanatory narrative. As Winterson herself said when commenting on the script for the BBC television adaptation of the novel, which, probably for dramatic reasons, featured more preaching than the novel itself does,

> I know that *Oranges* challenges the virtues of the home, the power of the church and the supposed normality of heterosexuality. I was always clear that it would do so. I would rather not have embarked on the project than see it toned down in any way.[58]

She uses the sermons in *Oranges* to probe her evidence for the abusive power of the church and to argue her case for a freer expression of religious and spiritual truth. Far from slowing the action or compromising her satire, they heighten her critical, satirical tone.

One question readers of *Oranges* must answer is precisely what Winterson's stance is with regard to religion. Some have said that the book is scurrilously irreverent about religion.[59] Is it indeed? Or is the author tracing an escape from literalist and fundamentalist religion by way of an open reading of the Christian story into the realm of wholesome spirituality based on acceptance, love, and loyalty? Is she reformulating biblical narratives so that they can continue to narrate and shape twenty-first-century people's lives, thus using her novel to achieve what preaching is intended to do? Is it not the case that this novel, by bringing together a range of story genres, including preaching, redeems meaning through memory of the Christian tradition and through imagining a possible alternative to the real experienced world? The preaching in *Oranges* is no exception to the continuously sustained role of preaching throughout its literary presence. It shapes readers' perception of Christianity; it conserves the tradition and refigures faith.

Except for the intentionally satirical, each instance of preaching in any novel further broadens and deepens the preaching schemata for readers. Readers construct the worlds of books through their use of memory and imagination. They do so to such an extent that past, present, and future are constructed entities. Similarly, theists make their theology, the church makes its *kerygma*, religious practitioners make their *ethos*, and preachers make their alternative worlds by acts of memory and imagination. This is not to say that they are imaginary or illusory, false or anachronistic, but it is to say that whatever fictional preachers create through such memory and imagination carries the potential to be the highest expression of truth as an alternative to the faulty worlds shown in novels and inhabited by people of the twenty-first century.

Epilogue

Gentle reader, as John Updike's Thomas Marshfield addresses you in *A Month of Sundays*, if you are naught but a reader, then the simplicity of your life is incredible. You are probably much more. You are probably also a Christian believer—or curious about religious belief. Why else would you be reading a book in the Making the Christian Imagination series, unless, as someone with a literary interest, you slipped in by mistake? Your understanding of what it means to be a believer might be no more than that, from a sociological perspective, you believe religion has something to offer to the well-being of humanity. Or it might mean that, from the perspective of the psychology of religions, you believe that either religious observance or personal faith contribute to a person's health. If you, gentle reader, are also this faithful, or religious, reader then this study has shown you that preaching in fiction takes the form of a wide range of sermons, both satirical and straight. Some bolster faith, whereas others problematize it. Some fictional preachers are untroubled, whereas others wrestle with belief. Some preaching in fiction subverts theism in general and Christianity in particular. Sometimes fictional preachers are conventional and adhere to traditional church and religious dogma, whereas others break away and forge new theology on the anvil of experience. Both in critique and support of Christianity, fictional preachers have shaped readers' various understandings of this world faith. In whatever way sermons are employed by writers, despite the clanging cymbals of their dissonances, there is yet no end to them in literature.

You, gentle reader, may also be a preacher, and if this book has any application outside the academic field of religion and literature, perhaps it encourages actual preachers to seek nonmanipulative, nonhegemonic, nonauthoritarian forms of communication in the pulpit. Effective preaching for the modern world comprises sermons that recognize the interdependence between preacher and hearer and in which both preacher and hearer move along a common pathway of empathic imagination. During the lengthy gestation period of this book, preaching in the real world has continued to change shape. Preachers think more carefully about the nature of authority and recognize that it is never to be assumed. Preachers know that the dominant voice should not be the preacher's but that of the silence in the gap between the speaker and the hearer, where truth is negotiated and agreed upon. This silence is reminiscent of and akin to the "still small voice" Elijah heard on Horeb. Effective preachers are, therefore, more careful about the language they use so that the poetry of theology resonates in hearers' hearts. Faithful preachers are more imaginative in their attempts to communicate religious experience, in their hope that hearers find God in the commonplace and the kingdom of God in the as-is world around them. And contemporary preachers have greater audience awareness than they once had. All preachers have much more to learn about the art of preaching, and there will always be those who continue to refine their art. They will be like so many contemporary novelists in that they will preach to fund the imaginative construction of a nonpresently real, godly world.

And if you, gentle reader, are also a writer, perhaps this book encourages you not to be as shy of using sermons in your work as was a popular romantic novelist who attended a British church. She would readily include extracts of lectures on veterinary practice in her books about a vet's clinic, but, as she said in casual conversation with her minister without full explanation, she would not presume to include sermons in her series about the rector of an English village. What opportunities she missed!

In a sermon preached in Berlin in 1932, Dietrich Bonhoeffer said:

> A proper sermon should be of the kind that holds out to a child a shining red apple or to a thirsty man a glass of fresh water and asks them, "Do you want it?" In this way, we should be able to speak about the things of faith so that hands are stretching out faster than we can fill them.

Sermons in fiction are equally powerful. Some can disrupt faith, and some show the redundancy of certain expressions of Christianity, yet others are capable of showing a remembered, imagined world for which humankind yearns. For this alternative world, readers will longingly stretch out their hands, hearts, and minds.

Notes

Introduction

1 Walter Brueggemann, *Cadences of Home: Preaching among Exiles* (Louisville, Ky.: Westminster John Knox, 1997), 40.
2 Cas Vos, "The Sermon as a Work of Art," *Expository Times* 116, no. 11 (2005): 371–73.
3 Mark Barger Elliott, *Creative Styles of Preaching* (Louisville, Ky.: Westminster John Knox, 2000).
4 This phrase, coined by Walter Brueggemann in *The Bible and the Postmodern Imagination: Texts under Negotiation* (London: SCM Press, 1993), 20, an eminent Old Testament theologian whose enthusiasm for his subject has led him into examining the nature of the preaching by which Christian theology is often communicated, helpfully uses the images of collecting and saving to express how imagination accumulates. Every penny counts!
5 Alan Bennett et al., *The Complete* Beyond the Fringe (London: Methuen, 1987), 104.
6 The established view is that "trade books" published in 1880 included 975 works of theology and sermons but only 580 novels (Richard Altick, *The English Common Reader: A Social History of the Mass Reading Public 1800–1900* [Chicago: University of Chicago Press, 1957], 108). This has been challenged by more recent research that suggests that by the 1870s more fiction than anything else was published. Nevertheless in the ten years between 1870 and 1879 more books on religious subjects were published than in the thirty-two years between 1814 and 1845 (Simon Eliot, *Some*

Patterns and Trends in British Publishing 1800–1919 [London: The Bibliographical Society, 1994], 47).
7   Jesse Matz, *The Modern Novel: A Short Introduction* (Oxford: Blackwell, 2004), 44.
8   This is the view expressed by David Lyle Jeffrey and Ronald B. Bond in their entry "Preaching" in the *Dictionary of Biblical Tradition in English Literature*, ed. D. L. Jeffrey (Grand Rapids, Eerdmans, 1992), 631–35.
9   Sabine Volk-Birke, *Chaucer and Medieval Preaching: Rhetoric for Listeners* (Tubingen: Gunter Narr Verlag, 1991).
10 Elizabeth Salter and Derek Pearsall, *Piers Plowman* (London: Edward Arnold, 1967); and Elizabeth Salter, *Piers Plowman: An Introduction* (Oxford: Basil Blackwell, 1963).
11 George Eliot, *Scenes of Clerical Life* (Harmondsworth, UK: Penguin, 1973; orig. pub. 1858).
12 Anthony Trollope, *Barchester Towers* (Harmondsworth, UK: Penguin, 1982; orig. pub. 1857); Charles Dickens, *Bleak House* (Harmondsworth, UK: Penguin, 1971; orig. pub. 1853).
13 Oliver Goldsmith, *The Vicar of Wakefield* (Harmondsworth, UK: Penguin, 1982; orig. pub. 1766).
14 Evelyn Waugh, *A Handful of Dust* (Harmondsworth, UK: Penguin, 1997; orig. pub. 1934); James Joyce, *A Portrait of the Artist as a Young Man* (Harmondsworth, UK: Penguin, 1960; orig. pub. 1916).
15 I explored some of the ideas in chapter 4 and used some of the associated critique of David Lodge's novel in an article written for *Homiletic* (32 no. 2 [2007]: 1–10). I am grateful for the opportunity to expound on that argument here in *The Novel as Church*.

Chapter 1

1   John Updike, *Pigeon Feathers and Other Stories* (Harmondsworth, UK: Penguin, 1965).
2   Parenthetical numbers within the text indicate page references in the novels under discussion as listed in the bibliography.
3   *Listener*, December 31, 1981, 817, quoted in Peter J. Conradi, *Iris Murdoch: The Saint and the Artist* (London: Macmillan, 1989), 145.
4   Conradi, *Saint and the Artist*, 167.
5   Conradi, *Saint and the Artist*, 176.
6   I have based this classification on the overview of early Christian preaching offered by George A. Kennedy, *Classical Rhetoric and its Christian and Secular Traditions from Ancient to Modern Times* (London: Croom Helm, 1980).

7   From *De praescriptione haereticorum* 7, quoted in Kennedy, *Classical Rhetoric*, 147.
8   For an assessment of Tertullian's preaching, see David Dunn-Wilson, *A Mirror for the Church: Preaching in the First Five Centuries* (Cambridge: Eerdmans, 2005), 36, 37.
9   See Robertson's translation of Augustine: D. W. Robertson, *St Augustine on Christian Doctrine* (New York: Prentice Hall, 1958), 161–62.
10 Melvyn Bragg, *The Adventure of English: The Biography of a Language* (London: Sceptre, 2003), 162.
11 Don H. Compier, *What is Rhetorical Theology? Textual Practice and Public Discourse* (Philadelphia: Trinity Press, 1999).
12 Lucy Lind Hogan and Robert Reid, *Connecting with the Congregation: Rhetoric and the Art of Preaching* (Nashville: Abingdon, 1999).
13 Hogan and Reid, *Connecting with the Congregation*, 73.
14 Theo Hobson, *The Rhetorical Word: Protestant Theology and the Rhetoric of Authority* (Aldershot, UK: Ashgate, 2002), 37.
15 Hobson, *Rhetorical Word*, 200.
16 Wayne C. Booth, *The Rhetoric of Fiction* (Chicago: University of Chicago Press, 1961), 20.
17 Booth, *The Rhetoric of Fiction*, 53.
18 Brueggemann, *Cadences of Home*, 35.
19 "And now to God the Father," he ends,
    And his voice thrills up to the topmost tiles:
    Each listener chokes as he bows and bends,
    And emotion pervades the crowded aisles.
    Then the preacher glides to the vestry-door,
    And shuts it, and thinks he is seen no more.

    The door swings softly ajar meanwhile,
    And a pupil of his in the Bible class,
    Who adores him as one without gloss or guile,
    Sees her idol stand with satisfied smile
    And re-enact at the vestry-glass
    Each pulpit gesture in deft dumb-show
    That had moved the congregation so.
    From Thomas Hardy, *Satires of Circumstance: Lyrics and Reveries* (London: Macmillan, 1914), 51.
20 Judith Butler, *Gender Trouble: Feminism and the Subversion of Identity* (London: Routledge, 1999), 180.
21 Butler, *Gender Trouble*, 33.

22 Mikhail. M. Bakhtin, *The Dialogical Imagination: Four Essays*, trans. Michael Holquist (Austin: University of Texas Press, 1981), 288–91.
23 Paul Ricoeur, *The Rule of Metaphor: Multi-disciplinary Studies of the Creation of Meaning in Language*, trans. Robert Czerny, Kathleen McLaughlin, and John Costello (London: Routledge & Kegan Paul, 1978; orig. pub. 1977), 11.
24 Ricoeur, *The Rule of Metaphor*, 324n6.
25 Richard Ward, "Performance Turns in Homiletics: Wrong Way or Right On?" *Journal of Communication and Religion* 17, no. 1 (1994): 2.
26 Alan de Lille, *The Art of Preaching*, trans. and introd. Gillian R. Evans (Kalamazoo, Mich.: Cistercian, 1981).
27 Claire M. Waters, *Angels and Earthly Creatures: Preaching, Performance and Gender in the Later Middle Ages* (Philadelphia: University of Pennsylvania Press, 2004), 49.
28 Barry Hannah, *Yonder Stands Your Orphan* (New York: Grove Press, 2001), 11.
29 Nigel Fabb, *Linguistics and Literature* (Oxford: Blackwell, 1997), 221.
30 Fabb, *Linguistics and Literature*, 240.
31 Richard Bauman, *Verbal Art as Performance* (Long Grove, Ill.: Waveland Press, 1977), 27.
32 Dell Hymes, *Foundations in Sociolinguistics*, quoted in Fabb, *Linguistics and Literature*, 225.
33 Reported in David O. Lose, *Confessing Jesus Christ: Preaching in a Postmodern World* (Grand Rapids: Eerdmans, 2003), 161.
34 Bauman, *Verbal Art as Performance*, 48.
35 Emily Brontë, *Wuthering Heights* (London: Heron Books, William Collins Sons, 1847), 20–21.
36 Robert H. Ellison, *The Victorian Pulpit: Spoken and Written Sermons in Nineteenth-Century Britain* (London: Associated Universities Press, 1998).
37 Ellison, *Victorian Pulpit*, 76.
38 Ellison, *Victorian Pulpit*, 126.
39 Ellison, *Victorian Pulpit*, 113.
40 George MacDonald, *Unspoken Sermons*, 1st, 2nd, and 3rd ser. (London: Alexander Strahan, 1867; Longmans-Green, 1885, 1889) are available as e-texts from Johannesen Publishing and Printing at www.johannesen.com.
41 Walter J. Ong, *Orality and Literacy: The Technologizing of the Word* (London: Routledge, 1982).
42 Ong, *Orality and Literacy*, 101.
43 Mikhail M. Bakhtin, "The Problem of Speech Genres," in *Speech Genres*

and Other Essays, trans. Michael Holquist (Austin: University of Texas Press, 1986), 60.

44 I use a variation of their practices and include here, chosen at random, a page of my script for Good Friday 2010, with its misremembered allusions and its delayed switch from necessarily gender-specific language to more inclusive terms. The visual cues on the page plainly foreground grammatical intonation.

"It stressed the notion that Jesus is representative man, man as man is meant to be,
    the man in whom our human frame reaches full maturity,
        the man whose integrity is such that there is no distinction whatsoever between the words he says and the deeds he does,
            the man who will not swerve from the path he intends to take,
                the man whose mind is clear, whose motives are pure and whose intentions are good, the exposed man.

Like William Shakespeare's creation, King Lear, on the stormy heath ripping off all his clothes to expose himself to the raging elements and describing himself as unaccommodated man—a man with nothing in the world, nowhere in the world to go and naked as the day he was born—so Jesus stood impassively in the middle of a stormy Jerusalem—for everyone to see.

The exposed, vulnerable man is someone we see too often in our newspapers:
- pictures of bloodied and battered commuters staggering away from bomb blasts in the Moscow underground
- pictures of Haitian earthquake survivors squatting outside their ruined homes
- pictures of long-term hospital patients staring into the bleak space of their wards
- and pictures of mourners at funerals weeping in the face of bleak futures.

In Jesus presented to the crowd by Pilate we see the naked truth about the human condition. We see human vulnerability;
    we see human frailty;
        we see human dependability both on God and on other people;
and we see the limits of human resourcefulness. 'Behold the man!'"

45 Bakhtin, *Dialogical Imagination*, 344.
46 Laurence Sterne, *The Sermons of Mr. Yorick* (Oxford: Basil Blackwell, 1927; orig. pub. 1760), 204.

47 I am indebted to the general editor of this series for reminding me of this literary antecedent of fictional sermons on which he comments in Stephen Prickett, *Origins of Narrative: The Romantic Appropriation of the Bible* (Cambridge: Cambridge University Press, 1996), 122–23.

Chapter 2

1 See David Seed, "The Voice of the Church: A Dialogical Approach to the Retreat Section of Joyce's *A Portrait of the Artist*," *Literature and Theology* 9, no. 2 (1995): 156.
2 See Louise Bentley, "Beyond the Liturgy: An Approach to Catholicism as Genre in the Work of James Joyce," *Literature and Theology* 12, no. 2 (1998): 165.
3 Seed, "Voice of the Church," 157.
4 Bentley, "Beyond the Liturgy," 165.
5 Origen, *On First Principles: Being Koetschau's Text of* De principiis, trans., intro., and notes by G. W. Butterworth (Gloucester, Mass.: Peter Smith, Torchbook Edition, 1973).
6 Damian Thompson, "Even the 'Messy Bits' Are Made in His Image," *Sunday Telegraph*, April 2, 2000.
7 I borrow a phrase from Matthew Fox whose best known book is entitled *Original Blessing* (1983).
8 John S. Spong, *Why Christianity Must Change or Die: A Bishop Speaks to Believers in Exile* (London: HarperCollins, 1998).

Chapter 3

1 Nicholas Lash, *Believing Three Ways in One God: A Reading of the Apostles' Creed* (London: SCM Press, 1992), 1.
2 Matt 9:6; 10:1; 28:18; 1 Tim 1:1, 18; Titus 2:15; Phil 2:5.
3 Mark C. Taylor, *Erring: A Postmodern A/theology* (Chicago: University of Chicago Press, 1984), 76.
4 Taylor, *Erring*, 81.
5 John S. McClure, *Other-Wise Preaching: A Postmodern Ethic for Homiletics* (St Louis, Mo.: Chalice Press, 2001), 14.
6 Ernest Best, *From Text to Sermon: Responsible Use of the New Testament in Preaching* (Edinburgh: T&T Clark, 1988).
7 Barger Elliott, *Creative Styles of Preaching*.
8 Jenny Diski, David Maine, and Anita Diamant are among the best known of these contemporary biblical novelists, but there are many others.
9 Michael Arditti, *The Celibate* (London: Minerva, 1993).
10 Sybil Steinberg, "Life and Death in Eyam," *Publishers' Weekly* 248, no. 33 (August 13, 2001): 279.

11 John Wroe, *Sermons Selected from the Scriptures: Being a Guide to the People Surnamed Israelites to Preach the Everlasting Gospel* (Ashton-under-Lyne, U.K.: Trustees of the Society of Christian Israelites, 1896), 42.
12 Wroe, *Sermons Selected from the Scriptures*, 16.
13 This was the title of an influential essay he published in 1931.
14 John Clifford, *Eyam Plague 1665–1666* (Eyam: John Clifford, 2003), 18. According to the novel's afterword, Brooks spent some time with Clifford when researching the novel and will have known that this is what he surmised.
15 Jane Rogers, *The Ice Is Singing* (London: Faber & Faber, 1987); *Promised Lands* (London: Faber & Faber, 1995); *Island* (London: Little, Brown, 1999); *The Voyage Home* (London: Abacus, 2004).
16 Hosea 9:8.
17 See James Schiff, *John Updike's Novels Revisited* (New York: Twayne, 1998), 147 for further elucidation of this point.
18 Robert Detweiler, *Breaking the Fall: Religious Readings of Contemporary Fiction* (London: Macmillan, 1989).
19 David R. Law, *Inspiration* (London: Continuum, 2001), 50–66.
20 Timothy Clark, *The Theory of Inspiration: Composition as a Crisis of Subjectivity in Romantic and Post-Romantic Writing* (Manchester: Manchester University Press, 1997), 42.
21 Austin M. Farrer, *The Glass of Vision* (London: Dacre Press, 1948), 53.
22 Clark, *Theory of Inspiration*, 3.
23 Clark, *Theory of Inspiration*, 42.
24 Clark, *Theory of Inspiration*, 139–40.
25 Clark, *Theory of Inspiration*, 149.
26 Derrida discusses this learning by heart (or, with more negative connotations, learning by rote) in his essay "Che cos'e la poesia?"
27 Joseph M. Bocheński, "On Authority," *South African Journal of Philosophy* 8, no. 2 (1988): 61–65.
28 Jean Goodwin, "Forms of Authority and the Real *Ad verecundiam*," *Argumentation* 12, no. 2 (1998): 267–80.
29 Maarten Wisse, "The Meaning of the Authority of the Bible," *Religious Studies* 36, no. 4 (2000): 473–87.
30 Bakhtin, "Speech Genres," 85.

Chapter 4

1 The gender-specific term is intended as few novelists have yet portrayed women preachers.
2 Hilary Mantel, *Fludd* (Harmondsworth, UK: Penguin, 1989).

3   Catherine Fox, *The Benefits of Passion* (Harmondsworth: Penguin, 1997).
4   Alan Isler, *Clerical Errors* (London: Vintage, 2001).
5   William Golding, *Rites of Passage* (London: Faber & Faber, 1980).
6   Margaret Forster, *Is There Anything You Want?* (London: Chatto & Windus, 2005).
7   Stephanie Johnson, *Belief* (London: Vintage, 2001).
8   Geraldine Brooks, *March* (London: Harper Perennial, 2005).
9   Peter Hobbs, *The Short Day Dying* (London: Faber, 2005).
10 David J. Taylor, "God's Odd-bods," *Guardian* (London), July 9, 2005, reviewing Jonathan Tulloch, *Give Us This Day* (London: Cape, 2005).
11 In his essay "An Essay on Cultural Criticism and Society," in *Prisms*, trans. Samuel and Shierry Weber (Cambridge, Mass.: MIT Press, 1967), 19.
12 John Updike, *A Month of Sundays* (London: Andre Deutsch, 1974).
13 David Lodge, *How Far Can You Go?* (Harmondsworth, UK: Penguin, 1980). Published in America with the title *Souls and Bodies*.
14 Tillich, Paul, *Systematic Theology*, vol. 1 (London: SCM Press, 1951), 10 (emphasis and gender-specific pronouns are original).
15 Quoted in McClure, *Other-Wise Preaching*, 35 (emphasis original).
16 Elisabeth Jay, "'Who Are You Gentle Reader?' John Updike—*A Month of Sundays* (1975)," *Literature and Theology* 19, no. 4 (2005): 351.
17 Victor Strandberg, "John Updike and the Changing of the Gods," in *Critical Essays on John Updike*, ed. William R. McNaughton (Boston: G. K. Hall, 1982), 175–93; Andrew Tate, *Contemporary Fiction and Christianity* (London: Continuum, 2008).
18 Penelope Brown and Stephen Levinson, "Universals in Language Usage: Politeness Phenomena," in *Questions and Politeness: Strategies in Social Interaction*, ed. E. N. Goody (Cambridge: Cambridge University Press, 1978), 256–89.
19 Gerald Parsons, "Paradigm or Period Piece? David Lodge's *How Far Can You Go?* in Perspective," *Journal of Literature and Theology* 6, no. 2 (1992): 174.
20 Beata Streichsbier, "Irony in David Lodge's *How Far Can You Go?*" in *A Yearbook of English Language and Literature*, ed. S. Korninger (Vienna: Braumuller, 1981), 105.
21 Bernard Bergonzi, "A Conspicuous Absentee: The Decline and Fall of the Catholic Novel," *Encounter* 55, nos. 2–3 (1980): 54.
22 David Lodge, *The Picturegoers* (Harmondsworth, UK: Penguin, 1960), ix.
23 Streichsbier, "Irony in David Lodge's *How Far Can You Go?*" 108.
24 Parsons, "Paradigm or Period Piece?" 176.
25 Parsons, "Paradigm or Period Piece?" 182.

26 David Lodge, *Consciousness and the Novel: Connected Essays* (London: Secker & Warburg, 2002), 42.
27 Marian E. Crowe, "Intimations of Immortality: Catholicism in David Lodge's *Paradise News*," *Renascence: Essays on Values in Literature* 52, no. 2 (2000): 152, making her assessment of Catholicism in *Paradise News*.
28 Crowe, "Intimations of Immortality," 149.
29 Jeremy Treglown, "Where Shall Wisdom Be Found?" *Times Literary Supplement* (London), May 2, 1980, 487.
30 Matz, *Modern Novel*, 35.
31 Matz, *Modern Novel*, 136.
32 Parsons, "Paradigm or Period Piece?" 174.
33 Parsons, "Paradigm or Period Piece?" 182.
34 Jean-Francois Lyotard, *The Postmodern Condition: A Report on Knowledge* (Manchester: Manchester University Press, 1984), xxiv.
35 J. Richard Middleton and Brian J. Walsh, *Truth Is Stranger Than It Used to Be: Biblical Faith in a Postmodern Age* (London: SPCK, 1995), 42.
36 This is the declaration in the Preface to the Declaration of Assent used at the induction of incumbents in the Church of England.
37 McClure, *Other-Wise Preaching*, 50.
38 David Lodge, *Thinks . . .* (Harmondsworth, UK: Penguin, 2001), 31.
39 Lodge, *The Picturegoers*, 105–7.
40 Iain McLean and Martin Johnes, *Aberfan: Government and Disasters* (Cardiff: Welsh Academic Press, 2000), 110.
41 Joan Miller, *Aberfan: A Disaster and Its Aftermath* (London: Constable, 1974), 29.
42 Anon., "Twin Towns That Know the Same Fear," *Times* (London), October 24, 1966, 8.
43 Miller, *Aberfan*; Paul Ballard, "Poverty and Change: The Churches' Response in South Wales, 1966–2000," *Expository Times* 116, no. 2 (2004): 43–48.
44 Walter Brueggemann, *Finally Comes the Poet: Daring Speech for Proclamation* (Minneapolis: Fortress, 1989), 10.
45 Terry Eagleton, *The English Novel: An Introduction* (Oxford: Blackwell, 2005), 3.

Chapter 5

1 Thomas Meaney, "Neuro-Stories," *Times Literary Supplement*, September 10, 2010, 29.
2 Lisa M. Siefker Bailey, "Fraught with Fire: Race and Theology in Marilynne Robinson's *Gilead*," *Christianity and Literature* 59, no. 2 (2010): 265.

3 This suggestion is made by Susan Petit in her "Finding Flannery O'Connor's 'Good Man' in Marilynne Robinson's *Gilead* and *Home*," *Christianity and Literature* 59, no.2 (2010): 306.
4 Quoted in Jennifer Holberg, "'The Courage to See It': Toward an Understanding of Glory," *Christianity and Literature* 59, no. 2 (2010): 284.
5 Marilynne Robinson, *The Death of Adam* (New York: Picador, 2005), 243.
6 In common parlance the terms "religious experience" and "spiritual experience" are often used synonymously. However, theologically speaking, there is a distinction in that "religious" implies bound up in or related to Otherness, while "spiritual" suggests something to do with an aspect of Self, or the ground of one's being whether expressed physically, mentally, or (tautologically) spiritually. In this chapter I am conscious of this distinction, but, as my discussion here is in terms of the psychology of religion rather than "pure" theology, I feel able to use both terms interchangeably without confusion.
7 "It is of the greatest importance to understand that religious truth is not a special kind of truth, nor religious experience a queer, unnatural kind of experience belonging to some strange and other world. Religious experience is normal experience, and we have religious experience every day, whether or not we recognise it as such. Religious truth is normal experience understood at full depth; what makes truth religious is not that it relates to some abnormal field of thought and feeling but that it goes to the roots of the experience which it interprets." M. V. C. Jeffreys, *Glaucon: An Inquiry into the Aims of Education* (London: Pitman & Sons, 1950), 118.
8 Chris J. Boyatzis, "A Critique of Models of Religious Experience," *International Journal for the Psychology of Religion* 11, no. 4 (2001): 247-58.
9 William James, *The Varieties of Religious Experience* (London: Fontana, 1960; orig. pub. 1902).
10 Boyatzis, "A Critique of Models of Religious Experience," 249.
11 Boyatzis, "A Critique of Models of Religious Experience," 252.
12 Boyatzis, "A Critique of Models of Religious Experience," 253, quoting Bruner.
13 This section of my book is heavily dependent upon Terry Eagleton's discussion of epistolary novels in *The Rape of Clarissa: Writing, Sexuality and Class Struggle in Samuel Richardson* (Oxford: Blackwell, 1982).
14 Eagleton, *Rape of Clarissa*, 19.
15 Eagleton, *Rape of Clarissa*, 25.
16 Eagleton, *Rape of Clarissa*, 44.
17 Eagleton, *Rape of Clarissa*, 51.

18 Terry Wright, *Theology and Literature* (Oxford: Blackwell, 1988), 94.
19 Callum Brown, *The Death of Christian Britain: Understanding Secularisation 1800–2000* (London: Routledge, 2001), 70.
20 See Krailsheimer for a rudimentary testing of the conversion formula and Bruce Hindmarsh for a comprehensive account of conversion narratives from the eighteenth century. Hindmarsh identifies a common pattern of a life crisis provoking a quest leading to an encounter with advocates of a new belief system, then a deeper exploration of the new option ultimately consummated in an act of commitment. His point that Wesley's control over his preachers makes Methodist narratives suspect is explored further by Isabel Rivers, who traces Scottish, French, Spanish, and American influences on Wesley in this respect. A. J. Krailsheimer, *Conversion* (London: SCM Press, 1980); D. Bruce Hindmarsh, *The Evangelical Conversion Narrative: Spiritual Autobiography in Early Modern England* (Oxford: Oxford University Press, 2005), 11; Isabel Rivers, "Strangers and Pilgrims: Sources and Patterns of Methodist Narrative," in *Augustan Worlds*, ed. J. D. Hilson, M. M. B. Jones, and J. R. Watson (Leicester: Leicester University Press, 1978), 189–203.
21 Rivers, "Strangers and Pilgrims," 60.
22 Rivers, "Strangers and Pilgrims," 80.
23 David Lodge, *The Art of Fiction: Illustrated from Classic and Modern Texts* (Harmondsworth, UK: Penguin, 1992), 23–24.
24 Wendy B. Faris, "The Question of the Other: Cultural Critiques of Magical Realism." In *Janus Head* 5, no. 2 (2002): 101–2.
25 Christopher Warnes, "Naturalizing the Supernatural: Faith, Irreverence and Magical Realism." *Literature Compass 2* 20C, no. 106 (2005): 1.
26 Faris, "Question of the Other," 107.
27 Don Cupitt, *Kingdom Come in Everyday Speech* (London: SCM Press, 2000), 48–49.
28 Tate, *Contemporary Fiction and Christianity*.
29 This is the claim made by Warnes, "Naturalizing the Supernatural," 1, 17.
30 Here I rely on Amaryll Chanady's taxonomy in a study distinguishing magical realism from fantasy, *Magical Realism and the Fantastic: Resolved versus Unresolved Antimony* (New York: Garland, 1985).
31 Chanady, *Magical Realism and the Fantastic*, 2, 4.
32 For instance, in "Naturalizing the Supernatural," Warnes cites Beloved who is simultaneously ghost and real person in Toni Morrison's *Beloved*.
33 Warnes, "Naturalizing the Supernatural," 129.
34 Warnes, "Naturalizing the Supernatural," 5–6.
35 Warnes, "Naturalizing the Supernatural," 6.

36 Updike, *Pigeon Feathers*.
37 See Detweiler, *Breaking the Fall*.
38 Paul Tillich, *Theology of Culture* (New York: Oxford University Press, 1959). See also Tillich, *Systematic Theology*, vol. 1.
39 Trustees for Methodist Church Purposes. *Hymns and Psalms* (Peterborough, UK: Methodist Publishing House, 1983), 282.
40 My comments on this work of art were enriched by Frank Whitford's discussion of the work in "Gauguin's Vision," *Sunday Times* (London), August 7, 2005, 6–7.

Chapter 6

1 Antonia S. Byatt, *The Virgin in the Garden* (London: Virago, 1978); *Still Life* (London: Virago, 1985); *Babel Tower* (London: Chatto & Windus, 1996); *A Whistling Woman* (London: Virago, 2002).
2 Despite Byatt's protestations, this is so clearly a function of the novels that a German critic used *The Virgin in the Garden* as a case study in his examination of the nature of Englishness in recent novels, (Kuno Schuhmann, "The Concept of Culture in Some Recent English Novels," in *Anglistentag*, ed. J. Hasler [Frankfurt: Peter Lang, 1982], 111–27), a British novelist described *A Whistling Woman* as a novel which anatomizes the sixties (Stevie Davies, "*A Whistling Woman* by A. S. Byatt," *The Independent* [London], September 7, 2002), and a newspaper reviewer's less than enthusiastic review of the same book suggested that Byatt was attempting to "encompass much of English cultural and social life in the late 1960s" (Jim Barloon, "Byatt's Latest Lacks Literary Inspiration," *Houston Chronicle*, March 28, 2003).
3 Byatt employs sermons to contextualize her narrative in a manner similar to that employed by some historical novelists who establish the religious context of their narratives by recounting a sermon. In the case of historical novels, this quickly and conveniently establishes for the reader the theological and spiritual presumptions shared by the characters and the prevailing religious mood of the period, as in Geraldine Brooks' account of Eyam in *Year of Wonders*. Here Brooks contrasted the preaching of the local clergyman who inspires the villagers to erect a cordon sanitaire around their village with both the words of the village's wise women who make herbal potions and his Puritan predecessor, so, on the one hand, he is seen to be preaching against the prevailing ethos and current mood of the time. On the other hand, during her research for the novel, Brooks visited the village and had access to copies of the actual rector's letters to family and friends and clearly employs the idioms and language of the time so that readers

encounter the sermons as authentic to the context of seventeenth-century Derbyshire. The main focus of discussion in this chapter, however, is not so much on the contextualizing capacity of sermons in historical fiction as the nature of the language in any fictional sermons.

4 None of the content of this sermon is reported to readers, although they are given to understand that, exaggeratedly following in the steps of Rudolf Bultmann, he was arguing against the historicity of supernatural elements in the four Gospels.
5 *Oxford English Dictionary*, 2nd ed., ed J. A. Simpson and E. S. C. Weiner (Oxford: Clarendon, 1989).
6 Emanuel Levinas. *Otherwise Than Being*. Translated by Alphonso Lingus. (The Hague: Martinus Nijhoff, 1981), 5–9, 37–38; cited by McClure, *Other-Wise Preaching*, 10.
7 See the originator of much thought about religious language, Ian T. Ramsey, *Religious Language: An Empirical Placing of Theological Phrases* (London: SCM Press, 1957).
8 Paul Simpson, *Language, Ideology and Point of View* (London: Routledge, 1993), 176.
9 Simpson, *Language, Ideology and Point of View*, 6.
10 Simpson, *Language, Ideology and Point of View*, 104.
11 Simpson, *Language, Ideology and Point of View*, 178.
12 Nicholas Lash, *Holiness, Speech and Silence: Reflections on the Question of God* (Aldershot, UK: Ashgate, 2004), 51.
13 Wright, *Theology and Literature*, 129.
14 Tillich, *Theology of Culture*, 66–67.
15 Henry L. Gates, *The Signifying Monkey: A Theory of African-American Literary Criticism* (Oxford: Oxford University Press, 1986), 22.
16 Gates, *Signifying Monkey*, 46.
17 Gates, *Signifying Monkey*, 82.
18 Mary Gerhart, *Genre Choices, Genre Questions* (Norman: University of Oklahoma Press, 1992), 121.
19 Sue Sorensen, "A. S. Byatt and the Life of the Mind: A Response to Jane Sturrock," *Connotations* 13, no. 1 (2003): 188.
20 See Janet M. Soskice, *Metaphor and Religious Language* (Oxford: Clarendon, 1985) for a more comprehensive discussion of classical Christian use of metaphor and analogy.
21 Garrett Green, *Imagining God: Theology and the Religious Imagination* (Grand Rapids: Eerdmans, 1989), 133.
22 George Lakoff and Mark Johnson, *Metaphors We Live By* (Chicago: University of Chicago Press, 1980), 5 (emphasis added).

23 Lakoff and Johnson, *Metaphors We Live By*, 160.
24 Because truth, rather than being objective and absolute, is based on understanding and is, therefore, both subjective and contingent, the following four assertions about truth follow:
   - Statements are true only in relation to some way in which they have been understood.
   - Understanding always involves categorizing the statement in terms emerging from human experience.
   - The truth of a statement always relates to the properties highlighted by the categories used in the statement.
   - These categories are neither fixed nor uniform but defined by prototypes and family resemblances to prototypes, thus adjustable and variable in context.

   Lakoff and Johnson, *Metaphors We Live By*, 165–66.
25 Lakoff and Johnson, *Metaphors We Live By*, 184.
26 Wright, *Theology and Literature*, 130; Soskice, *Metaphor and Religious Language*, 93.
27 Ricoeur, *Rule of Metaphor*, 221, 255.
28 Antonia S. Byatt, "A Life Less Ordinary," *Guardian Review*, July 2005, 16–17.
29 Alexa Alfer and Michael J. Noble, eds., *Essays on the Fiction of A. S. Byatt: Imagining the Real* (Westport, Conn.: Greenwood Press, 2001), 19.
30 Juliet Dusinberre, "Forms of Reality in A. S. Byatt's *The Virgin in the Garden*," *Critique: Studies in Modern Fiction* 24, no. 1 (1982): 55.
31 Dusinberre, "Forms of Reality," 56.
32 Dusinberre, "Forms of Reality," 56.
33 Dusinberre, "Forms of Reality," 57.
34 Dusinberre, "Forms of Reality," 59.
35 Dusinberre, "Forms of Reality," 61.
36 Julian Gitzen, "A. S. Byatt's Self-Mirroring Art," *Critique: Studies in Modern Fiction* 36, no. 2 (1995): 87.
37 Gitzen, "A. S. Byatt's Self-Mirroring Art," 89.
38 Paul Ricoeur, "The Function of Fiction in Shaping Reality," *Man and World* 12 (1979): 129.
39 Antonia S. Byatt, "Still Life / Nature morte," in *Passions of the Mind: Selected Writings* (London: Chatto, 1991), 9–20, 15.
40 Alexa Alfer, "Realism and its Discontents," in *Essays on the Fiction of A. S. Byatt: Imagining the Real*, ed. Alexa Alfer and Michael J. Noble (Westport, Conn.: Greenwood Press, 2001), 53.
41 Byatt, *Passions*, 11, 34; Byatt, "A Life Less Ordinary," 17.

42 Byatt, *Passions*, 17–18.
43 Michael Westlake, "The Hard Idea of Truth," *PN Review* 15, no. 4 (1989): 33.
44 Westlake, "The Hard Idea of Truth," 37.
45 Sallie McFague, *Speaking in Parables: A Study in Metaphor and Theology* (Philadelphia: Fortress, 1975), 22–23.
46 Brueggemann, *Cadences of Home*, 26, 74.
47 Brueggemann, *Cadences of Home*, 76.
48 Hobson, *Rhetorical Word*, 37.
49 Charles Pinches, "Proclaiming: Naming and Describing," in *The Blackwell Companion to Christian Ethics*, ed. Stanley Hauerwas and Samuel Wells (Oxford: Blackwell, 2004), 169.
50 Pinches, "Proclaiming," 176.
51 Pinches, "Proclaiming," 179.
52 John Vincent, "Imaginative Identification," *Epworth Review* 23, no. 3 (1996): 14–20.
53 Wayne G., Rollins, *Jung and the Bible* (Atlanta: Westminster John Knox, 1983), 104.
54 William H. Gass, *Omensetter's Luck* (Harmondsworth, UK: Penguin, 1997).
55 Ann-Janine Morey-Gaines, "Religion and Sexuality in Walker Percy, William Gass and John Updike: Metaphors of Embodiment in Androcentric Imagination," *Journal of the American Academy of Religion* 51, no.4 (1983): 595–609.
56 Carolyn J. Allen, "Fiction and Figures of Life in *Omensetter's Luck*," *Pacific Coast Philology* 9 (1974): 5–11.
57 H. I. Hix, *Understanding William Gass* (Columbia: University of South Carolina Press, 2002).
58 Richard Schneider, "The Fortunate Fall in William Gass's *Omensetter's Luck*," *Critique* 18, no. 1 (1976): 17.

Chapter 7

1 Benedict Anderson, *Imagined Communities* (New York: Verso, 1991).
2 David Buttrick, *Preaching the New and the Now* (Louisville, Ky.: Westminster John Knox, 1998), 99 (scare quotes in original).
3 David Buttrick, *Homiletic* (Philadelphia: Fortress, 1987), 26.
4 Buttrick, *Preaching the New and the Now*, 100.
5 Scott Bader-Saye, "Listening: Authority and Obedience," in *The Blackwell Companion to Christian Ethics*, ed. S. Hauerwas and S. Wells (Oxford: Blackwell, 2004), 158, 160.
6 Bader-Saye, "Listening: Authority and Obedience," 163.
7 Barger Elliott, *Creative Styles of Preaching*, 150.

8   Brueggemann, *Cadences*, 33.
9   Brueggemann, *Cadences*, 26, 27, 30.
10 Brueggemann, *Cadences*, 40.
11 Brueggemann, *Cadences*, 74.
12 Brueggemann, *Cadences*, 23.
13 James Muilenburg, "Form Criticism and Beyond," in *Journal of Biblical Literature* 88 (1969): 1–18.
14 Phyllis Trible, *Texts of Terror: Literary-Feminist Readings of Biblical Narratives* (Philadelphia: Fortress, 1984).
15 Brueggemann, *Cadences*, 76.
16 Brueggemann, *Cadences*, 32.
17 See McClure, *Other-Wise Preaching*, 105.
18 McClure, *Other-Wise Preaching*, 108.
19 McClure, *Other-Wise Preaching*, 113 (emphasis original).
20 McClure, *Other-Wise Preaching*, 111.
21 This remembering and forward-looking community is both anamnestic and eschatological, where anamnesis is a continuous process of re-remembering—a "cyclical return to an earlier moment, re-remembered in the present, in greater detail and with greater effect at each recurrence." Nicola King, *Memory, Narrative, Identity: Remembering the Self* (Edinburgh: Edinburgh University Press, 2000), 21.
22 King, *Memory, Narrative, Identity*, 103.
23 Raymond Plant, "Community: Concept, Conception and Ideology," *Politics and Society* 8 (1978): 81.
24 Keith Ward, *Religion and Community* (Oxford: Oxford University Press, 2000), 133.
25 Ward, *Religion and Community*, 157.
26 Frances Young, "School for Sinners," *Epworth Review* 23, no. 3 (1994): 66, 70.
27 Ward, *Religion and Community*, 183.
28 Ward, *Religion and Community*, 82.
29 Ward, *Religion and Community*, 233.
30 Thomas R. Lindlof, "Interpretive Community: An Approach to Media and Religion," *Journal of Media and Religion* 1, no. 1 (2002): 63.
31 Lisa Allerdice, "So Much for Freedom," *Daily Telegraph* (London), August 31, 2002.
32 This is contra Janet Soskice's warning that the historical facts of etymology are of limited value in determining the current significance of words, *Metaphor and Religious Language*, 81.
33 Dan Sperber and Deirdre Wilson, *Relevance: Communication and Cognition* (Oxford: Blackwell, 1986), 245.

34 The word "History" is capitalized in his sermon.
35 Ron Charles, "Frederica in Wonderland," *Christian Science Monitor*, December 19, 2002.
36 Allerdice, "So Much for Freedom."
37 Davies, "*A Whistling Woman*."
38 Byatt has written much critical appraisal of Iris Murdoch's novels, beginning with *Degrees of Freedom: The Novels of Iris Murdoch* (London: Chatto & Windus, 1965).
39 Iris Murdoch, *The Bell* (Harmondsworth, UK: Penguin, 1958), 135, 200.
40 Iris Murdoch, *The Time of the Angels* (Harmondsworth, UK: Penguin, 1966).
41 Conradi, *Saint and the Artist*, 175.
42 Ann-Janine Morey, "Margaret Atwood and Toni Morrison," in *Toni Morrison's Fiction: Contemporary Criticism*, ed. David Middleton (London: Garland Publishing, 2000), 261.
43 Bauman, *Verbal Art as Performance*, 44.
44 David Jasper, "In the Sermon Which I Have Just Completed, Wherever I Said Aristotle, I Meant Saint Paul," in *The Bible as Rhetoric: Studies in Biblical Persuasion and Credibility*, ed. M. Warner (London: Routledge, 1990) 142–43.
45 Gunther Bornkamm, *Paul* (London: Hodder & Stoughton, 1969), 194.
46 Michael De-La-Noy, "A Blast below the Bible Belt," *Evening Standard* (London), April 5, 2000.
47 Jasper, "In the Sermon Which I Have Just Completed," 147.
48 Detweiler, *Breaking the Fall*, 27.
49 Stanley Fish, *Is There a Text in This Class? The Authority of Interpretive Communities* (Cambridge, Mass.: Harvard University Press, 1994), 173.
50 Fish, *Is There a Text in This Class?* 171.
51 Lindlof, "Interpretive Community," 64.
52 Lindlof, "Interpretive Community," 69 (emphasis original).
53 Anderson, *Imagined Communities*, 6.

Chapter 8

1 Michael Grant, *Cicero: On the Good Life* (Harmondsworth, UK: Penguin Classics, 1971), 284.
2 Grant, *Cicero*, 280.
3 Grant, *Cicero*, 241.
4 Grant, *Cicero*, 242.
5 Buttrick, *Homiletic*, 179.
6 McClure, *Other-Wise Preaching*, 28.

7   Peter H. Nidditch, ed., *John Locke: An Essay Concerning Human Understanding* (Oxford: Clarendon, 1975), 342.
8   The preface of a collection of essays on cultural recall: Mieke Bal, Jonathan V. Crewe, and Leo Spitzer, eds., *Acts of Memory: Cultural Recall in the Present* (Hanover, N.H.: University Press of New England, 1999), vii.
9   Mieke Bal, Jonathan V. Crewe, and Leo Spitzer, *Acts of Memory*, xv.
10 Mieke Bal, Jonathan V. Crewe, and Leo Spitzer, *Acts of Memory*, 75.
11 King, *Memory, Narrative, Identity*, 6.
12 King, *Memory, Narrative, Identity*, 33.
13 King, *Memory, Narrative, Identity*, 22.
14 "The text we call present may be deciphered only at the bottom of the page, in a footnote or postscript. Before the recurrence, the present is only the call for a footnote." Jacques Derrida, "Freud and the Scene of Writing," in *Writing and Difference*, trans. Alan Bass (London: Routledge Kegan & Paul, 1978), 212.
15 McClure, *Other-Wise Preaching*, 31.
16 McClure, *Other-Wise Preaching*, 32.
17 Fish, *Is There a Text in This Class?* 173.
18 Fish, *Is There a Text in This Class?* 33.
19 David W. Price, *History Made, History Imagined: Contemporary Literature, Poesis and the Past* (Champaign: University of Illinois Press, 1999), 306.
20 Price, *History Made, History Imagined*, 46.
21 Price, *History Made, History Imagined*, 33.
22 Price, *History Made, History Imagined*, 34.
23 Price, *History Made, History Imagined*, 38.
24 Price, *History Made, History Imagined*, 35.
25 Robert Holton, *Jarring Witnesses: Modern Fiction and the Representation of History* (Hemel Hempstead, UK: Harvester Wheatsheaf, 1994), 251.
26 Holton, *Jarring Witnesses*, 257.
27 Holton, *Jarring Witnesses*.
28 Frederic M. Holmes, *The Historical Imagination: Postmodernism and the Treatment of the Past in Contemporary British Fiction* (Victoria: University of Victoria Press, 1997), 52.
29 Trustees for Methodist Church Purposes, *The Methodist Worship Book* (Peterborough, UK: Methodist Publishing House, 1999), 197.
30 Anne Michaels, *Fugitive Pieces* (London: Bloomsbury, 1997), 21.
31 Michel Foucault, "Nietzsche, Genealogy, History," in *The Foucault Reader: An Introduction to Foucault's Thought*, ed. P. Rabinow, trans. Donald Bouchard and Sherry Simon (Harmondsworth, UK: Penguin, 1977), 83.
32 Foucault, "Nietzsche, Genealogy, History," 88–89.

33 Foucault, "Nietzsche, Genealogy, History," 43.
34 Foucault, "Nietzsche, Genealogy, History," 43–44.
35 Foucault, "Nietzsche, Genealogy, History," 131.
36 Most notably, David Tracy, *The Analogical Imagination: Christian Theology and the Culture of Pluralism* (New York: Crossroad, 1981); Gordon D. Kaufman, *The Theological Imagination: Constructing the Concept of God* (Philadelphia: Westminster John Knox, 1981).
37 Green, *Imagining God*, 40.
38 Green, *Imagining God*, 9.
39 Basil Willey, "Imagination and Fancy," in *Nineteenth Century Studies: Coleridge to Matthew Arnold* (New York: Columbia University Press, 1949) 12.
40 Green, *Imagining God*, 19.
41 Willey, "Imagination and Fancy," 16.
42 Green, *Imagining God*, 20.
43 Green, *Imagining God*, 64.
44 Green, *Imagining God*, 64.
45 Green, *Imagining God*, 69, 78, 133.
46 Green, *Imagining God*, 145.
47 Liam Gearon, ed., *English Literature, Theology and the Curriculum: Theology in Dialogue* (London: Cassell, 1999), 59 (emphasis added, quoting Graham Ward).
48 Gearon, *English Literature, Theology and the Curriculum*, 198 (quoting Michael Wheeler).
49 Brueggemann, *Bible and the Postmodern Imagination*, 20.
50 Mick Short, *Exploring the Language of Poems, Plays and Prose* (Harlow, UK: Longman, 1996) 228.
51 Guy Cook, *Discourse and Literature* (Oxford: Oxford University Press, 1994), 191.
52 Winterson, *Lighthousekeeping* (London: Fourth Estate, 2004).
53 Recently, Winterson has published an intentionally autobiographical version of the events in the form of *Why Be Happy When You Could Be Normal?* (London: Jonathan Cape, 2011).
54 Elisabeth Jay, *Faith and Doubt in Victorian Britain* (London: Macmillan, 1986).
55 Hilary Hinds, "*Oranges Are Not the Only Fruit*: Reaching Audiences Other Lesbian Texts Cannot Reach," in *New Lesbian Criticism: Literary and Cultural Readings*, ed. Sally Munt (Hemel Hempstead, UK: Harvester Wheatsheaf, 1992), 170.
56 Amy Benson-Brown, "Inverted Conversions: Reading the Bible and Writing the Lesbian Subject in *Oranges Are Not the Only Fruit*," in *Reclaiming*

the Sacred: The Bible in Gay and Lesbian Fiction, ed. Raymond-Jean Frontain (New York: Haworth Press, 1997), 235.
57 Benson-Brown, "Inverted Conversions," 234.
58 Quoted in Hinds, "Reaching Audiences," 162.
59 Rebecca O'Rourke, "'Fingers in the Fruit Basket': A Feminist Reading of Jeanette Winterson's *Oranges Are Not the Only Fruit*," in *Feminist Criticism: Theory and Practice*, ed. Susan Sellers (Hemel Hempstead, UK: Harvester Wheatsheaf, 1990), 62.

Bibliography

Primary Sources

Arditti, Michael. *Easter*. London: Arcadia Books, 2001.
Brooks, Geraldine. *Year of Wonders*. London: Fourth Estate, 2001.
Byatt, Antonia S. *Babel Tower*. London: Chatto & Windus, 1996.
———. *Still Life*. London: Virago, 1985.
———. *The Virgin in the Garden*. London: Virago, 1978.
———. *A Whistling Woman*. London: Virago, 2002.
Gass, William H. *Omensetter's Luck*. Harmondsworth, UK: Penguin, 1997.
Lodge, David. *How Far Can You Go?* Harmondsworth, UK: Penguin, 1980.
Morrison, Toni. *Paradise*. London: Vintage, 1999.
Murdoch, Iris. *The Bell*. Harmondsworth, UK: Penguin, 1958.
———. *The Time of the Angels*. Harmondsworth, UK: Penguin, 1966.
Robinson, Marilynne. *Gilead*. London: Virago, 2005.
———. *Home*. London: Virago, 2008.
Rogers, Jane. *Mr Wroe's Virgins*. London: Faber & Faber, 1991.
Updike, John. *Couples*. Harmondsworth, UK: Penguin, 1970.
———. *In the Beauty of the Lilies*. Harmondsworth, UK: Penguin, 1996.
———. *A Month of Sundays*. London: Andre Deutsch, 1974.
———. *Of the Farm*. New York: Fawcett Crest, 1967.
———. *Pigeon Feathers and Other Stories*. Harmondsworth, UK: Penguin, 1965.
———. *Rabbit, Run*. Harmondsworth, UK: Penguin, 1964.

———. *The Witches of Eastwick*. Harmondsworth, UK: Penguin, 1985.
Winterson, Jeanette. *Oranges Are Not the Only Fruit*. London: Vintage, 1985.

Other Fiction, Poetry, and Plays Related to This Study

Arditti, Michael. *The Celibate*. London: Minerva, 1993.
Baldwin, James. *Go Tell It on the Mountain*. Harmondsworth, UK: Penguin, 1991. Originally published in 1952.
Barnes, Julian. *A History of the World in 10½ Chapters*. London: Picador, 1989.
Bennett, Alan, Peter Cook, Jonathan Miller, and Dudley Moor. *The Complete* Beyond the Fringe. London: Methuen, 1987.
Brontë, Emily. *Wuthering Heights*. London: Heron Books, William Collins Sons, 1847.
Brooks, Geraldine. *March*. London: Harper Perennial, 2005.
Chaucer, Geoffrey. *Canterbury Tales*. London: Dent, 1958.
Dickens, Charles. *Bleak House*. Harmondsworth, UK: Penguin, 1971. Originally published in 1853.
Eliot, George. *Adam Bede*. Harmondsworth, UK: Penguin, 1980. Originally published in 1859.
———. *Scenes of Clerical Life*. Harmondsworth, UK: Penguin, 1973. Originally published in 1858.
Eliot, Thomas S. *Murder in the Cathedral*. London: Faber & Faber, 1935.
Faulkner, William. *The Sound and the Fury*. London: Vintage, 1995. Originally published in 1931.
Forster, Margaret. *Is There Anything You Want?* London: Chatto & Windus, 2005.
Fox, Catherine. *The Benefits of Passion*. Harmondsworth, UK: Penguin, 1997.
Fuller, John. *Flying to Nowhere*. Harmondsworth, UK: Penguin, 1983.
Gaskell, Elizabeth. *Ruth*. Oxford: Oxford University Press, 1985. Originally published in 1853.
Golding, William. *Rites of Passage*. London: Faber & Faber, 1980.
Goldsmith, Oliver. *The Vicar of Wakefield*. Harmondsworth, UK: Penguin, 1982. Originally published in 1766.
Greene, Graham. *The Power and the Glory*. London: Vintage, 1940.
Hannah, Barry. *Yonder Stands Your Orphan*. New York: Grove Press, 2001.
Hardy, Thomas. *Satires of Circumstance: Lyrics and Reveries*. London: Macmillan, 1914.

Hawthorne, Nathaniel. *The Scarlet Letter*. Harmondsworth, UK: Penguin, 1970. Originally published in 1850.

Hobbs, Peter. *The Short Day Dying*. London: Faber, 2005.

Hurston, Zora Neale. *Jonah's Gourd Vine*. London: Virago, 1987. Originally published in 1934.

Isler, Alan. *Clerical Errors*. London: Vintage, 2001.

Johnson, Stephanie. *Belief*. London: Vintage, 2001.

Joyce, James. *A Portrait of the Artist as a Young Man*. Harmondsworth, UK: Penguin, 1960. Originally published in 1916.

Lewis, Sinclair. *Elmer Gantry*. Harmondsworth, UK: Penguin, 1967. Originally published in 1927.

Lodge, David. *The British Museum is Falling Down*. Harmondsworth, UK: Penguin, 1965.

———. *Paradise News*. Harmondsworth, UK: Penguin, 1991.

———. *The Picturegoers*. Harmondsworth, UK: Penguin, 1960.

———. *Thinks...* Harmondsworth, UK: Penguin, 2001.

Mantel, Hilary. *Fludd*. Harmondsworth, UK: Penguin, 1989.

Michaels, Anne. *Fugitive Pieces*. London: Bloomsbury, 1997.

Morrison, Toni. *Beloved*. London: Picador, 1987.

———. *Jazz*. London: Picador, 1993.

Murray, John. *John Dory*. Hexham: Flambard Press, 2001.

Rogers, Jane. *The Ice Is Singing*. London: Faber & Faber, 1987.

———. *Island*. London: Little, Brown, 1999.

———. *Promised Lands*. London: Faber & Faber, 1995.

———. *The Voyage Home*. London: Abacus, 2004.

Rule, Jane. *This Is Not for You*. Talahassee, Fla.: Naiad Press, 1970.

Shaw, George B. *Saint Joan*. Harmondsworth, UK, Penguin, 1946. Originally published in 1924.

Sterne, Laurence. *The Sermons of Mr. Yorick, Volume 1*. Oxford: Basil Blackwell, 1927. Originally published in 1760.

Trollope, Anthony. *Barchester Towers*. Harmondsworth, UK: Penguin, 1982. Originally published in 1857.

Tulloch, Jonathan. *Give Us This Day*. London: Cape, 2005.

Waugh, Evelyn. *A Handful of Dust*. Harmondsworth, UK: Penguin, 1997. Originally published in 1934.

Winterson, Jeanette. *Boating for Beginners*. London: Minerva, 1985.

———. *Lighthousekeeping*. London: Fourth Estate, 2004.

―――. *Sexing the Cherry*. London: Vintage, 1987.
Wright, David, ed. *The Selected Poems of Thomas Hardy*. Harmondsworth, UK: Penguin, 1978.

Secondary Criticism

Adorno, Theodor. *Prisms*. Translated by Samuel and Shierry Weber. Cambridge, Mass.: MIT Press, 1967.
Alfer, Alexa. "Realism and Its Discontents." In Alfer and Noble, *Essays on the Fiction of A. S. Byatt* 47–59.
Alfer, Alexa, and Michael J. Noble, eds. *Essays on the Fiction of A. S. Byatt: Imagining the Real*. Westport, Conn.: Greenwood Press, 2001.
Allen, Carolyn J. "Fiction and Figures of Life in *Omensetter's Luck*." *Pacific Coast Philology* 9 (1974): 5–11.
Allerdice, Lisa. "So Much for Freedom." *Daily Telegraph* (London), August 31, 2002.
Alter, Robert. *Canon and Creativity: Modern Writing and the Authority of Scripture*. New Haven, Conn.: Yale University Press, 2002.
Altick, Richard D. *The English Common Reader: A Social History of the Mass Reading Public 1800–1900*. Chicago: University of Chicago Press, 1957.
Anderson, Benedict. *Imagined Communities*. New York: Verso, 1991.
Anon. "Twin Towns That Know the Same Fear." *Times* (London), October 24, 1966, 8.
Arditti, Michael. "Frills and Thrills: High Camp at the High Altar." *New Statesman*, April 24, 2000, 32–33.
―――. "Satisfying Scenes from Provincial Life." *The Independent*, May 5, 2001.
Bader-Saye, Scott. "Listening: Authority and Obedience." In *The Blackwell Companion to Christian Ethics*, edited by S. Hauerwas and S. Wells, 156–68. Oxford: Blackwell, 2004.
Bakhtin, Mikhail M. *The Dialogical Imagination: Four Essays*. Translated by Michael Holquist. Austin: University of Texas Press, 1981.
―――. "The Problem of Speech Genres." In *Speech Genres and Other Essays*, 60–102. Translated by Michael Holquist. Austin: University of Texas Press, 1986.
Bal, Mieke, Jonathan V. Crewe, and Leo Spitzer, eds. *Acts of Memory: Cultural Recall in the Present*. Hanover, N.H.: University Press of New England, 1999.

Ballard, Paul. "Poverty and Change: The Churches' Response in South Wales, 1966–2000." *Expository Times* 116, no. 2 (2004): 43–48.

Barger Elliott, Mark. *Creative Styles of Preaching*. Louisville, Ky.: Westminster John Knox, 2000.

Barloon, Jim. "Byatt's Latest Lacks Literary Inspiration." *Houston Chronicle* (Houston), March 28, 2003.

Batson, C. Daniel, Patricia Schoenrade, and W. Larry Ventis. *Religion and the Individual: A Social-Psychological Perspective*. Oxford: Oxford University Press, 1993.

Bauman, Richard. *Verbal Art as Performance*. Long Grove, Ill.: Waveland Press, 1977.

Benson-Brown, Amy. "Inverted Conversions: Reading the Bible and Writing the Lesbian Subject in *Oranges Are Not the Only Fruit*." In *Reclaiming the Sacred: The Bible in Gay and Lesbian Fiction*, edited by Raymond-Jean Frontain, 233–52. New York: Haworth Press, 1997.

Bentley, Louise. "Beyond the Liturgy: An Approach to Catholicism as Genre in the Work of James Joyce." *Literature and Theology* 12, no. 2 (1998): 159–69.

Bergonzi, Bernard. "A Conspicuous Absentee: The Decline and Fall of the Catholic Novel." *Encounter* 55, nos. 2–3 (1980): 44–56.

Best, Ernest. *From Text to Sermon: Responsible Use of the New Testament in Preaching*. Edinburgh: T&T Clark, 1988.

Bocheński, Joseph M. "On Authority." *South African Journal of Philosophy* 8, no. 2 (1988): 61–65.

Booth, Wayne C. *The Rhetoric of Fiction*. Chicago: University of Chicago Press, 1961.

Bornkamm, Gunther. *Paul*. London: Hodder & Stoughton, 1969.

Boyatzis, Chris J. "A Critique of Models of Religious Experience." *International Journal for the Psychology of Religion* 11, no. 4 (2001): 247–58.

Bragg, Melvyn. *The Adventure of English: The Biography of a Language*. London: Sceptre, 2003.

Brown, Callum. *The Death of Christian Britain: Understanding Secularisation 1800–2000*. London: Routledge, 2001.

Brown, Penelope, and Stephen C. Levinson. "Universals in Language Usage: Politeness Phenomena." In *Questions and Politeness: Strategies in Social Interaction*, edited by E. N. Goody, 256–89. Cambridge: Cambridge University Press, 1978.

Brueggemann, Walter. *The Bible and the Postmodern Imagination: Texts under Negotiation*. London: SCM Press, 1993.
———. *Cadences of Home: Preaching among Exiles*. Louisville, Ky.: Westminster John Knox, 1997.
———. *Deep Memory, Exuberant Hope: Contested Truth in a Post-Christian World*. Minneapolis: Fortress, 2000.
———. *Finally Comes the Poet: Daring Speech for Proclamation*. Minneapolis: Fortress, 1989.
Burke, Kenneth. *The Rhetoric of Religion: Studies in Logology*. Boston: Beacon Press, 1961; reprint Berkeley: University of California Press, 1977.
Burman, Erica, and Ian Parker, eds. *Discourse Analytic Research: Repertoires and Readings of Texts in Action*. London: Routledge, 1993.
Butler, Judith. *Gender Trouble: Feminism and the Subversion of Identity*. London: Routledge, 1999.
Buttrick, David. *Homiletic*. Philadelphia: Fortress, 1987.
———. *Preaching the New and the Now*. Louisville, Ky.: Westminster John Knox, 1998.
Byatt, Antonia S. *Degrees of Freedom: The Novels of Iris Murdoch*. London: Chatto & Windus, 1965.
———. "A Life Less Ordinary." *Guardian Review*, July 2, 2005, 16–17.
———. *Passions of the Mind: Selected Writings*. London: Chatto, 1991.
Campbell, Karlyn K. *The Rhetorical Act*. Belmont: Wordsworth, 1996.
Chanady, Amaryll B. *Magical Realism and the Fantastic: Resolved versus Unresolved Antimony*. New York: Garland, 1985.
Charles, Ron. "Frederica in Wonderland." *Christian Science Monitor*, December 19, 2002.
Clark, Timothy. *The Theory of Inspiration: Composition as a Crisis of Subjectivity in Romantic and Post-Romantic Writing*. Manchester: Manchester University Press, 1997.
Clifford, John. *Eyam Plague 1665–1666*. Eyam: John Clifford, 2003.
Compier, Don H. *What is Rhetorical Theology? Textual Practice and Public Discourse*. Philadelphia: Trinity Press, 1999.
Conradi, Peter J. *Iris Murdoch: The Saint and the Artist*. London: Macmillan, 1989.
———. *The Saint and the Artist: A Study of the Fiction of Iris Murdoch*. London: HarperCollins, 2001.
Cook, Guy. *Discourse and Literature*. Oxford: Oxford University Press, 1994.

Cowart, David. *History and the Contemporary Novel*. Carbondale: Southern Illinois University Press, 1989.

Crowe, Marian E. "Intimations of Immortality: Catholicism in David Lodge's *Paradise News*." *Renascence: Essays on Values in Literature* 52, no. 2 (2000): 143–61.

Cunningham, David S. *Faithful Persuasion: In Aid of a Rhetoric of Christian Theology*. Notre Dame, Ind.: University of Notre Dame Press, 1990.

Cupitt, Don. *Kingdom Come in Everyday Speech*. London: SCM Press, 2000.

Davies, Stevie. "*A Whistling Woman* by A. S. Byatt." *The Independent* (London), September 7, 2002.

De Groot, Jerome. *The Historical Novel*. London: Routledge, 2010.

De-La-Noy, Michael. "A Blast below the Bible Belt." *Evening Standard* (London), April 5, 2000.

de Lille, Alain. *The Art of Preaching*. Translated with an introduction by Gillian R. Evans. Kalamazoo, Mich.: Cistercian, 1981.

Derrida, Jacques. "Freud and the Scene of Writing." In *Writing and Difference*, translated by Alan Bass, 196–231. London: Routledge & Kegan Paul, 1978.

———. "Che cos'è la poesia?" In *A Derrida Reader: Between the Blinds*, edited and translated by Peggy Kamuf, 221–37. London: Harvester, 1991.

Detweiler, Robert. *Breaking the Fall: Religious Readings of Contemporary Fiction*. London: Macmillan, 1989.

Dickinson, David. "Troubled Preachers: Keeping Faith." *Homiletic* 32, no. 2 (2007): 1–10.

Drummond, A. L. "The Sermon in Victorian Fiction." In *The Churches in English Fiction: A Literary and Historical Study, from the Regency to the Present Time, of British and American Fiction*, 308–17. Leicester: Edgar Backus, 1950.

Dunn-Wilson, David. *A Mirror for the Church: Preaching in the First Five Centuries*. Cambridge: Eerdmans, 2005.

Dusinberre, Juliet. "Forms of Reality in A. S. Byatt's *The Virgin in the Garden*." *Critique: Studies in Modern Fiction* 24, no. 1 (1982): 55–62.

Eagleton, Terry. *The English Novel: An Introduction*. Oxford: Blackwell, 2005.

———. *Ideology: An Introduction*. London: Verso, 1991.

———. *The Rape of Clarissa: Writing, Sexuality and Class Struggle in Samuel Richardson*. Oxford: Blackwell, 1982.

Edwards, Anthony C., and Mike J. Lowis. "The Batson-Schoenrade-Ventis

Model of Religious Experience: Critique and Reformulation." *The International Journal for the Psychology of Religion* 11, no. 4 (2001): 215–34.

Eliot, Simon. *Some Patterns and Trends in British Publishing 1800–1919*. London: The Bibliographical Society, 1994.

Ellison, Robert H. *The Victorian Pulpit: Spoken and Written Sermons in Nineteenth-Century Britain*. London: Associated Universities Press, 1998.

Fabb, Nigel. *Linguistics and Literature*. Oxford: Blackwell, 1997.

Faris, Wendy B. "The Question of the Other: Cultural Critiques of Magical Realism." *Janus Head* 5 no. 2 (2002): 101–19.

Farrer, Austin M. *The Glass of Vision*. London: Dacre Press, 1948.

Ferretter, Luke. *Toward a Christian Literary Theory*. Basingstoke: Palgrave Macmillan, 2003.

Fish, Stanley. *Is There a Text in This Class? The Authority of Interpretive Communities*. Cambridge, Mass.: Harvard University Press, 1994.

Foucault, Michel. "Nietzsche, Genealogy, History." In *The Foucault Reader: An Introduction to Foucault's Thought*, edited by P. Rabinow, 76–100. Translated by Donald Bouchard and Sherry Simon. Harmondsworth, UK: Penguin, 1977.

———. "What Is an Author?" In *Language, Counter-Memory, Practice: Selected Essays and Interviews*, edited by Donald B. Bouchard. Translated by Donald Bouchard and Sherry Simon, 124–27. Ithaca, N.Y.: Cornell University Press, 1969.

Fox, Matthew. *Original Blessing*. Santa Fe: Bear, 1983.

Gates, Henry L. *The Signifying Monkey: A Theory of African-American Literary Criticism*. Oxford: Oxford University Press, 1986.

Gearon, Liam, ed. *English Literature, Theology and the Curriculum: Theology in Dialogue*. London: Cassell, 1999.

Gerhart, Mary. *Genre Choices, Genre Questions*. Norman: University of Oklahoma Press, 1992.

Gitzen, Julian. "A. S. Byatt's Self-Mirroring Art." *Critique: Studies in Modern Fiction* 36, no. 2 (1995): 83–95.

Goodwin, Jean. "Forms of Authority and the Real *Ad verecundiam*." *Argumentation* 12, no. 2 (1998): 267–80.

Grant, Michael. *Cicero: On the Good Life*. Harmondsworth, UK: Penguin Classics, 1971.

Green, Garrett. *Imagining God: Theology and the Religious Imagination*. Grand Rapids: Eerdmans, 1989.

Greiner, Donald. *John Updike's Novels*. Athens: Ohio University Press, 1984.

Hindmarsh, D. Bruce. *The Evangelical Conversion Narrative: Spiritual Autobiography in Early Modern England*. Oxford: Oxford University Press, 2005.

Hinds, Hilary. "*Oranges Are Not the Only Fruit*: Reaching Audiences Other Lesbian Texts Cannot Reach." In *New Lesbian Criticism: Literary and Cultural Readings*, edited by Sally Munt, 153–72. Hemel Hempstead, UK: Harvester Wheatsheaf, 1992.

Hix, H. I. *Understanding William Gass*. Columbia: University of South Carolina Press, 2002.

Hobson, Theo. *The Rhetorical Word: Protestant Theology and the Rhetoric of Authority*. Aldershot, UK: Ashgate, 2002.

Hogan, Lucy Lind, and Robert Reid. *Connecting with the Congregation: Rhetoric and the Art of Preaching*. Nashville: Abingdon, 1999.

Holberg, Jennifer. "'The Courage to See It': Toward an Understanding of Glory." *Christianity and Literature* 59, no. 2 (2010): 283–300.

Holmes, Frederic M. *The Historical Imagination: Postmodernism and the Treatment of the Past in Contemporary British Fiction*. Victoria: University of Victoria Press, 1997.

Holton, Robert. *Jarring Witnesses: Modern Fiction and the Representation of History*. Hemel Hempstead, UK: Harvester Wheatsheaf, 1994.

Hymes, Dell. *Foundations in Sociolinguistics: An Ethnographic Approach*. Philadelphia: University of Pennsylvania Press, 1974.

James, William. *The Varieties of Religious Experience*. London: Fontana, 1960. Originally published in 1902.

Jasper, David. "In the Sermon Which I Have Just Completed, Wherever I Said Aristotle, I Meant Saint Paul." In *The Bible as Rhetoric: Studies in Biblical Persuasion and Credibility*, edited by M. Warner, 133–52. London: Routledge, 1990.

Jay, Elisabeth. *Faith and Doubt in Victorian Britain*. London: Macmillan, 1986.

———. "Introduction: The Return of the Culturally Repressed—Religion and Women." *Nineteenth Century Studies* 13, no. 17 (2003): 1–12.

———. "'Who Are You Gentle Reader?' John Updike—*A Month of Sundays* (1975)." *Literature and Theology* 19, no. 4 (2005): 346–54.

Jeffrey, David L., ed. *A Dictionary of Biblical Tradition in English Literature*. Grand Rapids: Eerdmans, 1992.

Jeffreys, M. V. C. *Glaucon: An Inquiry into the Aims of Education*. London: Pitman & Sons, 1950.

Kaufman, Gordon D. *The Theological Imagination: Constructing the Concept of God*. Philadelphia: Westminster John Knox, 1981.

Kearns, Michael. *Rhetorical Narratology*. Lincoln: University of Nebraska Press, 1999.

Kennedy, George A. *Classical Rhetoric and Its Christian and Secular Traditions from Ancient to Modern Times*. London: Croom Helm, 1980.

King, Nicola. *Memory, Narrative, Identity: Remembering the Self*. Edinburgh: Edinburgh University Press, 2000.

Krailsheimer, A. J. *Conversion*. London: SCM Press, 1980.

Lakoff, George, and Mark Johnson. *Metaphors We Live By*. Chicago: University of Chicago Press, 1980.

Lash, Nicholas. *Believing Three Ways in One God: A Reading of the Apostles' Creed*. London: SCM Press, 1992.

———. *Holiness, Speech and Silence: Reflections on the Question of God*. Aldershot, UK: Ashgate, 2004.

Law, David R. *Inspiration*. London: Continuum, 2001.

Levinas, Emmanuel. *Otherwise Than Being*. Translated by Alphonso Lingus. The Hague: Martinus Nijhoff, 1981.

Lindlof, Thomas R. "Interpretive Community: An Approach to Media and Religion." *Journal of Media and Religion* 1, no. 1 (2002): 61–74.

Lischer, Richard. *Theories of Preaching*. Durham, N.C.: Labyrinth Press, 1987.

Lodge, David. *The Art of Fiction: Illustrated from Classic and Modern Texts*. Harmondsworth, UK: Penguin, 1992.

———. *Consciousness and the Novel: Connected Essays*. London: Secker & Warburg, 2002.

Lose, David J. *Confessing Jesus Christ: Preaching in a Postmodern World*. Grand Rapids: Eerdmans, 2003.

Lyotard, Jean-Francois. *The Postmodern Condition: A Report on Knowledge*. Manchester: Manchester University Press, 1984.

MacDonald, George. *Unspoken Sermons*, 1st series. London: Alexander Strahan, 1867.

———. *Unspoken Sermons*, 2nd series. London: Longmans, Green, 1885.

———. *Unspoken Sermons*, 3rd series. London: Longmans, Green, 1889.

Matus, Jill. *Toni Morrison*. Manchester: Manchester University Press, 1998.

Matz, Jesse. *The Modern Novel: A Short Introduction*. Oxford: Blackwell, 2004.

McClure, John S. *Other-Wise Preaching: A Postmodern Ethic for Homiletics*. St Louis, Mo.: Chalice Press, 2001.

McFague, Sallie. *Speaking in Parables: A Study in Metaphor and Theology*. Philadelphia: Fortress, 1975.

McLean, Iain, and Martin Johnes. *Aberfan: Government and Disasters*. Cardiff: Welsh Academic Press, 2000.

Meaney, Thomas. "Neuro-Stories." *Times Literary Supplement*. September 10, 2010, 29.

Merrill, Thomas. *Christian Criticism: A Study of Literary God-Talk*. Amsterdam: Rodopi, 1976.

Middleton, David, ed. *Toni Morrison's Fiction: Contemporary Criticism*. London: Garland Publishing, 2000.

Middleton, J. Richard, and Brian J. Walsh. *Truth Is Stranger Than It Used to Be: Biblical Faith in a Postmodern Age*. London: SPCK, 1995.

Miller, Joan. *Aberfan: A Disaster and Its Aftermath*. London: Constable, 1974.

Morey-Gaines, Ann-Janine. "Religion and Sexuality in Walker Percy, William Gass and John Updike: Metaphors of Embodiment in Androcentric Imagination." *Journal of the American Academy of Religion* 51, no. 4 (1983): 595–609.

———. "Margaret Atwood and Toni Morrison." In *Toni Morrison's Fiction: Contemporary Criticism*, edited by David Middleton, 247–68. London: Garland Publishing, 2000.

Muilenburg, James. "Form Criticism and Beyond." *Journal of Biblical Literature* 88 (1969): 1–18.

Murdoch, Iris. *The Sovereignty of Good*. London: Routledge, 1970.

Newport, Kenneth G. C. *The Branch Davidians of Waco: The History and Beliefs of an Apocalyptic Sect*. Oxford: Oxford University Press, 2006.

Nidditch, Peter H., ed. *John Locke: An Essay Concerning Human Understanding*. Oxford: Clarendon, 1975.

Olson, David R., and Nancy Torrance. *Literacy and Orality*. Cambridge: Cambridge University Press, 1991.

Ong, Walter J. *Orality and Literacy: The Technologizing of the Word*. London: Routledge, 1982.

Origen. *On First Principles: Being Koetschau's Text of* De principiis. Translated, introduction, and notes by G. W. Butterworth. Gloucester, Mass.: Peter Smith, Torchbook, 1973.

O'Rourke, Rebecca. "'Fingers in the Fruit Basket': A Feminist Reading of Jeanette Winterson's *Oranges Are Not the Only Fruit*." In *Feminist*

Criticism: Theory and Practice, edited by Susan Sellers, 57–69. Hemel Hempstead, UK: Harvester Wheatsheaf, 1990.

Oxford English Dictionary, 2nd ed., ed J. A. Simpson and E. S. C. Weiner. Oxford: Clarendon, 1989.

Parsons, Gerald. "Paradigm or Period Piece? David Lodge's *How Far Can You Go?* in Perspective." *Journal of Literature and Theology* 6, no. 2 (1992): 171–90.

Pattison, Stephen. *Shame: Theory, Therapy, Theology*. Cambridge: Cambridge University Press, 2000.

Peters, Gerald. *The Mutilating God: Authorship and Authority in the Narrative of Conversion*. Amherst: University of Massachusetts Press, 1993.

Petit, Susan. "Finding Flannery O'Connor's 'Good Man' in Marilynne Robinson's *Gilead* and *Home*." *Christianity and Literature* 59, no. 2 (2010): 301–18.

Pinches, Charles. "Proclaiming: Naming and Describing." In *The Blackwell Companion to Christian Ethics*, edited by Stanley Hauerwas and Samuel Wells, 169–81. Oxford: Blackwell, 2004.

Plant, Raymond. "Community: Concept, Conception and Ideology." *Politics and Society* 8 (1978): 79–107.

Price, David W. *History Made, History Imagined: Contemporary Literature, Poesis and the Past*. Champaign: University of Illinois Press, 1999.

Prickett, Stephen. *Origins of Narrative: The Romantic Appropriation of the Bible*. Cambridge: Cambridge University Press, 1996.

Ramsey, Ian T. *Religious Language: An Empirical Placing of Theological Phrases*. London: SCM Press, 1957.

Reames, Kelly L. *Toni Morrison's Paradise: A Reader's Guide*. London: Continuum, 2001.

Ricoeur, Paul. "The Function of Fiction in Shaping Reality." *Man and World* 12 (1979): 123–41.

———. *The Rule of Metaphor: Multi-Disciplinary Studies of the Creation of Meaning in Language*. Translated by Robert Czerny, Kathleen McLaughlin, and John Costello. London: Routledge & Kegan Paul, 1978. Originally published in 1977.

Rivers, Isabel. "Strangers and Pilgrims: Sources and Patterns of Methodist Narrative." In *Augustan Worlds*, edited by J. D. Hilson, M. M. B. Jones, and J. R. Watson, 189–203. Leicester: Leicester University Press, 1978.

Robertson, D. W., trans. *St. Augustine on Christian Doctrine*. New York: Prentice Hall, 1958.

Robinson, Marilynne. *The Death of Adam*. New York: Picador, 2005.
Rollins, Wayne G. *Jung and the Bible*. Atlanta: Westminster John Knox, 1983.
Rzepka, Charles, and J. Rzepka. "Seeing into the Life of Things." In *Moral Cross-Dressing: Contemporary Trends in Liberal Preaching and Literary Criticism*, edited by J. Mahoney, 88–107. Bronx, N.Y.: Fordham University Press, 2000.
Salter, Elizabeth. *Piers Plowman: An Introduction*. Oxford: Basil Blackwell, 1963.
Salter, Elizabeth, and Derek Pearsall. *Piers Plowman*. London: Edward Arnold, 1967.
Salwak, Dale. "Review of *Souls and Bodies* by David Lodge." *Magil's Literary Annual* (1983): 761–63.
Schiff, James. *John Updike's Novels Revisited*. New York: Twayne, 1998.
Schneider, Richard. "The Fortunate Fall in William Gass's *Omensetter's Luck*." *Critique* 18, no. 1 (1976): 5–20.
Schuhmann, Kuno. "The Concept of Culture in Some Recent English Novels." In *Anglistentag*, edited by J. Hasler, 111–27. Frankfurt: Peter Lang, 1982.
Searle, John R. *Expression and Meaning: Studies in the Theory of Speech Acts*. Cambridge: Cambridge University Press, 1979.
Seed, David. "The Voices of the Church: A Dialogical Approach to the Retreat Section of Joyce's *A Portrait of the Artist*." *Literature and Theology* 9, no. 2 (1995): 153–64.
Seymour, Melody D. "The Pulpit in the Prow: The Voice of the Sermon in the Fiction and Culture of the United States." Ph.D. diss., University of Southern California, 1990.
Short, Mick. *Exploring the Language of Poems, Plays and Prose*. Harlow, UK: Longman, 1996.
Siefker Bailey, Lisa M. "Fraught with Fire: Race and Theology in Marilynne Robinson's *Gilead*." *Christianity and Literature* 59, no. 2 (2010): 265–80.
Simpson, Paul. *Language, Ideology and Point of View*. London: Routledge, 1993.
———. *Language through Literature: An Introduction*. London: Routledge, 1997.
Sorensen, Sue. "A. S. Byatt and the Life of the Mind: A Response to Jane Sturrock." *Connotations* 13, no. 1 (2003): 180–90.

———. "Death in the Fiction of A. S. Byatt." *Critique* 43, no. 3 (2002): 115–34.

Soskice, Janet M. *Metaphor and Religious Language*. Oxford: Clarendon, 1985.

Sperber, Dan, and Deirdre Wilson. *Relevance: Communication and Cognition*. Oxford: Blackwell, 1986.

Spong, John S. *Why Christianity Must Change or Die: A Bishop Speaks to Believers in Exile*. London: HarperCollins, 1998.

Steinberg, Sybil. "Life and Death in Eyam." *Publishers' Weekly* 248, no. 33 (August 13, 2001): 278–79.

Stockwell, Peter. *Cognitive Poetics: An Introduction*. London: Routledge, 2001.

Strandberg, Victor. "John Updike and the Changing of the Gods." In *Critical Essays on John Updike*, edited by William R. McNaughton, 175–93. Boston: G. K. Hall, 1982.

Streichsbier, Beata. "Irony in David Lodge's *How Far Can You Go?*" In *A Yearbook of English Language and Literature*, edited by S. Korninger, 97–110. Vienna: Braumuller, 1981.

Sturrock, Jane. "Angels, Insects and Analogy: A. S. Byatt's 'Morpho Eugenia.'" *Connotations* 12, no. 1 (2002): 93–104.

Tate, Andrew. *Contemporary Fiction and Christianity*. London: Continuum, 2008.

Taylor, David J. "God's Odd-Bods." *Guardian*, July 9, 2005.

Taylor, Mark C. *Erring: A Postmodern A/theology*. Chicago: University of Chicago Press, 1984.

Tew, Philip. *The Contemporary British Novel*. London: Continuum, 2004.

Tew, Philip, and Rod Mengham, eds. *British Fiction Today*. London: Continuum, 2006.

Thiel, John E. *Imagination and Authority: Theological Authorship in the Modern Tradition*. Minneapolis: Fortress, 1991.

Thompson, Damian. "Even the 'Messy Bits' Are Made in His Image." *Sunday Telegraph*, April 2, 2000.

Tillich, Paul. *Systematic Theology*. Vol. 1, *Reason and Revelation*. London: SCM Press, 1951.

———. *Systematic Theology*. Vol. 2, *Existence and the Christ*. London: SCM Press, 1957.

———. *Theology of Culture*. New York: Oxford University Press, 1959.

Toolan, Michael J. *Narrative: A Critical Linguistic Introduction*. London: Routledge, 1988.

Toulmin, Stephen. *The Uses of Argument*. Cambridge: Cambridge University Press, 1958.

Tracy, David. *The Analogical Imagination: Christian Theology and the Culture of Pluralism*. New York: Crossroad, 1981.

Treglown, Jeremy. "Where Shall Wisdom Be Found?" *Times Literary Supplement* (London), May 2, 1980, 487.

Trible, Phyllis. *Texts of Terror: Literary-Feminist Readings of Biblical Narratives*. Philadelphia: Fortress, 1984.

Trustees for Methodist Church Purposes. *Hymns and Psalms*. Peterborough, UK: Methodist Publishing House, 1983.

———. *The Methodist Worship Book*. Peterborough, UK: Methodist Publishing House, 1999.

Vincent, John. "Imaginative Identification." *Epworth Review* 23, no. 3 (1996): 14–20.

Volk-Birke, Sabine. *Chaucer and Medieval Preaching: Rhetoric for Listeners*. Tubingen: Gunter Narr Verlag, 1991.

Vos, Cas. "The Sermon as a Work of Art." *Expository Times* 116, no. 11 (2005): 371–73.

Ward, Keith. *Religion and Community*. Oxford: Oxford University Press, 2000.

Ward, Richard. "Performance Turns in Homiletics: Wrong Way or Right On?" *Journal of Communication and Religion* 17, no. 1 (1994): 1–11.

Warnes, Christopher. "Naturalizing the Supernatural: Faith, Irreverence and Magical Realism." *Literature Compass 2* 20C, no. 106 (2005): 1–16.

Waters, Claire M. *Angels and Earthly Creatures: Preaching, Performance and Gender in the Later Middle Ages*. Philadelphia: University of Pennsylvania Press, 2004.

Westlake, Michael. "The Hard Idea of Truth." *PN Review* 15, no. 4 (1989): 33–37.

Wheeler, Michael. "The Limits of Hell: Lodge, Murdoch, Burgess, Golding." *Journal of Literature and Theology* 4, no. 1 (1990): 72–83.

Whitford, Frank. "Gauguin's Vision." *Sunday Times* (London), August 7, 2005, 6–7.

Whittaker, John H. "Kierkegaard on the Concept of Authority." *International Journal for the Philosophy of Religion* 46 (1999): 83–101.

Willey, Basil. "Imagination and Fancy." In *Nineteenth Century Studies: Coleridge to Matthew Arnold*, 10–31. New York: Columbia University Press, 1949.

Williams, Raymond. *Marxism and Literature*. Oxford: Oxford University Press, 1977.

Winterson, Jeanette. *Why Be Happy When You Could Be Normal?* London: Jonathan Cape, 2011.

Wisse, Maarten. "The Meaning of the Authority of the Bible." *Religious Studies* 36, no. 4 (2000): 473–87.

Woodman, Thomas. *Faithful Fictions: The Catholic Novel in British Literature*. Milton Keynes, UK: Open University Press, 1991.

Wright, Terry. *Theology and Literature*. Oxford: Blackwell, 1988.

Wroe, John. *Sermons Selected from the Scriptures: Being a Guide to the People Surnamed Israelites to Preach the Everlasting Gospel*. Ashton-under-Lyne, UK: Trustees of the Society of Christian Israelites, 1896.

Young, Frances. "School for Sinners." *Epworth Review* 23, no. 3 (1994): 63–71.

Index of Biblical References

Genesis
  1–2   124
  2:18   57
  2:24   113
  22   86–87, 142
  32   85, 100–101
Joshua
  24:2–15   12
Isaiah
  14:12   32
  30:15–17   51
Matthew
  11:4–5   31–32, 114
Mark
  10:25–26   53–54
  14:22   85
Luke
  10:18   33
  12:35   25
  15:11–32   86
John
  8:1–11   69
  8:32   114
  15:13   51
  20:17   34
Acts
  2:14–36   12
  17:22–31   12
Romans
  8:12–13   113
  9:30–33   12
  10:11–17   12
1 Corinthians
  15:32   113
Ephesians
  5:28, 32   113
1 Peter
  1:6–7   51
Revelation
  7   25
  12:7–9   33
  21   145

General Index

"9/11," 44–45, 66

A Month of Sundays; *see* Updike
A Whistling Woman; *see* Byatt
Aberfan, 74, 75, 77, 80, 155
Adorno, Theodor, 66
allegory, 29
Allende, Isabel, 96
amen, 43, 31, 41, 59, 70
analogy, 74, 111, 113, 117, 118, 159
anamnesis, 36, 161
Anderson, Benedict, 127
anti-sermon, 11, 106, 144, 168
aptum, 61
Arditti, Michael, 28–41, 92, 95, 130, 138, 148–49, 156, 157–58, 161
Ardizzone, Edward, 23
Armistice Day, 156
atheist, 32, 11; *see also* preaching
attitude, 4, 20–22
audience, 27–28, 31, 41, 46, 53, 69–72, 74–76, 93, 120, 122, 133, 141–43, 174
audiobooks, 17, 19
Augustine of Hippo, 13, 89, 164
authenticity, 6, 37, 46, 89, 92
authority, 20, 28, 43, 45–46, 51, 62–63, 128, 174; assumed authority, 44, 57; attributed, 62; biblical, 62; of Christ, 44; deontic, 62; epistemic, 62; expressive, 56, 62–63
authorship, 33, 45, 56, 59

Babel Tower; *see* Byatt
Bader-Saye, Scott, 128
Bakhtin, Mikhail, 16, 153
Baldwin, James, 29
Bay Psalm Book, 13
Beloved; *see* Morrison
Bennett, Arnold, 3, 111
biblical fictions, 47
bifocality, 81, 112, 126, 162
bildungsroman, 166
bitonality, 73
body, 34, 36, 152
Bonhoeffer, Dietrich, 106, 175
book, 45
Books of Kings and Chronicles, 25
Booth, Wayne, 14
British Israelism, 49
Brooks, Geraldine, 47–48, 50–51, 61, 93, 156, 160; *March*, 65
Brueggemann, Walter, 14, 120, 128, 162, 164–65
Butler, Samuel, 3

Butterfield, Herbert, 50
Byatt, A. S., 103–9, 112, 114–18, 127, 131–44, 149; *A Whistling Woman*, 106–9, 112, 115–16, 131–44, 149; *Babel Tower*, 106; *Still Life*, 104, 105–6, 107, 114–15, 116–17, 118; *The Virgin in the Garden*, 103, 104, 114, 116

Calvin, John, 61, 88
Chaucer, Geoffrey, 5, 17, 49
Christian Israelites, 49
Chrysostom, John, 13
Cicero, 12, 13, 154
Clarissa; *see* Richardson, Samuel
Coleridge, Samuel Taylor, 163
community, 127, 129–31, 149–52; charismatic, 130–31; imagined, 127, 129; incomplete, 149–50; interpretive, 131, 150–51; moral, 131; organic, 130; religious, 152; response, 150; sacramental, 131; sectarian, 130; teaching, 130; virtual, 151–52
confessional theology, 20
countermemory, 161–62; *see also* memory
Cyril of Jerusalem, 43

"death of God" theology, 132, 143
de Lille, Alain, 4, 17
density, 14, 120
Detweiler, Robert, 150
dialogue, 79
Dickens, Charles, 4, 18, 134
disjunction, 14, 20, 86
dissonance, 2, 7, 11, 41, 47, 104, 174
Donne, John, 108, 137
double enunciation, 61, 126
double voice, 126; *see also* voice

e-book, 45, 79
"Eleanor Rigby," 2, 25, 73
Eliot, George, 4

ephlatus, 61
Epistle of Clement, 12
epistolary novel, 92–96
Esther, 49
experience, religious, 88–92, 101

faith, 65–66, 67–76, 78, 81, 90, 120, 129, 141, 153, 160, 162, 171, 173, 175
faithful imagination, 154, 164
fantasy, 29, 49, 97–98, 170
filtering, 134
Fish, Stanley, 150–51
focalization, 133, 135
forgiveness, 86
Forster, Margaret, 65
Foucault, Michel, 161
Fox, Catherine, 65
fundamentalism, 3, 30, 44–45, 166, 169, 170
funeral, 24, 35–36, 48, 55–56

Gaskell, Elizabeth, 23–26
Gass, William, 103, 121–26
Gauguin, Paul, 100–101
gender, 16
Gilead; *see* Robinson
Golding, William, 65
Goldsmith, Oliver, 3
Good Friday, 37
Green, Garrett, 163

Hannah, Barry, 17
Hardy, Thomas, 15–16
hegemony, 1, 74, 77, 120, 128
historical novels, 160
Hobbs, Peter, 65
holocaust, 154
Home; *see* Robinson
"honest to God" debate, 132
honesty, 5, 29, 38, 41, 52, 81
Hosea, 53
How Far Can You Go?; *see* Lodge

imagination, 2, 78, 82, 121, 126, 128, 129, 160, 162–65
incarnational theology, 40
inspiration, 59–60; biblical, 60; dictation theory, 59; levels, 60; plenary theory, 59; verbal theory, 59
integrity, 6, 22, 26, 37, 39, 87, 95, 103, 124, 142
intention, 4
interiorization, 61, 66
intertextuality, 14, 27, 31, 94, 120, 122, 129, 166
intonation, 19–20, 44
Isler, Alan, 65

James, William 88–89
Jeremiah, 89
Job, 75, 77–78, 81
Johnson, Stephanie, 65
Joyce, James, 26–28, 73

Kierkegaard, 108, 136
kunstleroman, 166

Langland, William, 4
language, 103, 109–11, 117, 121, 125, 126; differentiated, 103; metaphorical, 111, 117, 121, 125, 126; religious, 109–11
lexis, 31, 114–15
"Lifeguard"; *see* Updike
lifewriting, 94, 156, 166
liturgy, 29–30, 39, 43, 56, 78–79, 82, 125, 128, 158, 165
Locke, John, 155
Lodge, David, 66, 72–81, 96, 155–56, 161–62; *How Far Can You Go?* 66, 72–81, 155–56, 161–62; *The Art of Fiction*, 96; *The Picturegoers*, 73, 79; *Thinks…*, 79–80
logology, 109–10

MacDonald, George, 19

magical realism, 96–98
Manson, Charles, 133
Mantel, Hilary, 65
March; *see* Brooks
memory, 129, 154–62; countermemory, 161–62; inherited, 160; kerygmatic, 158–59; mimetic, 159–60
metaphor, 111–12, 121, 163
Michaels, Anne, 161
midrash, 29, 33
Milton, John, 10, 33; *Areopagetica,* 10; *Paradise Lost*, 33
mimesis, 4, 159–60
missionary sermon, 12
Morrison, Toni, 26, 127, 144–48, 149; *Beloved*, 144; *Paradise*, 26, 144–48
Mr Wroe's Virgins; *see* Rogers
Murdoch, Iris, 9, 10, 11, 37, 143–44, 148; *The Bell*, 10, 143–44; *The Time of the Angels*, 11, 37, 144

naming, 158
narrative, 90–91
natural disaster, 66
New Homiletic, 2
Newman, John Henry, 19
Nietzsche, Friedrich Wilhelm, 115, 143
nomenclature, 5–6
normality, 88

Of the Farm; *see* Updike
Omensetter's Luck; *see* Gass
Ong, Walter, 19
orality, 4, 18–20, 93, 103
Oranges Are Not the Only Fruit; *see* Winterson
Origen, 33, 130

Paradise; *see* Morrison
Pepys, Samuel, 48
performance, 3, 15–18, 140
performance frames, 34, 68, 70, 71

perfunctory performance, 18; *see also* performance
pluralist, 75, 76, 81, 130–31
politeness phenomena, 68
polyphony, 81, 119–20, 121
postmodernity, 79, 81
preachiness, 4, 6, 83
preaching, 1, 3, 11, 20, 28, 30, 31, 37, 38, 45, 46, 54, 56, 58, 73, 79, 144, 128, 158; absolutist, 45; atheist, 11, 37, 144; biblical, 46, 54; comedic, 3; fascistic, 28; formulaic, 158; honest, 38; monological, 20, 28, 79, 128; oppressive, 28; parodic, 31, 54, 58, 73; redundant, 30, 158; satirical, 54, 56; univocal, 1
preaching at wedding, 74–75, 145
prodigal son, 86
pulpit, 13–14, 25, 93, 95, 99, 106, 121, 125–26, 138, 144, 165

quadrilateral of authorities, 1

Rabbit, Run; *see* Updike
readership, 131, 141–44
realist novel, 107–16
religious reading, 150
Remembrance Sunday, 155
resurrection, 36
rhetoric, 3, 6–7, 12–15, 51
rhetorical narratology, 6, 133
rhetorical theology, 13
Richardson, Samuel, 92–96
Ricoeur, Paul, 16, 68, 76, 159–60
Robinson, Marilynne, 83–101; *Gilead*, 85–87, 92, 93, 100–101; *Home*, 87–101; *The Death of Adam*, 88
Rogers, Jane, 48–50, 51–25, 61, 156, 160; *Island*, 52; *Mr Wroe's Virgins*, 48–50, 51, 61, 156, 160; *Promised Lands*, 52; *The Ice is Singing*, 52; *The Voyage Home*, 52
Ruskin, John, 164

Ruth; *see* Gaskell

satire, 4, 5, 29, 30, 33, 41, 54, 70, 132, 149, 170
schema breaking, 34, 165
schema theory, 165
schemata, 68, 70, 165, 171
sermon; *see* preaching
sermon, unspoken, 19, 68, 85, 146–48
setting, 137–39
silence, 16, 17, 21, 25–26, 38, 54, 66, 80, 123, 137, 142–43, 146, 155, 168, 174
Sodom and Gomorrah narrative, 53
speech act, 18, 139–42
Spong, John, 41
Spurgeon, Charles, 19
Sterne, Laurence, 21
Still Life; *see* Byatt
stratification, 20
styles of preaching, 46

Tertullian, 12
testimony, 61, 91, 94, 156, 160
theatricality, 15–17, 18, 124
The Bell; *see* Murdoch
The Picturegoers; *see* Lodge
The Time of the Angels; *see* Murdoch
The Virgin in the Garden; *see* Byatt
The Witches of Eastwick; *see* Updike
Thinks...; *see* Lodge
Tillich, Paul, 67, 99
Timothy, letter to, 44
Titus, letter to, 44
trinity, 106, 114
Trollope, Anthony, 4
troubled preachers, 23, 65–82
truth, 1–2, 16, 41, 45, 56, 63, 89–91, 95, 97–98, 104, 109, 112, 114, 119–21, 130, 135, 163, 170, 174
Tulloch, Jonathan, 65
Tŷ Toronto, 81

unlimited conversation, 129–30, 162
Updike, John, 9, 54, 55, 56–57, 58, 61–62, 66–67, 68–72, 92, 98–100, 173; *A Month of Sundays*, 54, 66–67, 68–72, 173; *Couples*, 54, 56; *In the Beauty of the Lilies*, 54; "Lifeguard," 9, 54, 58, 92, 98–100; *Of the Farm*, 54, 56–57; *Rabbit, Run*, 54, 55; *The Witches of Eastwick*, 54, 58

Vatican II, 73, 76, 78
voice, 20–22, 79, 119–20, 126, 129

wedding, 74, 77, 145
Wesley, Charles, 99, 119
Wesley, John, 39
Wesley, Susanna, 39
whig interpretation, 50
Winterson, Jeanette, 154, 166–71; *Lighthousekeeping*, 166; *Oranges are not the only fruit*, 154, 166–71

Year of Wonders; *see* Brooks